55

Inside My Life Outdoors

A memoir of woods and waters

Douglas Arthur Dohne

Inside My Life Outdoors

By Douglas A. Dohne

ACKNOWLEDGMENTS
&
FOREWORD

In the beginning we are all reporters. Our dispatches are recorded not in words but in the sounds every baby makes to signal joy, hunger, fatigue, pain, fright, etc. This instinct to report is reinforced by what follows, i.e., a bottle of milk, a dry diaper and so on.

Most of my adult life was spent in the news business, which runs on our collective hunger to know what's going on in the world. To the extent that this appetite is satisfied, we are better equipped for life. Every day is a learning experience, revealing that the more we know the more there is to find out, and communication is what paves the way forward.

Studying French led to the realization that, *Mon Dieu*, this thing called English is simply one exception piled atop another, condemning its users to the drudgery of memorization while providing too little relief via form *à la* the Romance languages. I noticed that the rhythm of poetry teaches discipline in prose, and that keeping a diary can help boost one's recall.

Autobiography has been a humbling experience, impressing upon me the huge debt owed to those who helped out along the way. Some of their names are among the more than 200 that appear in this book, while others are not. The latter group includes Charles Schaeffer, a boyhood neighbor and high school math teacher who pried open many young eyes to the vastness of the universe; Lionel Hall,

Fred Eisenhard, Wayne Grube, Paul Opitz, Marlin Klinger and Mister Brosius, coaches whose lessons about life spiraled in importance far above those that unfolded on the gridiron; and John Harrison, my favorite prof at Penn State, whose writing standards served to stretch mine.

At The Patriot-News, principal players in my personal/professional development included reporter Harry McLaughlin, the scars of whose relentlessness I will always carry; copy desk chief Leon Baden, my main editing mentor, who never tired of toying with the written word; and fellow copy editor Bill Blando, whose fiery sense of justice has helped to define his life, mine and many others privileged to know him. For reminding her editor of the essence of teamwork by treating him as a co-captain, I cheer columnist Nancy Eshelman.

For their encouragement and technical assistance in producing this work, I am indebted to my brother, Steve, and close friend and fellow wordsmith Don Sarvey. A special thank-you is due The Patriot-News for granting permission to reprint the columns and several photos contained herein.

I also appreciate the cooperation of the U.S. Fish and Wildlife Service in allowing republication of its American eel image.

For their collaborative artistic efforts on this book's cover, I applaud Holly Blyler and Carlton Hoke. As a retirement gift, graphics artist Holly created a wonderful watercolor, "Still life with trout," from which former elementary school art teacher Carlton so cleverly netted her fish and released it into his design. He also flew in the wild turkey gobbler from a photo by Andrew Edris and landed it nearby. Friend Carlton has remained my faithful guide and companion throughout the twists and turns of modern book publication, his devotion to the project at times eclipsing my own.

About the photos inside: Some of them include handwritten notes – usually setting the date and place, or sometimes introducing a touch of humor. Dad was a camera bug and filled about a dozen family picture albums. In time, we came to cherish his notations as much as the images they adorn.

In the interest of flow and readability, I tried to avoid excessive punctuation and attribution. When recording unspoken thoughts, for example, I followed the lead of other authors and simply italicized that part without further clarification. Except where otherwise noted, the poetry herein is original.

A great deal of information was gleaned from these state departments and agencies: Agriculture; Conservation and Natural Resources; Environmental Protection and its Bureau of Deep Mine Safety; the Fish and Boat Commission and its capable press secretary, Eric Levis; Game Commission, and the Hardwoods Development Council. Penn State also assisted.

And now the feds: Agriculture; Energy Regulatory Commission; Environmental Protection Agency; FWS; Geological Survey; National Marine Fisheries Service; Weather Service; and the Susquehanna River Basin Commission, which combines state and federal powers but has sovereign strengths all its own.

For his friendship and willingness to weigh in on all topics watery, I am indebted to the SRBC's retired skipper, Paul O. Swartz, who enlisted early on in this labor of love, as he so aptly tagged it.

Special thanks are due my friend in the castle a.k.a. the PA State Library, Eileen Kocher, a research assistant who briefly but brilliantly brought local history to life one spring day in 2016.

Not least, I give thanks to the Author of all for my life and that of the little lady who helps run it. Special Kay gave me the freedom to roam and write, then pitched in like a seasoned pro as my editor.

Finally, my sincere thanks to everyone along the way who took time out for one little boy who never really quite grew up, at least re: asking questions.

I began as a reporter and will proudly finish as one, too; but first, this account of my life outdoors. It's been like writing a letter home.

December 2016

Inside My Life Outdoors 1
Chapter 1 - Shush! 15
On to Michigan..19
Back to Pennsylvania 20
First the surgery, then they called Doc 22
Grandfather, you have such big ears..................................24
Learning about the birds and the bees 26
Father was a papermaker 29
Trees were piling up 30
Journey into journalism started right out front 32
This time the attack was provoked 33
Not a good match next door 34
I was in love with Daisy, but now she was gone 36
Adventures in archery...37
My closest pal was Alfie...41
Lake Harmony, here we come 44
Panther Lake still owned a piece of our heart 48
Rainy days on the porch 50
Uncle Abe's woodlot 52
Ontario beckons...52
Welcome to Canada: Day I, Part II.....................................53
Lake Harmony was more populous 54
The last time I saw Butch 55
Cousin Karen takes the towrope..57
So long, Alfie...57
My first shotgun cost $5 58
A living monument to flexibility 60
Three of us skipped school 63
One final stone..64
Picking up the javelin 66
Yes, there was a dark side...68
Where are they now 70
Chapter 2 - Bang! 73
My first turkey hunt..79
New job, new faces...82

A taste of hunting camp 84
Mountainside mystery 86
Red Wolfe, a blue hen and the forest aflame 88
Ah, springtime vacations 92
Mimicking the wild turkey's voice 93
Woods wisdom 95
Some do's and don'ts 96
It's listen up or lose out 96
Calling on the coconut 97
Failing a pop quiz 98
Bamboo takes center stage 99
The real experts live in the woods 101
'Let's … see what happens' 102
My bluff is called 103
Look, ma, no hands 104
Diving into the diaphragm 105
Calls of the wild aplenty 106
Pummel Rock 109
Morning in the mountains 111
The lunch bunch 113
Electrical malfunction follows the mental kind 115
A man called Tank 116
Aw, the trailer lights ain't workin' 117
Our longest walk 118
Can turkeys tell time? 119
We don't shoot strangers 121
Finding Ditchmo 124
King of the Road 126
Pincushion Knob 128
Big Boy, Part I 130
Into each life some rain must fall 135
The wild leek revisited 137
Doing Hobo Suppers like an Indian 139
Sawyer's Rest and Big Boy, Part II 140
Lou Hoffman Memorial Highway 141

Chang Hollow....................145
Lonely Boy....................151
Favorite Son....................154
The game of itsy bitsy....................155
A typical turkey hunt....................157
When it comes to shooting....................164
Bullets vs. hooks....................165
Eventually you wind up on Blue Dot....................165
Nightlife in the woods....................169
A light in the forest, a fisher on the run....................171
Champion chewer....................173
Porkies have a taste for camp....................174
Wily and wary....................176
Still going up....................179
A big ol' boy....................183
That empty feeling....................184
Oh, just humor me....................186
Lost!....................188
Deerly beloved....................190
Rest of the story....................192
THE DEER THING....................193
A clutch shot with Chauney's F-150....................196
A very chilly hunting trip....................198
The Wild Boy and Old SOB....................203
A mile away lived another hermit....................206
The flood within....................208
Chapter 3 - Splash!....................211
Catch of the day: Trout pans out as gift of the gods......214
A memorable fishing trip....................217
Why we fish often dictates where....................227
From a land of lakes to the riverside....................228
The rhythm of the river....................230
Living near a dam....................231
Teatime in Cly....................233
Getting upset....................234

A flourishing fishery 236
Night of the cereus..237
Two different kinds of fishing 238
The perils of hook and bullet.......................................239
Tiny hook, huge hurt 240
A regular patient 241
A winged one 242
Ray, ray, ray your boat...244
Sometimes it's where you get hung up … 247
… and sometimes it's how 248
Know your knots, sailor 250
Near Davy Jones' locker...252
The danger below 256
Sharking..257
Another finned opportunist...258
The bass are always up for a snack 261
Night falls as the bass rise 263
Watch your step 265
Sickness in the Susquehanna 266
Doing the write thing..268
The hunger to know...270
The bass seem to be bouncing back 272
Meanwhile, back at the office.......................................273
Are we seeing end of the American eel? 275
Enlisting in the eel effort 280
On the campaign trail 282
On the comeback trail..283
River cleaners ride the eel express 285
Killing one eel might wipe out 20 million....................286
Taking it personally 288
The season of relicensure 288
Location, location, location 289
Full to the brim 290
Water wisdom 292
FOR ANGLERS, IT'S TIME TO GO ON LINE 295

Rod 'n' reel create family bond 300
Christmas Eve call 311
The beauty of brevity..311
Church connections 315
Fisherman's prayer 319
A tense day at the office and same on the stream 319
To every rule there is an exception 322
The day panic punctured the peace 322
Seeing things through eyes of a wise man.....................324
TROUT FISHING IN AMERICA.................................326
What makes trouting special 329
The world of all things trouty.......................................332
Still life with fishermen 333
Special delivery 335
Rain Dance Weekend...340
The Sarvey story 343
A river in rebirth 346
A lesson on the road 349
Still more to learn out west 350
IF TROUT COULD TALK ... .352
The Answers 357
My best keepers 359
A man of the woods 359
Hunter/angler/computer guru smiled through it all 367
Just between friends at the trout stream 371
Chapter 4 - March! 375
Walking's greatest attribute 377
Catching up with a trailblazer.......................................378
$ome other dividend$ 380
Passing newspapers versus weed whacking in the
cemetery 381
Two routes to knowledge...382
History by the acre..385
Digging in on the eastern front 386
A flock of funerals 389

Figuring it all out 393
Walkin' in the rain 395
Life and times of the lowly leaf....................................397
Tracks reveal drama in the snow … 401
… as wind puts the tooth in winter's bite 403
Spring comes a-calling 405
Viva la fleur 408
City stroll reveals nature's glory // Wildwood Lake lotus colony a spectacular sight...411
Nature struts on an urban stage 413
1) The state of Penn-saw-drill-ia 414
2) Briefly, a little relief at DEP.....................................417
3a) This lady can take a punch 419
b) Our ticket to change at camp.....................................420
4) Predators are on the rise 422
5) Best offense is still a good defense 424

To Kay, my last wife, and in memory of Danny, a first-rate farmer

Chapter 1 - *Shush!*

Picking things up

At first they can't lift a thing,
including their tiny selves;
then overnight, it seems, they're
grabbing car keys off the shelves.

In between what comes to hand
oft directs what pops to mind,
and good guidance at such times
can be oh so hard to find.

Thus it is our young must learn
that a pitcher poorly versed
might yield a run, shatter glass
or do something even worse.

Doug, put that down -- it's someone else's!

Impromptu backyard tents were all
the rage in post-World War II America.

I WAS ABOUT a year old, according to Mother, when my first word came forth – "oudoo," uttered with face pressed to windowpane, a finger pointing outside our Great Barrington, MA, home. All my life I've been in love with and fascinated by the blue-domed laboratory that is the great outdoors. For a few summers as a child, I slept almost as many nights under stars as under roof.

Every kid picks things up and, eventually, puts them down. Some children like to throw objects, and I was in that group. Most often my favorite objects to toss, flip, skip or drop were rocks.

It all started in Pennsylvania with mud balls and a neighbor boy as the target. I honestly don't remember who lobbed the first messy missile, but we traded shots regularly – until the day it became apparent that he had the better aim. A mud ball containing a piece of glass sliced through an eyebrow and gave my new woolen jacket a blood bath.

Once the necessary stitches were in place, Mother marched to the thrower's front door and unleashed a verbal barrage heard all the way up the street at our house. This effectively ended the mud-ball war.

Brother Steve, 3 ½ years my junior, was another regular target. I was about 6 and we were playing in a creek close to our house in Rosemont, near Philadelphia, when I dropped a stone on his head from a bridge. I had selected a flat piece of sandstone and still can visualize it breaking cleanly in half upon impact and causing three splashes, one for each piece of rock and the third for Steve's face. We were very lucky little boys that day as he wasn't seriously hurt.

Not far from the scene of the sandstone drop was a fence that bordered land I later learned was controlled by Villanova University. It held free-ranging cattle and a stream and pond, which I explored with the much older Jeff McMullen. He coached me to climb a tree should any bulls get too close.

Near the stream we kept hidden a glass gallon jug to contain the snakes we caught. You kept the jug plugged with a just-the-right-sized stick or they'd escape. Jeff had a bow and strange arrows that suddenly stopped in mid-flight and fell to the ground for easy pickup. Called flu flu arrows, they were designed for launching at birds, and that's just what we did.

After scaling the fence one day, I was bitten between the thumb and forefinger by a squirrel that got upset when my supply of peanuts ran out. Which led to my first tetanus shot.

It was the pond, however, that provided my clearest memory of this haunt. One day Jeff and I lugged our fishing rods over the fence. About 10 years older, he could wade faster and farther – you know, out where the big ones were. I did my best to keep up, but it was getting too deep. Green pond scum was soiling my clothes and I knew Mom would blow a gasket. Then I lucked into a large submerged rock. Scrambling up on top, I had a better view of Jeff, now catching a fish.

And then – whoa! – the rock moved. I was standing on a turtle, probably a snapper, and getting off meant going back into that yucky water (which happened) and maybe being bitten in the process (which didn't). I don't remember how Mr. Turtle got out of the pond or over the fence. What I do recall is how he seemed to fill the trunk of the McMullen family car, where he was stowed for a one-way trip to the Philadelphia Zoo.

On to Michigan

Shortly after that Jeff enlisted in the Marines and we moved to Kalamazoo, where I broke a window at South Westnedge School, probably with a baseball, and paid the replacement cost, $1. The receipt is dated March 12, 1952.

My Michigan memories are few because our stay was brief. I recall snow, lots of it, and tobogganing within walking distance of home. My closest pal in K-city, as Dad called it, was Frankie Moss, who lived down our street and had the toboggan. Next-door playmate Johnny Sorensen completed the crew for the toboggan run that I remember best.

Our hill of choice was dotted with evergreens, about Christmas-tree-sized and planted haphazardly – perhaps to discourage tobogganing, we theorized. The trees made it tough to navigate a speedy descent, and that was key to having a good run out on the lake ice that began at the bottom.

On a great run you went so far that you only had time for one trip after school because already it was getting dark. We had a dandy like that the previous time out and were anticipating a repeat. It would be our last ride together.

I think I was up front but I'm not positive. In any event, we took a slightly different course than usual and went airborne – wow, this was going to be our best run ever! Then we landed on a rock, right under whoever was in the middle – Frankie, I guess, because he yelled loudest – and the toboggan got busted up. Well, at least no one was hurt.

Back to Pennsylvania

I was 9 when our family moved to Palmer Twp. in Northampton County, PA, where I discovered that touching the ceiling of an old Army tent while you're inside on a rainy day is like turning on a faucet. The spot you touch is where water seeps in, especially if there's a Monopoly board set up and the moola accumulated in a game now stretching into its fourth day is stacked neatly on the floor.

Can't remember who won the game, but I can still picture my opponent, Bobby Wetmore. He had red hair and freckles, and the tent was pitched in his backyard. The game had begun in an upstairs bedroom of the Wetmore home, which we fled one very humid August afternoon. I remember thinking later that our choice of canvas had been a dumb move. I mean, what did we think was going to happen when it got so sticky you could cut the humidity with a knife, as Mom loved to say. It was guaranteed to rain and that old canvas was going to leak.

But we were young and oblivious in a simpler era with a more relaxed parenting style. Hey, sometimes it was like they were downright unaware of us. Thus no adult intervened to save Bobby and me from the leak that not only ended our Monopoly match but also ruined the game and the box it came in. But we did learn our lesson, largely because the adults allowed us to make a mistake.

First the surgery, then they called Doc

Dr. Arthur M. Loope went to work in
the year of the Spanish-American War.

Neither of my grandfathers was much of a talker – especially Grampa Dohne – so I don't remember them telling many stories. One notable exception offers a glimpse of small-town life in the Gay Nineties.

Mother's father, Arthur M. Loope, started out in medical practice just as a new apple variety was being raised at the NY State Agricultural Experiment Station. The apple was named for Cortland, where Doc Loope was living in 1898.

One of his earliest calls, just weeks after hostilities ceased in the Spanish-American War, was to a Cortland County apple orchard. Someone, evidently tired of picking apples, had instead picked a fight with a co-worker.

"These men were gypsies, part of a large group traveling from orchard to orchard to take in the crop," Doc told us. "They had their own language, and they had their own ways.

"If you were challenged you had two options: turn and walk away or take out the large bandanna that every one of them seemed to have in a pocket or around the neck. To accept a challenge, a man clenched one corner of the bandanna in his teeth and extended another corner to his adversary.

"If it was accepted and placed in the mouth, the two men would be at arm's length and the knives came out. The slashing lasted until one of them was too seriously hurt to go on – or lost his nerve. Either way, someone would let go of the bandanna.

"This particular time there were lots of cuts on their arms and stomachs – and enough blood on the ground that they slipped and fell in it – that's what ended the fight. One fella needed six stitches and the other, three.

"The next day I received three live chickens in payment. They were tied together at the neck and handed over in a bushel basket."

Grampa Charles Dohne at 92.

Grandfather, you have such big ears

Grampa Dohne's ears seemed so large that as a boy I wondered if he could eavesdrop on my thoughts. No matter, I loved being at his elbow, learning to understand and respect my elder.

Most of my close friends in life have been older, a pattern no doubt deriving from the esteem for age and experience that I developed in childhood, mainly in the company of Grampa D.

My maternal great-grandfather lived down the street from the Dohnes in Syracuse. I'm unsure how Herman Roese earned a living, but he was an accomplished outdoorsman who regularly sold his best fish and game. Surely at least some of my outdoors inclinations came from him.

Another man I looked up to was the charismatic scoutmaster of the troop at nearby Palmer Moravian Church, Dr. Underwood. His love of long marches – into rural Palmer Twp. and beyond – dovetailed with my sense of adventure.

He had a knack for handling the grumbling that sometimes marked the troop's marches. Just as open revolt seemed imminent, our leader would be rescued by a deer or turtle crossing our path or maybe the shrill cry of a hunting hawk. It was amazing how often this happened.

The Underwoods had twin sons who were in our troop, and it puzzled me that they didn't look or act anything alike. One was short and chummy, the other tall and quiet. The only thing they had in common that I could see was their hair color (brown). Mother explained that the Underwood boys were fraternal twins, formed from separate eggs. She further informed me that fraternal twins, therefore, also could be brother and sister or two sisters.

Learning about the birds and the bees

Here was an opportunity for a mother to educate her 12-year-old son about the birds and the bees, and to her everlasting credit Mom dove right in. Recognizing my curiosity as natural and healthy, she knew she had my attention since I had raised the issue.

Her excellent timing was matched by a presentation that flowed smoothly yet included many pauses for questions. And boy did I fire away! Mother's handling of this delicate subject gave me a solid foundation for life. Somehow she took away most of the mystery without tarnishing the magic, and I have always admired and respected her for that special gift.

I knew several sets of identical twins, too, and with one of them, the Rissmillers, shared Scouting and gridiron connections. A year ahead of me in school and bigger, Don and Ron were linemen who blocked for the ball carriers (including me) in our midget football league. I think one of them and maybe both were doing exactly that earlier on the day my brother Carl was born. The umbilical cord was wound around his throat, and the doctor blamed Mom's jumping up and down on the sidelines as her eldest scored 1-2-3 touchdowns that October 1955 afternoon.

Carl W. Dohne

I was assigned sleeping quarters with the Rissmillers during a winter Scouting retreat at Camp Weygadt in Delaware Water Gap. We three were bunking in a cabin that was big enough for at least six. It was cold (8 degrees inside) and snowy outside, so much so that most of the planned activities never happened. The weekend amounted to a crash course in survival.

Someone didn't want to cook the steak his mom had packed, and I offered my hamburger in trade. Tasted great to me. Another clear memory is that the eggs froze in their shells – inside our cabin – and we were so counting on bacon and eggs that morning.

A greater problem: We were fresh out of wood and had to brave the elements to get more. Out we went – like the self-reliant young men we were in training to become – for all of about five minutes.

I don't know how much snow was down, but there was enough to complicate our task. At last finding a few paltry pieces, I looked up to check on the twins and could see only one of them. Not sure whether it was Ron or Don – I never could tell them apart for sure – but whoever it was had even less kindling than me. By the time we dragged our half-frozen butts back inside, his twin had unsheathed his trusty handsaw and cut most of the way through the 4-by-4 overhead support beam running the length of the cabin.

"It's oak!" he shouted, in the tone of a miner striking the mother lode. I don't remember whether we had bacon and eggs that day, but I do recall worrying if the cabin, minus that main support beam, could withstand the gale that persisted all day and night. Inside there was a whole lot of creaking going on. As far as I know, no one else ever mentioned that missing timber.

Father was a papermaker

The mere mention of wood brings to mind my father, William P. Dohne, who was our family's first collegian. He was a humble man who earned a baccalaureate degree and then a master's from Syracuse University's College of Forestry. Dad was the 50th person to receive an SU master's in forestry, and it happened during the school's golden anniversary year.

He worked as a paper chemist for Dixie Cup in Wilson Borough, a job that took him to Southern mills producing paper to hold the company's products. His job included formulating and then testing paper pulp – on the spot, early in the production run – to ensure it would perform adequately once turned into containers.

Dad won modest acclaim for his work, and there was a steady stream of social events at our house that attracted the Dixie papermaking fraternity.

Turns out that Father's mastery of all things woody had some grainy spots, one of which came to light dramatically in the early 1950s. The holidays were drawing near when Bobby Wetmore and I got an idea, a stroke of brilliance that would outshine even Christmas.

The Dohne homestead bordered on a farm field, which we saw as the perfect place to pile up Christmas trees that neighbors would discard after the holidays; then we'd torch 'em. Wow! This would be huge!

Trees were piling up

I don't recall much of any discussion about this adventure, maybe because it never really was formally presented to Mom and Dad. Remember, this was not the era of parental supervision so pronounced that many were living vicariously through their kids. No, this was the period that helped give rise to all that.

Out back the trees started accumulating, thanks in part to Terry Gibbs and Rich Brasefield, my football, pinochle and table tennis buddies from down the street. Rich's folks ran a hardware store, where he sometimes worked, and Terry's Dad drove a potato chip delivery truck.

Terry and Rich were early recruits to the cause, chipping in with their family trees and spreading the word about what was fast shaping up to be a memorable bonfire. Mt. Evergreen, as someone dubbed it, now had tree No. 21 at its summit, and some folks were bringing trees without even being asked.

Blaze Day plainly was drawing near. Though he never said so, at least to me, Dad must have realized that things were getting out of hand. A quiet man of action accustomed to meeting life head on, he announced at the table one afternoon that "Tonight is the night!"

It happened so quickly there was no time to contact Bobby. Or Terry, Rich or anyone else. No matter: This was a news event that would announce itself to all simply by happening.

Dad obviously had given some thought to igniting Mt. Evergreen – the how-to part, I mean. By the light of our Coleman kerosene lantern, he climbed among tree boughs, dousing here and there with gasoline from the lawn mower fuel can. Finally, he pulled back, put down the can and picked up a ball of newspaper he had prepared in advance. Putting match to paper, he tossed the ball underhand onto Mt. Evergreen.

There was a loud hissing sound, then a deafening whoosh! as Mt. Evergreen was transformed into Mt. Vesuvius. I never dreamed the fire would be so noisy – or that dried evergreen needles and small branches would shoot into the sky like Roman candles. With our attention riveted on the roaring flames, we didn't notice right away the ones racing in a line along the ground – in our direction!

Dad evidently had spilled some gas while retreating from Mt. Evergreen. Some apparently got on his trousers, too, because the flames ran right up one pant leg. Fortunately, his preparations had included drawing a pail of water, which he now put to use.

As the roar of the fire subsided slightly, other sounds crept in, such as voices in a crowd that now seemed to be everywhere. And sirens, lots of them, and they were getting louder.

In hindsight, there must have been repercussions from this risky stunt, but I honestly don't recall hearing about any. Most likely the adults involved simply accepted the consequences without whimper. How refreshing.

As an enduring reminder, I have a burn scar on the left thumb from carelessly grabbing the lantern during the bonfire. For his part, I think, Dad seemed to suffer more from embarrassment than physical injury. Whenever the incident popped up in conversation, even years later, he would flash a look of pure pain.

Journey into journalism started right out front

My language skills came from Mother, who dabbled in art – mostly ceramics – and poetry. Ruth Eleanor Loope Dohne was college educated (SU) and produced illustrated pamphlets packed with details of the Loope and Dohne clans, such as: One of our ancestors was an aide to Gen. George Washington and slept in his tent (before being hanged for horse thievery). Mom's handiwork gave me a personal appreciation of history and likely provided a push toward journalism.

A 51-year association with newspapers – like so many parts of my life – began outdoors and had a football flavor. I was barely 11 but tall for my age, big enough that the local newspaper carrier recruiter thought I was 12, the youngest allowed, when he saw me passing the ball with Rich and Terry in the yard. He never asked my age, and I never bothered to say.

Among the original 44 customers on my route lived a teen-age bully who threw stones or turned a garden hose on me, or both. Most days he didn't do anything but smile in an odd sort of way.

One afternoon I was getting stoned – using my (luckily still nearly full) paper bag to absorb the hits – when Don Gibbs intervened. Terry's dad was done with his daily deliveries, had parked the truck in his driveway and was probably looking forward to a cold beer. But his sense of justice delayed happy hour.

I don't recall the conversation, but I do remember the elbow he shoved into my tormentor's stomach to reinforce the message: Time to knock it off! Never did a darned thing to him that I know of, but the next week he beaned me with a golf ball when my back was turned. I showed it to Dad, and thereafter the bully's family was served via motor delivery.

This time the attack was provoked

If someone gets needled often enough, sooner or later he's going to fly off the handle – like brother Steve did one hot summer afternoon.

I loved to dig – just for the exercise, I guess – and was working on a hole worthy of use as a gravesite (in size if not location) out behind the garage. Steve was in the garage fixing his bicycle, and I had taken a break from digging to annoy him. Apparently I was succeeding because little brother now had a big claw hammer (it's always big when the other guy has it) in his hand and a nasty look in his eye. And he was staring at me.

Around and around the two-car garage we went. On my third trip past the picnic table – where years later Mom made me chew the pack of Red Man she caught me with till I was green in the face – I split for the house. Made it as far as the second porch step before something struck me high in the back, and suddenly I was falling into a black pit.

I imagined that hole out back had turned into my grave. The next thing I remember was Mom shoving something smelly (probably cotton soaked with ammonia) under my nose.

Regaining consciousness is a strange experience. My brother's tears of contrition contrasted greatly with his earlier angry glare. Then the claw hammer flew to mind and I knew I had it coming – and had gotten it. No serious injury resulted and, once again, the Dohne boys were very lucky.

Not a good match next door

One family whose Christmas tree did not wind up on Mt. Evergreen was the Folkensons' right next door. Those last three words of the previous sentence are telltale. Honestly, our two families were not well suited to be neighbors.

There were five of us – three being active boys – and a cat, a dog and a basketball hoop mounted on a garage that hugged the Dohne/Folkenson property line. Joe Folkenson, a house painter, and his wife, Marie, had no children and seemed to stay indoors a lot.

But one of them, usually Mr. F, always seemed to be around when a basketball, baseball or football came sailing in from Dohne land. Sometimes – probably after the game had been going on for what the Folkensons felt was long enough – he'd keep the ball. Later we'd find it resting just barely on our side and the time-out was over.

But it wasn't the occasional errant ball that really lit up the Folkensons; nope, it was BBs.

Birds had become a big part of life shortly after I got my first Daisy Red Ryder BB gun at about age 8. At first, target practice was restricted to a metal bird – the rooster weathervane atop our garage. The resulting ping of a BB striking metal was music to this young shooter's ears. Only thing was, the ricocheting pellets might rain on Folkenson property. That didn't seem like a big deal to me – until the night Mr. F came knocking on our kitchen door.

After Mother got up from the table and let him in, he reached out as if to shake hands, then instead let a bunch of BBs drop onto our linoleum floor.

"Now," he said, turning to leave, "you can pick them up just like we did, one at a time."

When Miss Daisy was the apple of Doug's eye.

I was in love with Daisy, but now she was gone

I lost the use of my BB gun for what seemed an eternity – almost a week. And of course when I got her back in my arms it was with strict instructions never again to shoot “in that direction.”

Truth was, that old weathervane was a pretty easy shot anyway, so I began taking Miss Daisy on walks that threaded through the tree rows bordering nearby farm fields. No more metal birds; it was time for the real thing. I have no idea how many winged targets fell to our BBs, but in sum probably a sizable flock.

By summer 1953, the BB gun was less apt to be in my hands and the bow and arrow more so – or maybe the handlebars of my Columbia. I adored that old bicycle – especially after taking off the fenders, thinking it would go faster. No fenders meant no protection against water streaming off the tires when gliding over wet surfaces. But it was dry the day I coasted into the driveway and heard Dad's excited but hushed greeting at the door.

Adventures in archery

"Hey, Doug, there's a rabbit out front," he said. "Get your bow!"

The bow in question was made of lemon wood, and the handgrip was honest-to-gosh-real alligator hide, which was showing wear in testament to my dogged pursuit of accuracy.

A cornstalk (from the field of the friendly farmer who hadn't objected to the rise or demise of Mt. Evergreen) was placed over the bull's-eye on the circular straw target in the backyard. The idea was to focus on something smaller than the target's 4-inch yellow center. And it worked: In no time the stalk was taking regular hits, and once an arrow was even split in Robin Hood fashion.

Back to the rabbit out front: It was sitting on the lawn, confident of its camouflage in the shade of a sycamore. Peering around a corner of the house, I judged the distance to Mr. Rabbit as about equal to my normal practice range. It was a broadside shot – hot dog! I pulled back and let ’er go right into my quarry.

Knocked down by the impact, the rabbit regained its feet and high-tailed it into a big azalea bush. Failing in my attempts to find or flush it, I gave up and headed in for supper. End of story.

More like the beginning, really. Next day, subscribers to The Easton Express (where later I would become a cub reporter) were reading:

Boy, 10, Admits Accuracy, Loses Bow To Police

A 10-year-old Palmer Township boy who wouldn't tell a lie is minus his archery equipment today.

Yesterday afternoon the boy, Douglas Dohne, son of Mr. and Mrs. W. R. Dohne of 153 Greenwood avenue, picked off a field rabbit with his bow and arrow. Acting on the complaint of a neighbor, Officer Bernard Hoffmeier, of the Palmer Township police, went to the Dohne home.

"Did you shoot that rabbit with a bow and arrow?" asked Officer Hoffmeier, somewhat sceptically.

"Yes, sir," replied Douglas.

Officer Hoffmeier confiscated the bow. He didn't take any arrows from the boy. The rabbit, stunned but not killed by the blow, ran off with Douglas' last arrow.

Douglas, who usually confines his shooting to a target his parents have set up in their yard, has been using the bow and arrow for about a year. He received the 70-inch bow as a gift last summer.

Steve & Doug, the early years.

I loved listening to Paul Harvey on the radio, and heard what he would have called "the rest of the story" a few days later from the township police chief.

Chief Wenner told us that the wounded rabbit had taken refuge in bushes by the Folkenson front porch, apparently just before Mr. F came out to read his evening newspaper. The rabbit was going through its death throes, a noisy thrashing event that upset its human witness. Spotting the arrow was the last straw; Mr. F called the cops.

The chief had white hair and a stern, direct manner, but my focus was on the bow – my bow – standing in the corner behind him. To get it back, he demanded my promise never again to aim an arrow at a living thing. He heard a barely audible "yes," but was deaf to the shouts of *No! No! No!* within.

My closest pal was Alfie

Rather than the windup, the rabbit incident was more like the launch of my archery escapades. Another one of them involved a big bird and a small fish; the former I tried to kill, the latter to rescue.

My closest friend at this point was Alfie Maleski, who had given me a deer-antler-and-rawhide necklace he claimed would make my chicken pox go away. I thought the necklace helped, but Mom threw it out when I came down with mumps, on both sides, even before the CP cleared up. She said we couldn't take any chances, but she never revealed what the chances were that we were taking.

Never mind, Alfie loomed large in my eyes. About a head taller, he had straight, jet black hair and high cheekbones. I was convinced he was at least part

American Indian and thus had certain innate abilities that I obviously didn't.

One day during archery practice when he suggested we take turns holding the cardboard target for each other, I volunteered to lead off. He got me dead center in the left wrist with his first shot, but I couldn't believe what happened next.

I think I stopped breathing for a moment as Alfie drew his hunting knife and rushed over in such a way that I instantly knew how little boys must have felt during Indian attacks on the frontier.

His dark eyes met mine as he came right up and plunged the knife into – look out – his left wrist! Then he pressed our wounds together, produced a hunk of rawhide – Alfie was real big on rawhide, never left home without it – and bound our wrists. He pronounced us "blood brothers, forever," completing our quick climb from imaginary adversaries to true friends.

Adding to Alfie's allure was his artistic ability. He could draw or sketch anything – which, at our age (12-13), meant girls! The fact that his parents let him have a .22-caliber rifle didn't hurt either.

Our rifle era was initiated by the simplest of invitations: "Wanna go rat shootin' at the dump?" Once we racked up 51 rat kills, taking turns with his little single-shot rifle at the Easton city dump. The best time for ratting was late in the day because they got bolder in fading light. The action really picked up right before dark.

Not far from the dump, on the same city-owned property about a mile from my home and even closer to his, was Hackett Pond. Once frozen over, its surface was soon packed with skaters. Then a warm spell would melt enough ice to chase the skaters and attract winter-weary waterfowl – and our attention.

One day we visited the pond with bow and arrow in hand. My memory is hazy about who was responsible for it, but a mallard was paddling around in tight circles, an arrow sticking out one side. The plan was for someone to crawl out on the receding ice, wait for the wind to push the duck close enough, then hook it by the neck with his bow.

Being smaller, I got the nod as retriever. All was going well – the bird was close enough to make the grab – when we heard a siren, then another. Easton Hospital wasn't too far away, but the sirens were getting louder, not softer as they would if an ambulance were headed up there.

A driver on nearby Route 22 must have spotted us and reported two boys in trouble on the ice. That was correct: There would be trouble if we got caught! Our retreat was reluctant but hasty.

Nearing shore, I spied a little catfish frozen in the ice a few inches below the surface. I knew even as I ran that I'd be back to rescue the fish and satisfy my curiosity. *Are you really alive?*

Returning the next day, without Alfie, I chopped out a chunk of ice containing the fish, deposited it in a canvas bag and headed home. *This is better than if the duck had wound up in the bag!*

Along the way I considered how best to revive the fish – if it was alive. *If you are, I'll take care of you, forever.* By the time I reached Five Points, "Finny" had surfaced from the pool of potential names swimming around in my head.

Even in the mid-Fifties this was a bustling, dangerous intersection that marked the main entrance to Palmer Twp. from the east. It had no traffic light. What it did have was five intersecting streets. As I scampered across one of them the bag slipped from my grasp and fell right in front of a truck which ran over it, crushing ice, fish and – temporarily, thank goodness – my adventuresome spirit. I can still visualize the pinkish spot.

Lake Harmony, here we come

In 1955, Mom and Dad acquired a two-unit cottage on Lake Harmony in Pennsylvania's Pocono Mountains. Less than an hour's drive from our home, the new cottage quickly replaced Grampa D's cabin in upstate New York as our regular getaway spot. It was about 6 hours by car to Panther Lake – a long trip, even with the Animal Crackers that Mom always packed.

So, we were happy about the shorter-travel-longer-visit aspect of Lake Harmony, but there was a price to pay.

The original owner was a minister, and he named the larger of the two units Merry Land and the smaller, which he rented out (as did we), Sky Pilot.

But there was an owner between the pastor and us, and that fellow – a Mr. Youse of Lehighton – let the place run down before selling out.

There were several Fibber McGee's closets – and enough stuff left behind to fill a few more. There was a collection of 78 rpm Guy Lombardo records. The stack – originally 20 inches high, at least – had melted into one big blob of vinyl, now 15 inches tall, thanks to improper storage. Obviously, Mr. Youse (who quickly became "Yousie" to us, as in the rhetorical "Yo, Yousie, what's this for!") was a guy who spent too much time collecting and not enough taking care of what he already had.

So the promise of more lake time was, well, maybe a little misleading. There was something in need of attention everywhere we looked:

The floors needed to be re-covered, walls inside and out (of course I only wanted to do the latter) were begging to be scraped and repainted, the docks screamed for repair, trees reached out for a trimming (including one with a big limb that Dad later sawed off while standing on it, the 20-foot fall from which he somehow survived without a scratch), and a boathouse so dilapidated we'd have to replace it.

Steve and I were hot to tackle the boathouse – primarily because Dad had just bought a 14-foot Aluma Craft and 18-hp Johnson outboard motor – but the other more mundane jobs were assigned higher priority.

It turned out Dad was right about that because while dismantling the old boathouse would be easy, removing the big hemlock butt snug against it would not. That tree should have been taken out – stump and all – before the original boathouse was erected, as its presence had dictated a structure so narrow it was difficult to use.

What youth lacks in finesse and understanding it tries to make up for with brute force applied relentlessly. When it was time to remove the stump, I got the job and went at it with vigor.

That old stump, its roots sunk as deep in the lake bottom as (Uncle Chuck liked to say) the government's hands are in your pockets, was as tough and sinewy as any living tree. It seemed to laugh off the ax blade, and I took it personally, pressing the attack. Eventually it capitulated, but not before its conqueror learned to slow down and think his way forward, a good lesson for life.

The author at age 11.

Panther Lake still owned a piece of our heart

Meanwhile, with all the work at Lake Harmony, Grampa's cottage regained some magnetism. In truth the two places were quite different.

At Panther Lake, for instance, all the neighbors knew one another and did things together. There was a Memorial Day Regatta, and just about everyone on the lake would decorate and enter a boat in the parade. Prizes and friendly side wagers marked the event, which launched the summer boating season.

Once the lake was closed to boating after a drowning. It took three days for a diver to locate and recover the body. A father dove to save his young son's life, but lost his own. The boy had fallen in while they were crossing the lake to O'Connell's Point.

The roughly rectangular lake was half a mile wide, three times as long, and quite deep in spots. I remember all this because of occasional swims across the lake with my water-rat cousins (always led by Alice Ferris, who was older than us), and crossings by rowboat – just as the dead man had, to purchase Mrs. O'Connell's fresh homemade bread.

Panther Lake's cottages went only about halfway around, so one end was quiet and abounded in lily pads and fish. We sometimes saw deer on the shoreline. Grampa's cottage was the next to last one on our side of the lake before you came to the stone wall that marked the farmer's property line.

This was a place where you lived very close to nature, meaning raccoons, loons, frogs and, of course, snakes. On bright days while lunching on the front porch, we watched as water snakes sunned themselves on the docks from which we had been fishing only minutes before.

After dessert the challenge was to vanquish the invaders, a task which delighted the boys but daunted the girls – except for Alice, who would join right in. She became my hero. Her brother, Warren, built a birch-bark canoe and could skipper a sailboat. He was high on my list, too.

One day we found a huge bullfrog struggling in the water near the docks. The frog couldn't quite swallow the snake it had taken on, literally head to head. In fact, the job was only about half done.

Grampa used a boat oar to guide the combatants toward shore and then flipped them up on land. He yanked the snake from the frog's mouth and – in the spirit of fair play – turned both loose. The frog made it back into the water, but the snake just lay there, by all appearances dead.

Next morning Mr. Bullfrog was belly up on the shoreline, waves rhythmically banging his swollen carcass against the rocks, and the snake was gone. Grampa said that didn't necessarily signal survival – it could have fallen prey to a raccoon overnight.

Rainy days on the porch

Rainy days – and you always had lots of those in New York – were special, too. Father's sisters, Helen Ferris (Alice and Warren's mom) and Laura Kohles, with help from the latter's daughter, Janet, maintained a big box of comic books.

We crowded with our younger cousins – Allen, Brian and Judy Dohne, and Linda and Robby Raleigh and later on their brother, Peter Hess – into gliders on the big porch out front overlooking the lake to pore over the latest adventures of Superman, Red Ryder, Roy Rogers, *et al*. Under roof and screened in, it was the next best thing to being outdoors, but you had to lean in from the screen so the drizzle wouldn't get down your neck.

If you tired of comics, you could reach for a fishing rod. There were always plenty of those at camp, and when the line on one got balled up during use you simply reached for another. Those with fouled lines were parked in a corner of the porch. Somehow the challenge to untangle them was more acceptable on those damp days when you had nothing better to do than on sunny ones when you did.

The adults logged a lot of porch time playing pinochle, often dealing in Alice and Warren or our other senior cousins, on mother's side, Karen and Donny Zimmerman. On sunny days, sometimes accompanied by their parents, Aunt Irma and Uncle Zim, they played a hand to see who would wash the dishes, but on rainy days it might take a whole game. Well, at least they weren't untangling fishing lines.

P.L. 54

Cousins admire … hey, wait a minute, that looks just like the fish Doug had!

Uncle Abe's woodlot

Aunt Helen's husband, Abraham, was a quiet man, an electrician by trade. He was a guy who liked to get away from it all – so much so that he bought 250 forested acres a few miles from Panther Lake. Uncle Abe regularly disappeared for most of the day, and everyone knew where he was, though he never said much upon returning.

One day – I might have been or 10 – he invited me to go along huckleberry picking. You picked into a tin can attached to a string draped from your neck so the container would hang at belt level, just right to drop in the berries.

It was nice having both hands free to work, but it was suddenly even more meaningful when a snake slithered between my sneakers and I instinctively grabbed tree branches to help stay upright.

Uncle Abe calmed me down by pointing out nearby signs of bear and deer and the feather he said was from a wild turkey. It began to make more sense when he explained that we were visitors who had not been invited by "the locals," as he called the animals. We had to step quietly and carefully, he said, adding "Remember, they didn't know we were coming, right?"

Ontario beckons

Lake Harmony was shaped like a frying pan, and most of the fish we caught there – unlike many taken from Panther Lake – easily fit in a skillet. Too easily.

Though they were about the same size, LH had more motorboats and far more water-sport activity than PL, and it was obvious that the fish – and therefore the fishing – were affected by it. That registered with me because, at about 13, I had been spoiled by my first fishing trip to Canada.

Mom and Dad took us to a lake in Ontario where a Dixie co-worker, Bill Laudermilch, had rented a cabin. Dad took me fishing the first afternoon, even though someone told us, “The fish up here don’t bite at midday.”

Well, he was right, there wasn’t much action – except for one cast. My surface lure took a powerful slam, the fish darting all over the place before yielding to net. With a belly that smacked of sunrise, it measured 12 ¼ inches, still my biggest sunny.

Welcome to Canada: Day I, Part II

More adventure and another lunker awaited us that night, this time with a different outcome. Dad was in the middle, rowing, and I was in the bow with Steve at the stern.

We were using nightcrawlers on the lake bottom and not having much luck. Dusk was settling in and Dad decided it was time to pull up and head home. The words were no sooner off his lips than a fish was on my line, a real rod-bender that wasn’t coming up easily.

Finally the fish gave in a bit and came toward the surface. Then he dove and hugged bottom again.

Next he surprised me with a charge and came right up where we could see him. His mouth looked big enough to chomp a grapefruit!

That's when Dad stood up (a mild violation of the rules he had laid out for us) and committed the cardinal sin – grabbing the line. He was more excited than we were.

When the line snapped and Mr. Bigmouth sped off, Dad sat down, head in hands like he was about to bawl. Then he apologized so profusely that both of us promised never to tell anyone about it. He died in '93, so I'm thinking it's OK now.

Another highlight of the trip came as Mr. Laudermilch returned one night from fishing. He had an old noisy outboard motor and somehow was unaware his fishing lure was in the water and the line had run off down to the knot.

So he was quite surprised when the rod sprang nearly out of the boat. Quickly slowing and coming about, he discovered that a fish apparently had been hooked (in the mouth, indicating it had attacked the lure, not vice versa) and soon was giving him quite a tussle. The bass stretched out exactly 20 inches on the picnic table.

Lake Harmony was more populous

Lake Harmony, in contrast to Panther Lake, was shallower in depth but deeper in residential development. Cottages – some of them beautiful year-round residences – dotted most of its perimeter, and it had popular hotel resorts at either end.

You could – and we did on occasion – walk around the lake. It took an hour and a half, give or take 15 minutes, and was one of my favorite pastimes. Most often I made the trip solo. Looking back, one difference from Panther Lake was that you knew fewer of the folks whose cottages you passed. The sense of community was stronger at PL.

Our motorboat was powerful enough for water skiing, in which we reveled. After making a model steam engine – and yes, by cracky, it worked – Steve talked Dad into "shaving the head" of the outboard motor so we could go faster.

However, for a really speedy trip you wanted my several years older buddy in the camp next door, Ralph "Butch" Hechler, to tow you on skis. His wooden boat had a 25-hp Evinrude and, besides being superior for towing skiers, it was great for picking up girls.

The last time I saw Butch

My enduring memory of him has nothing to do with the fairer sex or my first taste of beer, which came in his boat and made me sick the whole next day. It was Labor Day and bye-bye day all rolled into one for Butch and me.

A recent Navy enlistee, he was off to marry the beautiful Annette, but first we were going to water-ski one last time – all day, we vowed, or until we ran out of gas. We had 10 gallons of that and were brim full of teen-age enthusiasm.

One thing we did not have was ideal weather. It was cold and windy and whitecaps greeted the eye that September 1959 morn. One thing in our favor was that practically no other boats were on the water. *Gee, I wonder why.*

Against adult advice, we launched our mission. Butch would ski for half an hour while I piloted his boat, then we'd swap places. By lunchtime our 30-minute shifts had collapsed to 15.

We were determined young men deaf to warnings of danger, delivered over lunch, by my parents and, in Butch's case, his grandparents. "You're getting wind burned!" "You can't go back out there after eating for at least half an hour or you'll get cramps!" "When you're tired is when you make mistakes!"

Back out on the water, the first gas can was empty in half an hour, restoring our confidence. My cheeks felt fiery but, glancing at Butch and noting his cherry-red glow, I reached for the second can anyhow.

On and on through the afternoon wind and waves we skied, gritting our teeth as we whacked along over the whitecaps. Whether we were up to the challenge to finish what'd started hours ago now seemed in doubt.

We were down to switching from skier to driver about every five minutes when the engine finally sputtered and quit (still the only time I can ever remember being happy to run out of gas).

Now all we had to do was paddle – and the wind, all day our adversary, now lent a homeward drift. My last memory of that day – and of Butch – is of how similar in color his legs and the gas can were as he walked off with it. Hey, I was in the same boat.

Cousin Karen takes the towrope

I recall one other scarlet-skinned water skier, but hers was no case of sunburn. Karen is the only cousin I can remember visiting at Lake Harmony. And of course, she wanted to go water-skiing. Her Uncle Bill tried and tried, but each time she wound up on her back in the water, skis pointed at the boat, the towrope once again raking her legs.

Finally, sheer grit lifted her briefly atop the lake in skis. Bright red thighs screamed the price was too high, but her silent smile denied it. Bob Karnei was not yet a doctor, Karen's husband or even present; still, this old man can imagine him nodding to the patient, then prescribing – and yes, *dispensing!* – a congratulatory kiss, just as if it'd really happened.

At the time, a boy said, "Welcome to the club, cuz!"

So long, Alfie

By now Alfie Maleski and I were headed in opposite directions: He was off to school in Easton, while I chose Wilson High.

Kids in Palmer Twp. – Steve and little Carl included – would lose the right to choose under the pending school district jointure. They'd all be going to Easton. The last to have a say was my gang, the Wilson Borough High School Class of 1961.

We were 14 or 15 the last time I saw Alfie. He tackled me – with gusto – in the Easton vs. Wilson jayvee football game. We led at halftime but they walked away winners. The long (and lopsided, in their favor) grid rivalry also ended with the jointure.

My first shotgun cost $5

Another neighbor, Allen VanHorne, stepped into my life at this point. He was two years my junior but way ahead when it came to hunting because his uncle took him afield.

While deer hunting in Connecticut, the uncle found a double-barreled 16-gauge shotgun leaning against a tree. He gave it to his nephew, who sold it to me. Rust had obliterated the gun-maker's markings, so its origins were a mystery.

I was able to restore some of the finish with a bluing kit, then took it to a gunsmith in Easton. He tightened the action but warned against overuse.

Of course I had to try it out just a few days later. It was after school – and after passing my papers, too – that Allen and I set out into a cornfield in search of ring-necked pheasant.

Our late start darkened the whole outing. How I mistook the stately great horned owl for a noisy ring-neck is hard to imagine. All you really need to know is that the former is active at night, the latter by day.

Allen abhorred my blunder because I had broken some of the basic rules of hunting that his uncle had drilled into him. I was hunting after hours, unlicensed, and failed to properly identify my target, which was a protected species. Allen didn't say anything and he didn't have to. I was deeply ashamed and already off on a guilt trip.

Birds have played a big role in Doug's life.

A living monument to flexibility

There was another event – much less public, mercifully, than the Mt. Evergreen episode – involving Dad and a tree.

In our back yard was a willow whose roots seemed to be everywhere and complicated grass mowing considerably.

The worst verbal abuse, however, was aimed at the tree during family croquet games. Its roots were forever re-routing those colorful wooden game balls and thus distorting the outcome. Dad would utter a "dammit!" and immediately receive Mom's curt "William!"

Mother Nature came to the rescue when a late-winter storm coated our world with 3 inches of ice, forcing the willow parallel to the ground and eventually flattening it.

The tree grabbed our attention that spring by slowly righting itself. This performance won the willow a certain star status, and the griping about the inconvenience of its roots withered.

All of that began to change the day a man came to pump out our septic tank and found – horrors! – roots from our monument to flexibility where they shouldn't be, couldn't be. He said willows were notorious for invading septic systems and almost certainly it would recur.

In a brief after-dinner discussion Mother made it clear that any sentiment in favor of preserving the willow could not be allowed to override practicality.

Mom was good at accenting her words with body language:

"If it happens again," she said, then fell silent. But she was wagging an index finger, which obviously did not bode well for friend willow.

Despite the tree's apparent reprieve, Steve and I were not surprised when Dad declared the next Saturday morning that the tree would come down that very day.

Reading reluctance in our faces, he knew he had to bring us on board for the project. After all, that was how our family did everything – together. His approach was to assign us specific duties. My job was to wield the hatchet at those hated surface roots while Steve was handed a rope and directed to climb up and tie one end fast to the tree.

The severing of the roots was proceeding so slowly that Dad and Steve had to help. The idea was, once the willow was minus the support of its roots we'd tie the other end of the rope to the bumper of our 1954 Mercury and pull it over. For some reason, pitting car vs. tree excited Steve and me. Dad was delighted that finally we were 100 percent into the task.

Everything went as forecast: The willow wobbled a bit once those roots were cut, and yes, by golly, the Merc had the power to topple the tree. But Dad's moment of triumph was fleeting because he had come up short on one detail: The rope wasn't long enough, and the tree fell on the car, knocking him to the ground.

Trapped at the wheel by branches that held her captive, Mom frantically barked out the orders:

"Ye gods and little fishes! Don't just stand there! Help your father! Get me out of here! Now!"

Father suffered a sprained shoulder and, of course, more bruising of the ego. For a forester, the poor guy suffered a lot of psychological splinters. Much easier to fix was the dent in the car roof from the willow's wallop: We simply pushed it out from inside.

The brothers Dohne at the wheel. Behind them is the car that wound up beneath the willow.

Pulling down the willow tree with the family car backfired when the tree landed on the vehicle.

Three of us skipped school

Playing hooky was a rare thing in my boyhood, with one notable exception. I don't recall whose idea it was or how we got to Bushkill Creek, but it must have been opening day of trout season because the stream was jammed.

I remember there were three of us, but I'm unsure who was along. I thought one of them was Bobby Aber, but years later my former classmate was unable to confirm it. Abe lived with his grandparents, the Cregars, who were customers on my paper route, and his granddad ran the potato chip operation where Terry's father worked.

What I recall vividly is the image of Gordon Hicks glaring down from the Bushkill Park Bridge. Yes, Mr. Hicks wore a fishing vest and carried a rod, but he wasn't just another fisherman. He was the dreaded truant officer of Wilson High.

Mr. Hicks locked eyes with me briefly, then smiled broadly and moved on. I'd never before seen the stern ex-football coach come anywhere close to smiling. Neither, so far as I knew, had anyone else. *Uh-oh, this could end very badly.*

I visualized myself standing in the corner of his office for endless hours on sunny afternoons when I could be fishing. Then I pictured myself on a street corner, cleaning vehicle after vehicle and wondering just how many free car washes Mr. Hicks (everyone called him that, every time) had promised. He was known for innovative punishment.

With both of those alternatives so unappetizing, I chose instead to interpret Mr. Hicks' smile as a good thing. Now I saw it as a signal that somehow everything was OK because fishing was such a special endeavor and we were all members of the esteemed, ahem, Trout Brotherhood. Which, apparently, was pretty close to the truth because – as best I can recall – our fishing trio went unpunished, and Mr. Hicks even flashed me another smile, albeit years later.

One final stone

Another victim of my rock-throwing – the last as it turned out – was Roger Boger. Somewhat serious and quite focused as a youth, Roger was a neat guy and belonged to DeMolay International.

Rog tried to recruit me into DI, an organization dedicated to helping young men develop into leaders. Lord knows I could have benefited from membership, but I chose not to join, just as I declined Mother's invitation of piano lessons.

My relationship with Rog was built primarily on athletics: We were sprinters on the Wilson track squad and backfield teammates on the gridiron. I recall one heat – it was only a practice run, darn it – when we finished the hundred neck and neck in 10.1 seconds.

Rog was our quarterback and I was a halfback. He had really good ball-handling skills, which off the field he put to use as an amateur magician. In contrast, my hands too often seemed to do the kinds of tricks that all the rest of me eventually regretted.

The Bogers invited me along one weekend to their summer home in the Poconos, and Rog was showing me around a neighborhood that included cottages in various stages of construction. With no workmen present, it was time for us to explore. Just as our adventuresome spirit hit full stride, Rog announced he had to take a break and dashed off into some bushes.

I was such an active kid that sometimes boredom was a problem – in this case all it took was a few moments. I hollered that break time was over and, getting no reply, picked up a rock and lobbed it in there to prod him a bit. Rog didn't reappear for quite awhile, and when he did he came staggering toward me, hands to forehead. Over and over he said, "It's OK – I'm all right."

But he couldn't see the size of the lump (about half an egg) and probably didn't know how big a rock (whole egg) I'd heaved. We found a well and turned a T-shirt into a cold compress. I nearly threw up a very good breakfast before coming to accept as true what Rog kept repeating, "It's OK – I'm all right."

The first thing he said – after that last "It's OK – I'm all right" – was, "Mom's gonna cry," which in turn made me weepy. *Too late, Doug, you dummy. You had better knock it off!*

The Bogers handled the incident in private – shades of Mt. Evergreen/Mt. Vesuvius – and none of them ever mentioned it – to me, at least. In his own special way and long before he became Dr. Boger, Rog cured me of the nasty habit of throwing things at people. We remain close friends to this day.

Picking up the javelin

A season of change was under way as I began to drive the family car. I was learning a lot behind the wheel and maturing in other ways, too.

Recognizing that I was unprepared to hunt safely, I put down my weapons, and Mom gave away the shotgun at first chance. In what seemed even worse punishment, she put my complete Elvis Presley record collection (each still in its original jacket) in the church rummage sale. *Wonder what those little 45s would fetch today?*

By now I was running and throwing on the track and field team, which set the stage for a casual acquaintance with an upperclassman to mature into friendship.

A year older and at least a foot taller than me, John Telepo once scored 53 points for Wilson High on the basketball court. His coach encouraged him to try out for track and field that spring.

Sizing up the new recruit, T&F coach Frank Martenis decided unofficially to entrust me with his development. As the anchor on the javelin squad, I would help this lanky prospect learn to chuck the stick, as Coach liked to say.

John and his brother lived at the Easton Children's Home. I couldn't imagine what their personal lives were like, but there probably was no Mt. Vesuvius or bird hunting with a BB gun in their background.

When it came to throwing things, John T. was all about basketballs and baseballs, certainly not the javelin. Starting out, he was strong but stiff, athletic yet strangely awkward and anemic at the throwing line.

It struck me that JT no doubt could throw the javelin – hey, he could hold a basketball with one hand and toss a baseball from deep center to home plate with the other. All it would take was a little instruction and encouragement. I was less confident about the assignment than Coach seemed to be, but after all, he was an ex-Marine.

Big John's initial progress came quickly but stalled when his throws began equaling mine in competition. I told him that failing to test his full potential would be the most embarrassing thing of all

– for both of us. He responded by beating me and every other opponent by at least 10 feet in the next meet.

We took our dates to the prom, which fell the night before the district T&F competition, and stayed out late partying, then competed the next morning against spear throwers from several dozen other schools. Wilson was first up and, by now the anchor of our squad, Big John's first toss was a respectable effort – and so was mine, about 3 or 4 feet behind.

After the initial round we were leading the field. Coach came over and asked whether we wanted to know our distances. Shaking our heads in unison, we led off the second round, neither able to best his first attempt.

And that's how it went the rest of the way. We failed to exceed our initial efforts – and so did everyone else. We collected gold and silver but for some reason never went on to the state finals. I guess it just would have been anticlimactic.

Yes, there was a dark side

My largely positive view of boyhood springs from a natural bent. It's in my DNA, and I'll be the first to admit that at times the can-do approach has led me directly into deep doo-doo.

Throughout life I've paid the dues of a confirmed optimist, just as the perennial pessimist renders his. I mention this only to help clarify the overall impression that you, dear reader, might be getting.

Indeed, there was a Dohne dark to contrast with the Dohne lite, and no account of my boyhood outdoors would be complete without mention of its lowest point: I was sexually abused at age 9.

It happened only once and never seriously dented my psyche. In golf they call it a mulligan; in life it's known as getting a second chance. I gave the offender an opportunity not to do it again, and so far as I know it worked. The perpetrator died before I was old enough to grasp the main reason to report abuse: to protect yourself and others. I should have spoken up but didn't.

Dad maintained various handwritten files, one of which came to light only recently. While focusing on the Folkensons, it offers a view of Mom and Dad that conflicts with my recollections.

The Dohne/Folkenson relationship that emerges from this source is not very pretty. Dad specified what to do "if they phone and are angry": "Hang up immediately." If they "come on our property," we are to "order them off and, if they don't leave, call police." Under no circumstances, he wrote, "are we to go on their property."

The word "lawsuit" pops up, and his notes indicate that he and Mother discussed the situation with Chief Wenner and the Rev. Floyd Petersen, our minister. And at least once Dad called for police help to retrieve Allen's basketball from the Folkensons. So much for my portrait of relaxed parenting!

Mother and Father had a penchant for secrecy regarding health issues. Both underwent cancer surgeries and other medical procedures that somehow always came to light after the fact – in some cases years later.

I guess they were just trying to let us lead a carefree childhood. In my case, it worked out splendidly, if temporarily.

Where are they now

Some of my childhood chums have vanished like blackbirds on a moonless midnight. Here's what I know:

Dr. Robert Aber directs the Department of Medicine at Penn State University's Hershey Medical Center. Abe and his wife, Karen, live near Hummelstown, PA.

Dr. Roger Boger put down his dentistry tools and, in midlife, picked up the pen. As an entrepreneur in the wellness industry, he travels widely to promote proactive health choices. His second book is due out this year. Rog and his wife, Karen, live in Dublin, Ohio.

Richard Brasefield had a rewarding career with DuPont. Typically quiet as a kid, Rich the man is an entertaining emcee, as demonstrated at the WHS Class of 1961's 50th anniversary reunion. This ardent boater and his wife, Nancy, reside in Elkton, MD.

***Carl Dohne** is a dental lab technician, a magician in the medium of porcelain and rare metals. He and his wife, Susan, and their large family live in Eustis, FL.

***Steven Dohne** worked in three states and traveled abroad as a mechanical engineer for Armstrong. Now retired, he and his wife, Lynn, live near Lancaster, PA.

D. Terry Gibbs, after a career blending beverage sales and counseling, lives with his wife, Joanne, in Glenside, PA.

Alfred Maleski's artistic ability eventually led him to the U.S. Mint and a career in engraving.

John Telepo bounced into a successful business career in the Chicago area following his days as player and coach.

**What's in a name: Grampa Dohne's parents named him Karl William, but he didn't care for it. On the first day of school he told the teacher his name was Charles Dohne, to which he answered the rest of his life. Carl's middle name is William, honoring our father and grandfather, but the Karl/Carl thing came to light only after Carl's baptism – which followed Steven Charles Dohne's birth by eight years. Douglas Arthur Dohne, born less than 15 months after the Pearl Harbor bombing, was named in a shared salute to Mother's father, Dr. Arthur M. Loope, and Gen. Douglas MacArthur. The family of Doc Loope's mother, Catharine R. Crysler Loope, inserted an "h" before sharing their name with the automobile.*

Chapter 2 - *Bang!*

Why we hunt
To loose an arrow
or pull the trigger
is but one small part
of something bigger.

Nimrod takes to woods
not just blood to spill,
but from instinct deep
that he must fulfill.

His re-acquaintance
with nature's beauty
brings satisfaction
to age-old duty.

THE WILD TURKEY was a thriving species under American Indian rule. The big bird was relatively easy prey for the red man and, later, the whites, but the Colonists and their descendants abused the privilege and relentlessly depleted the stock. Nor were the deer in any better shape.

By the time the Pennsylvania Game Commission came along in 1895, the woods were nearly fresh out of venison and drumsticks.

Bringing law and order to the forest was the crucial first step, but it didn't come easily: Three state game wardens were shot dead in 1906, and seven more were wounded. There was no such thing as a hunting license in those days. That started in 1913, at a price of $1. In the end, the protectors prevailed and the animals responded by staging an astonishing comeback.

The turkey chapter of my life began in the spring of 1966 right next to a big pink-and-white chunk of quartz in front of our home in York New Salem. My wife had decided this rock that glistened in sunlight was the ideal piece to accent the entry to our property, further determining that the perfect spot to display it was about 10 feet from where it sat. But no matter what I tried or how hard I struggled the stone stood its ground. Words were being exchanged, and things were not going well.

We had just moved in, so at first I didn't recognize the cavalry riding to my rescue. There were no galloping horses and/or blast of bugle, just a family arriving by station wagon at their home across the street. I sensed help was at hand when G. John Martin strode our way. Bless his heart, he was well over 6 feet tall, and would you just look at those shoulders!

That blasted rock got moved in about 5 minutes, and although neither of us knew it, this simple act of neighbor helping neighbor was the foundation for a friendship that would span more than half a century and take us thousands of miles together.

Our wives had met when Peg Martin brought over a homemade pie in welcome. As our families mingled and summer stretched toward autumn, I began using the Dutchified version of Johnny, "Chauney," a good fit in a neighborhood where German descent was common.

Other tongues were heard there, too, of course. One rather outspoken and unabashedly gaudy resident was an Asian immigrant with a decidedly Greek-sounding name, Phasianus C. Torquatus. Chauney had a dog, and one day we tracked this fellow down in a field and shot at him.

Nor were we alone: Shotgunners everywhere had been welcoming the ring-necked pheasant with open bores since shortly after his 1880s arrival in North America.

The ring-neck, classified as a game bird here in 1902, favors a habitat of open fields and weedy/ brushy fence lines, which Pennsylvania farms had plenty of in the 1960s. The iridescent copper-and-gold plumage of the male is twinned with a red face and a crisp white collar. His stentorian, rooster-like crowing can be heard up to a mile away.

The flush of a cockbird is a furious and raucous event usually preceded by a lot of walking and running as the bird shows his true colors: A stand-his-ground kind of guy the pheasant is not. Provided he has enough cover, his instinct is to run first and flush later and – to the consternation of gundog and hunter – he's very good at it.

Hunting over a dog was new to me, and I loved the learning experience. Chauney's German shorthaired pointer, Sugar Babe, brought a marvelous work ethic and what seemed like unlimited stamina to the task of leading hunter to quarry. She did everything but pull the trigger.

Our hunting time was curtailed, however, because my new friend was a state game protector and, especially during autumn, he was busy monitoring other hunters. His days off in the fall were as scarce as elephants running wild in the York County district he patrolled. Most often when setting out to hunt we wound up answering not the call of the wild but the call of duty.

Pennsylvania's launch of spring turkey hunting was a godsend for two wannabe hunting buddies separated by terms of employment. With no turkey flocks in his district, Chauney was free to hunt them elsewhere.

By Christmastime 1967 our womenfolk were weary of hearing about plans for the upcoming wild turkey chase.

Doug and Gold Strike with a daily
limit of ring-necks in the 1960s.

Doug and Dave Dohne head home after a day in pursuit of
pheasant. Photo by Jim Bradley of The Patriot News, 1973.

Father and son with bounty of woods and field.

My first turkey hunt

Our May 1968 hunt was staged out of the Martin family's station wagon near English Center, Lycoming County.

I can still recall that first morning and Jack Frost's fingers knifing through the blankets while scrawling his signature coat of white. We had parked along a creek and left the rear window open. The next night, trying to avoid a repeat creek-side chill, we were jack-lighted like deer by pranksters who spotted our vehicle on a hillside.

Not long after sunup two uniformed men (game protectors, I think) approached and told us we were parked illegally. Then the more talkative one, whom Chauney seemed to know, gave us an impromptu turkey-talk lesson using a diaphragm-style mouth call.

Shortly after that we got more company as father-and-son Realtors Ben and Mike Sweigart of York showed up. Rain drove our foursome into the tight quarters of Chauney's car with the newcomers sitting up front.

Someone suggested poker, and we used a hunting hat to hold the pot. I wasn't doing very well; in fact, I was losing badly.

We were parked by a decent sized trout stream which, in spite of a light rain, succeeded in luring me into trying my luck at fishing.

Pulling on hip boots, I waded in, turning my back against a breeze as I worked upstream. When the rain picked up it made hearing difficult, and I wasn't watching where I was going very closely either – until a sudden movement nearby grabbed my attention.

Carelessly wading to within five steps of a black bear that also wasn't staying very alert gave us both a jolt. Bruin was intent on finding whatever snack lay beneath the huge flat rocks that he (she?) was flipping like pancakes.

Suddenly full of, um, courtesy, I made the first move to clear the watery path over which our eyes now briefly met. My retreat was casual enough to avoid being described as running away, but somehow I did manage to slip and fall in.

Back at camp, the poker players took a break to have a good laugh. When I got back on my feet and sneaked a peek, the bear was still looking for lunch in the rocks.

Ben, Mike's dad, won the award for compassion that day, lending me a pair of bib overalls, donned in the men's room of a small-town restaurant while my companions chowed down at the counter.

The cook, apparently near his quitting time, turned surly after one of the Sweigarts ordered a second round of pork chops with applesauce – "and this time put the cinnamon on like you're not paying for it." I was lucky to get a hamburger and never said a word when there was no ketchup.

Yes, there was a wild turkey encounter that trip. It came toward the end of the week, just in time to spare us from depression.

We had brought along one Lynch box call – Chauney's – but the sounds it made in no way even remotely resembled the sweet, seductive imitation of a turkey hen's voice that our hillside instructor had produced.

What we had is what we used, as we lay on the ground listening to a gobbler sound off from a safe distance. This went on for close to an hour. Then a hen half-circled us, approaching from the rear. I couldn't see her, but by the chirping and clucking she had to be getting close.

The bird halted about six feet in front of me, then stepped closer and bent down for a better look. I blinked, she flew, and ol' tom hurried off on foot. In baseball terms: no runs, no hits, countless errors. More importantly, of the roughly 800 species of birds found in North America, the wild turkey had soared into my life with top billing.

Professionally speaking, the next few years of the Dohne/Martin friendship were tinged with irony as he sought my help via the newspaper in making the Game Commission's case for mandatory hunter education. In a series of stories – no doubt simultaneously involving other reporters and newspapers – the point was made that introducing youngsters in a classroom to the rules of the woods would boost safety once they went afield. Eventually, of course, hunter ed became law.

This was pretty heady stuff for a young newsman and budding bird hunter – and a quite personal matter as well. *If only you'd had this kind of training as a kid, things might have been very different. You never would have been hunting with Allen VanHorne in the dark, and a certain great horned owl might still be hootin' it up somewhere out there.*

John Martin with Doug after a Canada goose hunt.

New job, new faces

The violent Sixties were winding down as a new phase began in my news career, working on the copy desk.

Among my fellow employees was the gregarious Gilbert "Red" Wolfe, a linotype operator at The Patriot-News main plant in Harrisburg, where we met in August 1969. His huge machine was near the coffee pot in the Composing Room, a destination frequented by reporters, editors and others.

My first impression was that this guy resembled a pianist, his fingers gliding over the keys as he sat straight-backed, the hint of a smile playing across a pasty face.

Wolfe was a carrottop, known to all as Red. I soon learned that this interesting and lively conversationalist was a fellow hunter. With the gift of gab and an infectious laugh, Red exuded the enthusiasm of a grade-schooler though then in his 50s.

He had a roller-coaster speech pattern and a favorite wind-up comment – as in what happened after he fired three quick shots at a black bear:

"Well, bruin made a "lickety-split escape – ohmagod, did he ever!"

Hearing that I was a trout fisherman, Red said he'd once run a sporting goods store in nearby New Cumberland, and still could get certain equipment at discount. Through him I bought a Fenwick fly rod for $30 that to this day remains my favorite for trout, outranking even the $300 Orvis magic wand I received as a retirement gift.

We weren't fishing buddies, however; in fact, we never wet a line together that I recall. No, it was hunting that held our common interest. In the end, our collaboration resulted in a lucrative business deal that paved the way to early retirement for one of us. As Red would say, "Ohmagod, did it ever!"

It turned out that, as with fishing, Red and I were never destined to be hard and fast hunting buddies either, though each would host the other for an occasional hunt.

A taste of hunting camp

He and three brothers belonged to a camp near Blossburg, Tioga County, where he invited me to hunt. We were after turkey, while the rest of the guys had dogs along and spent that fall day rabbit chasing. What I recall about this hunt is how frustrating it was being unable to locate a turkey flock, a fact that the successful rabbit hunters took delight in reinforcing.

It was dark when we returned to camp, our headlights reflecting off a large galvanized tub now gracing the front porch. Peering into the container we found it brimming with fresh-skinned cottontails, several of whose legs protruded through a thin layer of ice.

Red's older brother, Claude, was just serving up a supper of roasted rabbit, mashed potatoes and gravy with all the extras. Claude earned a living selling real estate, but he could have worn a chef's hat at The Hotel Hershey.

While the excellent cuisine earned kudos for Claude, the rest of the table talk had a less lofty flavor. At first, I thought perhaps the purpose of the determined detractors was to get us to join in their rabbit hunt, which obviously was going well. Then I noticed the brothers' heckling seemed to be singling out Red, and I recognized this as simply good old sibling rivalry.

Red was holding his own well enough that I stole a glance around the camp. Yes, several nice deer racks were on display, but only a few. *What on earth is that collection of crimson fabric scraps tacked to the wall? Looks like a name and a date under each one. And no doubt a memory, too, but of what?*

After closer inspection, I concluded that these guys treasured their memories of the woods, but with a twist. Rather than a deer rack or bear head on the wall, the Wolfes favored trophies earned not through loss of life but loss of face.

In other words, some of the camp's most cherished memories marked mistakes made in the field. And when half of the members are your brothers, there's a good chance it's someone you've ribbed (and vice versa) all your life who will be next to miss a shot, maybe at a big buck, and surrender a bit of his shirttail to the Wall of Shame.

Sure, this is about hunting, but it's also about being part of a family with a healthy perspective on its chosen sport. Some of their best trophies are gathered and displayed not by those who earned them but by the, um, witnesses. They celebrate not animal deaths in the woods, but rather a balanced family life, accenting humility over braggadocio. These guys have figured out how to preserve one of the best parts of childhood and enjoy it as adults.

Well, this is all well and good, but why are you feeling so poorly about today's hunt? It's probably just part of the failure-as-trophy phenomenon. Of course, that's it. With their code of the woods, these rabbit hunters have done a bang-up job of jabbing your ego.

To be sure, I was young and, outside of pheasant and rabbit hunting, inexperienced. Not only was this my initial autumn turkey chase, but it also was my first taste of life at hunting camp. The Wolfe pack's perfectly delivered potshots revealed their way of enjoying the great outdoors, but my biggest takeaway was a renewed determination to succeed at this thing called turkey hunting.

Mountainside mystery

My turn to host a turkey hunt didn't arrive until a few years later. Along with Red and me that trip was my oldest son, David, then 15, and we lodged in a large inn at Carter Camp, Potter County.

The proprietor was a lumberman who spoke in such a high pitch that a little voice in my head objected when he did. *There's no way that voice could come from a grown man.*

But it had, and the message was that as his hotel business was light – we were his sole customers – he would be sawing in the morning. He volunteered having spotted a large turkey flock yesterday (I swear his voice actually went up a notch when he spoke the next four words) "just over the mountain." We thanked him and said we'd give it a try.

The next day, dropping Red off at the base of said mountain, Dave and I proceeded to a likely looking spot farther on. Mother Nature having completed her annual strip tease act, the trees were bare of leaves. That meant a noisy walk, plowing through the dry debris.

Woods minus their leaves are easier to see through. But that works both ways, and the advantage is the turkey's.

Such conditions dictated that we keep watching for game as far out front as possible. Which is to say we weren't careful enough where we stepped and were vulnerable to falling. Fortunately, Dave wasn't hurt when the inevitable occurred, and I silently chided myself for not having warned him.

There was something odd about his fall, but at first I didn't pick up on it. My ears came to the rescue – a dull click had accompanied his landing. Metal on metal? Brushing aside leaves, we uncovered a rusty length of chain. Apparently, Dave's gun had contacted its heavy links.

Gentle tugging extracted a 4-foot length of chain from the rocky soil. At either end was attached a large handcuff. They were flat, about ¾-inch thick in a figure-8 shape. The top oval of the 8 was slightly smaller than the bottom one, with the rivets still intact. The duff also yielded the head of a double-bladed ax, one cutting edge missing a chunk. There was no evidence of a handle.

A thick patina of rust signaled an old secret had just come to light. But what exactly was it? The handcuffs were in closed position, but were they locked? Too much rust to tell. Clearly we no longer were hunting for turkeys; now we wanted answers to questions flowing like a storm-swollen trout stream:

Had a fugitive from justice shed his shackles on this spot? In the impromptu court of public opinion, now in special mountainside session, this was the unanimous finding.

What was his crime? How and where had he obtained the ax, and how had it (and presumably him) gotten here? Maybe there was an accomplice! Where did he (or was it they or perhaps even he and she) go next? And how had it all ended – in capture after a short taste of freedom, or years later of natural causes, or somewhere in between?

I don't remember how long we lingered, as if the answers would arrive in payment for patience, but I do recall Dave grabbing a stick and thoroughly poking the ground to find anything we might have missed. No dice.

Our hiatus from hunting was shattered by the distant blast of a shotgun, reminding us that somewhere in these woods we had a hunting companion. Had Red shot a turkey? Having more questions than answers is a recurring theme in the forest, and we had about an hour's wait before spotting Red as he descended from the ridge opposite ours.

Red Wolfe, a blue hen and the forest aflame

The only thing Red was carrying was his shotgun. Once we were reunited, he confirmed with one word that indeed he had fired at a turkey. His tale unfolded over ham sandwiches and coffee back at the car:

"It happened right on top of the mountain. I climbed most of the way up before I began to see fresh scratching in the beech. That's a favorite turkey feed, of course, and the sign was pretty fresh – maybe even from this morning. I hung around that spot a bit, then continued uphill.

"Boy, your beech leaves sure are a treat for the feet, just like little cushions. You Potter boys are lucky; over in Tioga it's so oaky. No big beech stands like this. Anyway, the wind had swept the leaves off the mountaintop, so that last leg was nice quiet walking.

"Which probably accounts for me walking right up on about 20 turkeys smack at the crest! Just then it got real bright – you know how the sun's been in and out all morning – well, suddenly it was sunny. It was like a light comin' on in my brain, too. 'C'mon, Red, ya gotta pick out one bird to aim at,' I told myself.

"Just that quick my eyes went to a big hen in the middle of the flock. She was slate blue, so stunning I couldn't take my eyes off of her. I pulled up but at the last second shot at another bird. Heck, I don't even know why I did that because right after I shot I was looking for my blue hen, but she was gone. Ohmagod, was she ever!"

After lunch we should have climbed right back up to where he'd likely split the flock, but we didn't. Instead we chose to hunt the next hill to the north, which was even higher ground. Driving a dirt road in that direction, we began the long ascent, complete with several switchbacks.

Along the way we passed hunters in another vehicle proceeding downhill. Nodding to the passersby, I noticed someone smoking in the backseat –

probably because of my longtime battle with cigarettes, a struggle I had yet to win.

Not much farther on the road went down, but we wanted to hunt the top. Turning around, we retraced our route, passing a section of stone wall on the uphill side of the road. Likely the wall was the handiwork of a CCC crew, whose purpose was to ensure a clear drainage path for water pooling at its base before passing under the road and downhill.

Using a nearby pull-off spot, I climbed out and instinctively checked the drainage pipe on the downhill side. Yep, everything was in fine working order, just waiting for storm water to come charging down the mountainside. Glancing uphill, it occurred to me that right now would be the perfect time for a deluge because – holy Toledo! – the hillside was on fire!

Red and Dave, who had been donning hunting coats to resume the turkey chase, wheeled around to see what I was hollering about. In a wink they had those coats off and, at Red's shouted command, were emptying the pockets of ammunition, apples, etc. As they charged uphill, using their coats to swat flames, I ran back to the car and grabbed a hatchet, tucked it under my belt and followed the other volunteer firemen to work.

After a short climb we could see that the blaze had a good head start. A quick glance at an adjacent mountain showed we were about halfway up. The unspoken question was, could we get to the fire line above and halt its advance before things got out of control? There was a gentle breeze, steady enough to lift dry leaves as it climbed the mountainside. This literally was going to be an uphill battle.

Just climbing taxes the lungs. Trotting and slapping down flames with every step is exhausting. Mix in the smoke and, well, it's just about impossible to stay with the fight. With handkerchiefs covering mouth and nose, somehow we managed to reach the head of the blaze.

But all that bending over to beat down flames had exacted a toll. I remember thinking my back felt like it, too, was on fire. Chopping off hemlock branches for use as rakes allowed us to stand upright – and rest those aching backs – while continuing the fight.

I have no idea how long it took, but the battle was won when we looked up and saw that we were all working with our backs to the mountaintop and the flames below. Which is about when we heard distant sirens and spotted a chopper circling our position. As a threat to the woods, the fire had ceased to exist.

Returning to the car, we crossed perhaps a 5-acre plot of blackened forest. No mature trees appeared to have been damaged. The downhill extremity of the charring was in a V shape, with the point of the V right atop that old stone wall. Clearly the fire had started there.

And just as obviously, the likely cause was carelessness by the smoker in that passing vehicle. The guilty party probably flicked his butt at that stonewall, assuming it would fall and be extinguished in a wet ditch below.

Wrong on all counts: The butt didn't fall; somehow (the wind?) it landed above the wall and ignited dry grass and leaves. Even if it had fallen, the ditch was dry, as Mr. Butthead – had he paid attention to woods conditions – should have known. Makes me wonder if he ever even got out to hunt.

Passing no firefighting crews on our way out, we decided to head home. About an hour into the trip, three exhausted listeners caught a radio report on the fire, which was attributed to "careless smoking by a turkey hunter." Our response – blurted out in near unison – was "Hey, it was turkey hunters who put it out, too!" Ohmagod, did we ever!

Ah, springtime vacations

By the early Seventies, my favorite vacations had become turkey hunts with Chauney and tent camping in Florida with David and his brothers, Daniel and Dennis, and their mother. Our return usually coincided with the spring green-up around our rural York County home, signaling the start of another busy season for our ag-oriented family.

We brought home fresh citrus fruit and sometimes a few coconuts to eat, and bamboo shoots for staking garden plants. Two of these commodities later would answer a very different calling.

Originally the spring hunt was restricted to the morning hours to protect hens, which stay on the nest overnight and well into the next day until the air warms and they can take a break from incubating eggs to eat and drink. All-day hunting has been allowed in recent years mainly, I think, because of milder weather and the good conduct of spring turkey hunters (relatively few hens shot in mistake for toms). And accidents resulting in human injury or death also have fallen.

Actually it's the spring hunt's no-rifle rule that deserves a lot of credit for that last part. Using a shotgun means you have to get close to the bird. The nearer the turkey, naturally, the better the chance to identify your target. But every step he takes your way raises his odds of detecting danger.

This is a hunt for gobblers – only bearded birds are legal targets – and it takes place during the windup of the turkey mating season. The quarry typically is a wily and experienced creature, in his second year or older, and knows exactly what he's after.

Mimicking the wild turkey's voice

Man had a love-hate relationship with artificial wild-turkey calls in the first half of the 20th century. A ban on such devices, enacted in 1909, was lifted in 1937. Thirty-one years later, game managers came full circle on the turkey-call issue when they mandated its use in the spring hunt.

The result was to place a premium on Nimrod's ability to lure his prey into range by imitating springtime turkey talk. His objective now was to duplicate the calls a hen makes when receptive to a visit from the gobbler. Success would depend less on one's ability to ambush and more on his fluency in turkey love lingo – for most humans, a very foreign language indeed.

All of which made spring gobbler hunting a whole new challenge for hunters, including me, a guy who had absolutely no idea what he was doing. If it's true that one learns more by failing than succeeding, I should have been an expert after those first few spring hunts. But there I was, still stuck in student mode.

I learned that *Meleagris gallopavo* sees in color (so it's best to swap that orange hat for a camo one before he shows up). I found out that unless you can imitate the immobility of a rock it doesn't matter how well you can talk turkey (often still a struggle for me) or how good your setup is.

I determined that a stream might mark the boundary between one gobbler's territory and another's, and that while calling over such a waterway might ignite a turkey gobbling duel in which I could see one, both or neither of the adversaries, most often no shooting would result. The birds focus on shouting each other down, then typically work away from that spot (and me) after making their point.

Along the way, I came to know the wild turkey as a worthy challenge. He can see and hear better than me, and worse yet he has zero curiosity about anything even the least bit suspicious. In contrast, a white-tailed deer will bound away then stop and, statue still, study your approach.

I have yet to see a turkey do that. Invariably he exercises his one-size-fits-all reaction to any hint of danger – he vamooses. When this occurs after you've invested several hours in careful and sometimes tiring maneuvers to set up in a favorable position from which to call the bird, you need to learn from it.

Woods wisdom

If you talk to the animals they will talk with you and you will know each other. If you do not talk to them you will not know them, and what you do not know, you will fear. What one fears, one destroys.

– Chief Dan George (1899-1981) of the Tsleil-Waututh Nation, actor, poet and author

Since he lives in Charlotte, NC, we don't often get to hunt with Dr. Remus "Ret" Turner, but something our friend wrote illustrates perfectly what Chief George was driving at.

In an e-mail exchange about the spring 2016 gobbler hunt, this Southern gentleman reported that he "… had a great season talking with intelligent birds – lots of fun, but no meat in the freezer."

The wild turkey rates as a teacher par excellence when the subject is stealth. Pass his final exam and you have arrived as a woodsman. While still very much the student, I've come a long way since the days of committing every faux pas hinted at in the following.

Some do's and don'ts

To speak with turkeys wild
just get to know their talk,
then observe their customs
and too close never walk.

With hearing excellent
and sight superior,
they abide no approach
that ranks inferior.

Smart hunters choose to use
the privy back at camp
and take snacks well before
through trees they dare to tramp.

If circumstance allows
this tactic to employ,
in a woods thin and bright
place well a hen decoy.

But first lay down the gun –
might fall if you lean it,
leaving this hill turk-free
as you've ever seen it.

It's listen up or lose out

One big lesson I took from those early errors is the importance of stopping to listen, especially when stalking big woods gobblers in the spring. While his voice might carry a mile, you likely won't hear a tom if there's anything – and the littlest hill is enough – between the two of you. Unless you're really lucky, you won't hear a gobbler while walking. Your chances of hearing a turkey rise when you are stationary.

Sound travels best in a straight line; its intensity and clarity fade as the waves bounce off a hillside or ravine, for example. In a mountain setting you hear the call of the gobbler clearest – and from the greatest distance – when you're both on the same level. *Father, thank You for teaching me to be a better listener in the woods. And elsewhere.*

To me, "shotguns only" is what makes the spring hunt special. Because of its range-reducing impact, this rule reinforces the communication aspect that is at the heart of the hunt. Nothing else compares to the don't-blink-now-he'll-spot-you experience of calling in a gobbler on a May morn. Nothing else, that is, except maybe doing it with your own homemade call. Talk about making a personal call!

Calling on the coconut

Back to those coconuts and bamboo stalks we lugged home from the Sunshine State:

After removing the husk and sawing the shell roughly in half, the coconut meat was harvested. Either piece of the shell then formed the foundation of a turkey call. A section of roofing slate, ground in a circular shape, nested neatly inside the shell.

A pencil-shaped pick was fashioned from two pieces of wood, a thin one embedded in a larger block, serving as the handle. The protruding end, once rounded off and charred lightly, produced sounds closely resembling a turkey voice when drawn across the slate.

The contraption's weight and bulk, however, detracted from its audio achievement. Another disadvantage: It would take both hands to operate and require too much movement. That last part was causing misgivings and eroding my confidence in the choice of coconut.

Soon I was mentally revisiting my body's first solo encounter with wild turkeys. I refer to it that way because my mind really wasn't along that spring day in 1971.

I was scouting toward sunset, heard a roosting gobbler and, next morning, climbed the mountain in the dark and sat down to wait for birdsong to begin. I carried a box call and a 16-gauge Savage.

This is your fourth spring hunt – soon you'll have a baccalaureate in turkey hunting. It's time to join the ranks of successful turkey hunters!

Failing a pop quiz

Well, this almost Turkey College grad didn't do very well in class that day because there was still so much to learn. My first mistake was crouching next to a tree for concealment – because it also blocked my view of the approaching turkeys, laying the groundwork for what happened next.

Guessing them to be close enough for a shot, I scooted to the other side of the tree just in time to see three turkeys, heads down, scampering away. Which one was the gobbler? By the time I figured that out Turkey 101 was over for the day. Once again I'd been flummoxed, still an undergrad.

Not so fast! Let's be cerebral about what just happened. Well, dummy, you have to be able to see the gobbler to make a positive ID. OK, I'd been shut out on that point and paid the price. *No more hiding behind trees!*

But I had heard everything, so now I'd have to rely on my ears. *Well, exactly what did you hear?*

Suddenly, in that special theater in which an audience of one is a full house, I was listening to the soundtrack of my encounter with the turkey trio. The gobbler's voice was magnificent, powerful, penetrating. There was the rustling of dry leaves as he dragged his wingtips. It reminded me of a snare drummer when he sucked air in and pumped himself up for the incomparable display of iridescent beauty that (even after this encounter) I'd seen only in pictures.

The putt-putt-putting of the hens now and then was interspersed with a yelp, purr, cluck or toot. Aside from the gobbling, it sounded so much like a kazoo that to me they became the Little Kitchen Band of the Big Woods.

Bamboo takes center stage

Sensing that somehow it could be tooled to talk turkey, the arborescent grass a.k.a. bamboo now stole my attention. It was such a lightweight! I was surprised to find that those handsome knuckles grew all the way through so that, for instance, you could not look through a length of bamboo as though it were a telescope.

Curiosity was in full gallop as I worked the hacksaw between two knuckles of bamboo. A peek inside revealed the knuckle was paper thin at the center of the stalk.

I'd been careless with the blade, resulting in perhaps a 25-degree angle cut, and the section of bamboo now resembled in size and shape the mouthpiece of a clarinet. Soon the Little Kitchen Band of the Big Woods was doing an encore in that special theater as I stared at what now loomed as a potentially instrumental piece of equipment in my next turkey hunt.

Selecting a bamboo shoot about a ring-finger in width, I made a cut on a 45-degree angle between two knuckles. Another slice, this one straight through and just past the next nearest knuckle, left a hunk about 4 inches long.

With the edges sanded smooth, part of a balloon was stretched and taped over three-quarters of the angled opening, tightening the chamber. A small hole was drilled in the tube's knuckle, to let sound escape.

Before long the little trumpet was producing what seemed like realistic turkey sounds. I was satisfied enough to share my crude invention with Red, who was immediately enthusiastic – ohmagod, was he ever! He contributed several revisions and refinements, including a lanyard to which the call was attached and carried like an athletic official's whistle, ready for quick access.

The real experts live in the woods

A popular pastime in some quarters of the turkey hunting fraternity is the calling contest. There are scads of them, some offering nice prizes. Once I attended a competition in Harrisburg but came away unimpressed. *Why should people be the judges? Why not the birds themselves?*

I decided to delay trying out my call until I was with the savviest turkey hunter I knew. His name was Roscoe Stiles, and he was the captain of our camp; indeed, he was its chief architect. I met him at Moon Valley Lodge a few years after he and seven relatives and hunting buddies built it in the early Sixties in Potter County's East Fork Twp.

Roscoe quickly earned my respect as a student of the wild turkey. He used CDs and tapes and was well read, having bought, pored over and saved every issue of the PA Game News magazine.

Though at the time he was still fairly new to it, Roscoe's focus on and knowledge of turkey hunting was impressive. In the next 40 years of hunting in three states, he would bag dozens upon dozens of them.

Roscoe had at least a dozen box calls – his favorite was a Lynch – but he was a minimalist when it came to their use.

"I play the feeding call, and not real loud or very often. Call softly and a whole flock might show up. Turkeys hear very well – better than we can," he told me.

And where you set up is more important than the call you carry, according to Roscoe, who once confided:

"I like to be under a hemlock or pine tree, if possible, because it cuts the light. You sort of melt into the shadow. Or, find two trees close together and sit between them. Pretend you're a statue: no feelings, no movement."

'Let's ... see what happens'

On this day of experimentation Roscoe didn't seem to want to hear my new bamboo turkey call. Heck, he didn't even ask to see it. Instead, in his very direct way, he said:

"Let's go try it out in the woods – see what happens."

And that's what we did. As it was a Sunday morning – by law since 1873 a day of rest for the hunted and the hunter in Pennsylvania – I carried no firearm as Roscoe dropped me off near a favorite ridge.

The reward for a 10-minute walk into the forest was hearing the thunderous but distant sound of a turkey gobbler. Three crisp yelps on my bamboo call evoked an immediate answer, and then another and another.

Within minutes the bird appeared in the shadowy edge of a clearing about 30 yards off. He was in full strut, fan spread, all pumped up to dazzle the hen he felt was near.

Concealed between a tree and a large rock, I clapped my hands to send tom on his way. My turkey call had passed muster with a master, and I left the woods with a bounce in my step.

Roscoe's reaction was somewhat deflating. All he said was:

"The call's just one part of turkey hunting, probably the most overrated part."

In time I learned how right he was, but just then it wasn't registering.

My bluff is called

Meantime, Red was conducting his own research. His confidence shot way up after using one of our calls to lure and bag a gobbler. While I reveled in it as a special hunting triumph, Red's thoughts were running the retail trail.

"We should be making these calls to sell," he was arguing, even before the hunting season ended. "To do that, we'll have to start making them out of plastic, so they're uniform. Then we can get a patent …"

As the father of three youngsters, I knew it was time to fold my hand in this turkey-call poker game.

Red went straight to a machinist. Soon I was shown a sample – plastic, as promised – that functioned as well as our bamboo prototype.

And, yes, he was in consultation with the only patent attorney in central PA at the time – coincidentally a man whose children were schoolmates of my kids. Bottom line: Startup would cost about $2,500. I told my friend he was on his own and wished him well.

Red's investment produced a patent and ultimately a six-figure settlement with an established call manufacturer that let him retire in comfort from the newspaper. Best of all, under terms of the deal, he could continue tinkering in the garage/workshop behind his home, making and selling calls.

While Red pressed on down the inventor's path, I turned back to my hunting roots – mentally, at least. A reminder about the importance of practicality came from Red and Ida's middle son, Dave.

Look, ma, no hands

An accomplished craftsman in his own right, Dave Wolfe used a brass bullet casing to join the wing bones from my first wild turkey, resulting in a handsome call resembling a trumpet. I found it hard to play and, like the coconut model, it required both hands to achieve peak performance.

More practical by far was the diaphragm call that Dave made out of aluminum sheeting (meant for use in roofing) and part of a balloon – the same style of call that was demonstrated for Chauney and me on our maiden turkey hunt.

Apparently I'd needed some seasoning in the woods to appreciate the huge advantage of this design. About the same shape as a silver dollar cut in half, this device, once concealed in the mouth, requires minimal motion to operate. Perhaps best of all, both hands are free.

Diving into the diaphragm

My conversion to the diaphragm-style call was swift and complete: Out with the bamboo, in with aluminum sheeting and balloons. Once more family members were rolling their eyes and voicing opinions:

"He's at it again!" "Spends more time making turkey calls than he does hunting them!" "Yeah, and he never brings any home!" Etc., etc., etc.

Undaunted by the naysayers, I busied myself in the basement cranking out an array of experimental calls. Differing sizes and shapes of aluminum frames were outfitted with assorted balloon cuttings. Pieces snipped from latex gloves designed for surgical and other purposes entered the mix. I've stuck with the resulting design ever since.

Here, I owe a tip of the hunting cap to Roscoe because, as he told me back in my slate and bamboo days, calling is just one part of the hunt. Woods skills and knowledge, stealth, patience and weather count heavily.

As for luck, let's just say successful turkey hunters have two things in common with American Indian rain dancers who get drenched: Both have chosen fortuitously when and where to go at it.

In practice, turkey hunters often overdo the calling thing, and after one annoyingly noisy spring hunt with Chauney, this story appeared:

Calls of the wild aplenty

(Sunday, June 6, 2004)

When it comes to spring turkey hunting, a whole flock of folks seems to think it's all in the call.

Early in last month's hunt, my partner and I were swapping calls with a gobbler on a ridge not far from our camp in Potter County. Suddenly a chorus of turkey calls erupted downhill.

There were more yelps in 20 minutes than a wild turkey would let go in a week. These were decidedly not the calls of the wild. For a few minutes it was so unreal I thought the local PETA chapter was paying us a call. Guys – and gals, too, thank you, Shirley Grenoble* – it's the turkeys we want to call in, not one another.

The technical triumph that is the modern turkey call is marketed by dozens of makers. All of them seem to sell diaphragm and box calls, but there are more kinds of devices on the shelf than a gobbler has tail feathers.

A popular one is the push-peg call, which several makers design to be attached to your shotgun. It sometimes is referred to as a push-button or push-pin call. One outfit, touting its version's shape, calls it The Egg.

There are various friction calls, usually utilizing slate, as well as wing-bone models, trumpet or tube-type jobs, shaker models, etc.

It seems pretty obvious that many of these calls are designed more for hunters than turkeys. One manufacturer claims its box call will "work flawlessly under all weather conditions," while the producer of a certain slate call promises it will "bring longbeards looking for you!"

With gadgets that are nearly foolproof to operate, many hunters seem to have been seduced by their own calling, overdoing it in frequency and volume, as we witnessed on that ridge.

During our days afield this spring, we encountered extreme cases, in which calling seemed to take the place of traditional hunting. These folks were calling incessantly, as if believing wild turkeys can be created out of thin air – provided it's filled with enough yelps, clucks, putts, whines and, of course, gobbles.

While 36 spring hunts in Pennsylvania have taught me the importance of the call, I'd have to rank woods skills, persistence, physical conditioning and shooting ability as equally critical to success. Fail in one of these areas and you'll quickly be calling it a day in the turkey woods.

As misinformed as these over-callers might be, their malnourished turkey tactics are eclipsed at times by those of yet another hunting contingent, people using locator calls. Mostly they imitate the voices of owls, crows, ravens and hawks.

The owl is active at night, so a blast from a barred owl at 10:30 a.m. is likely a fake. That will raise the suspicions of any turkey within earshot, the last thing a hunter wants.

One maker promises its "Hoot Flute" will produce four distinct copycat pitches of the barred owl or the great horned owl, touting it as the loudest and most versatile on the market.

Ah, but the four-hole Super Hooter's maker calls it "the loudest and most realistic in the industry," reaching 400 yards, while another model claims to pack the voices of the owl, coyote and woodpecker into a single call.

No doubt imitating the call of his enemy will cause a gobbler to announce his presence, but at what cost? Now he's upset, on the defensive, bracing for battle with an adversary he feels is calling his bluff.

You could switch to a turkey hen call, but in old tom's mind a foe still lurks. He's going to be extra cautious about coming to any call.

In spite of such woods logic, some owl, crow, raven and hawk imitators persist in audio-assaulting the gobbler, apparently convinced he can be called out to fight. I'd never say never, but I would say an exchange of calls between a gobbler and someone imitating one of his enemies is a long shot, at best.

One challenge call that could be effective is the gobble, especially if employed over a decoy. A lusty gobble might lure tom forth to defend his territory, but this is a risky tactic in the increasingly crowded spring woods.

It boils down to a matter of personal safety, and that's definitely your call.

**Ex-president of the former PA Wild Turkey Federation*

Nowhere was Roscoe's reasoning – less is more when it comes to calling the wild turkey – better illustrated than at a place we call …

Pummel Rock

About five miles from our camp a large rocky outcropping rises from a narrow, hog-backed mountaintop. Downhill from there one foggy spring morning I heard a distant gobbler. Chauney's older son, Brad, caught it, too.

We judged the bird too far off for us to try calling; we weren't even on his level. The fog thickened and thunder cracked, triggering a barrage of crow calls as if in protest to the prospect of rain. *My sentiments exactly.*

It seemed to work as no raindrops came and soon the crows fell silent – well, almost. One pesky individual persisted.

Crows and turkeys are enemies, so maybe this fellow was protesting not the likelihood of rain but the presence of that distant gobbler, which had shut up during the crow cacophony. The turkey likely had moved away from us and the crows, which is why we no longer could hear him. It was time for us to move as well.

Before we crested the mountain the noisy crow had departed and once again we could hear gobbling. We set up with a pickup-truck-sized rock between us and the bird. Brad's position would let him cover one end of the formation, while I took the other. In theory, the bird would come to our call, traveling around the rock to provide someone a shot.

Just three successively softer yelps with the mouth call – directed away from the bird – was all it took. Somehow tom chose a path that led right down over the rock – and into shooting range for both of us. This was Brad's first chance for a spring gobbler, and I was a happy witness. *Wish you were here to see this, Chauney.*

Bang! Down went the gobbler, his head driven hard into rock by the impact of Brad's pellets. I couldn't believe it when the turkey jumped up, shook himself like a dog coming out of a creek, and staggered into a small bramble patch bordering the lip of the mountain. Brad's second shot didn't seem to faze the bird at all.

My gun barked once as tom went airborne, set his wings and hit glide mode headed downhill.

We rushed over, expecting to see our prey sprawled below. The only movement to greet our eyes was the nodding of wildflowers as a gentle breeze kissed the hillside. But we were nowhere near ready to kiss the turkey good-bye.

While I stayed atop studying the mountainside through binoculars, Brad spent most of an hour searching below. Surely after taking such a pummeling the bird at least would leave a feather or two behind, but none was found. Nor did any leaves appear to have been ruffled by his landing far below. Tom had vanished.

While the survival skills of wild animals are remarkable, sometimes they live only to suffer a slow death. Thus a deer, hit by a car, might crawl under a downed tree just a few yards off road, enduring that day but succumbing the next. Our crippled gobbler lived long enough to elude pursuit, but chances are he never saw another sunrise.

Around our camp, Pummel Rock is regarded as a monument to the toughness of the wild turkey.

Morning in the mountains

Sunrise is special, the focal point of Nimrod's day. The hour preceding it and the one right after form the core of a spring turkey hunter's day. Rising at 4 a.m., he's busy dressing for the occasion – weather appropriate, so he has what's needed and nothing extra – and getting breakfast and a snack to go.

The first spoken words of the day might be: "Hey, next man up the hill (to the privy) better take a roll of paper."

The goal is to be at the takeoff point for the hunt – sometimes requiring a lengthy car ride – by 5 o'clock. It's still dark – make that very dark – in the turkey woods. It might be just a short walk to high ground to listen for a gobbler. But with any luck Nimrod will have a much longer tramp – to an area far off-road where he heard a tom roosting last night.

Either way, birdsong trumpets the coming of day well before the fact. Suddenly the forest sounds like a building site as nearby a woodpecker hammers out his breakfast order on a dead tree. Today's special (he hopes): Fresh insects (same as yesterday).

Dampness invades your jacket and the temperature sinks slightly as gathering light signals sunrise is near. *This is prime time. Where are you, tom?*

The rise of the sun lifts the temperature with it. The shivering is over; now get ready to sweat. Soon the deer will drop into bed as the owls go quiet and turkey hens leave the nest.

If you are someplace other than hilltop at sunrise under a clear sky, it might be a long wait to see your shadow. More importantly, the lower your position, the less likely you are to hear ol' tom. Sure, you could get lucky and hear him as you climb the mountain, but a lot will have changed by the time you crest it.

Another factor is fog. When it carpets the valleys and hugs the hollows, you have to know the woods well enough to navigate without benefit of the big picture. And fog-decapitated mountains are a challenge regardless of whether you're on top of one or at its base.

Turkeys are on the ground with the arrival of sufficient light. A bird can melt away in a big woods as fast as the wind changes direction. If the gobbler enters a hollow or walks around a hill, the last time you heard him might turn out to be just that. You are left to find the spot from which you think he called, then try to read the landscape and guess which way he went. Good luck!

Brad Martin with the author after a spring hunt in Potter.

The lunch bunch

For various reasons, spring turkey hunting is best practiced as a solo sport. Even when together in the woods, you don't want to be too close to your companion(s) – certainly not shoulder to shoulder on the same path, which is how Chauney and I were walking one day.

Hearing a gobbler, we instinctively pivoted in unison toward the sound. The gun barrel of One of Us contacted the head of the Other, propelling the latter headfirst into a mud puddle. It wasn't a knockout, but the Other later reported having witnessed a star-filled performance by the Keystone Kops.

Lunch at spring turkey camp is a feast of stories of the morning's hunt shared with buddies you haven't seen in some cases since before sunup. There are relatively short (one-beer) stories (in which the gobbler usually lives to fly another day) and longer ones, perhaps describing the discovery of a mammoth marijuana patch or the weathered wreckage of a small airplane (no human remains) deep in the forest.

These days some of our younger hunters are getting in on the storytelling that always follows a hunt, any hunt. Brad's son, Shane, and one of my grandsons, Tyler Hoffman, bagged their first gobblers in spring 2014.

Our repertoire of outdoor lore includes several incidents with electrical connections, one of which occurred right at the camp table. Jawing with Chauney and Brad, yours truly was peeling potatoes while seated beneath a fluorescent fixture when the lights went out.

In and of itself, a power outage is a routine thing in the big woods. Storms take down wires regularly, and lapses in electrical service, sometimes lengthy, are to be expected. But not this time, because there was no storm and the only lights that went out were mine.

That happened when the 4-foot fixture – a sturdy old-timer made of steel – somehow broke free and fell on my head. I recall sliding off the chair and, later, waking up in bed as my companions were about to eat supper – yes, with mashed potatoes!

Wearing the then-mandatory orange hat while hunting proved painful but helped to protect the wound. On the plus side, most of the so-called floaters that had clouded my vision for years now disappeared. By the end of the week my headache was gone, but those pesky floaters were back.

Electrical malfunction follows the mental kind

During an especially soggy spring hunt, One of Us had a brand new Pontiac, and the Other was at the wheel on what ordinarily was a dusty dirt road. This day it was slippery and deeply rutted.

The woods were so soaked we couldn't bring ourselves to traipse them. Instead, we stopped once in a while and stepped out, hoping to hear a gobbler. The idea was, if we did hear one it would motivate us to pull our shotguns out of the case and get into the forest to hunt.

But the only thing we heard was a barred owl – and each other's grousing about the endless ding-ding-dinging because we weren't bothering to buckle up between stops. Finally, the Other said, "Want me to fix that ding?"

Authorization by One of Us was short and sweet – "Sure" – but, as we would soon find out, wholly ill-advised.

At the next listening point, the Other jumped out, reached under the driver's seat and mumbled a few, um, unintelligible words. Moments later he straightened up, triumphantly holding a hunk of cable and wearing a coast-to-coast grin. Couldn't have been any happier if he'd just killed a big old longbeard.

Detecting no gobbling at that spot either, we got back in and drove off as the drizzle grew into rain. Our next discovery was, yeah, no more ding,-ding-ding was nice, but what happened to the windshield wipers? Uh-oh!

First the rain kept us out of the woods, now it was making car travel uncomfortable, not to mention unsafe. What became an unmercifully long, wet week was punctuated by the tail-between-the-legs return of One of Us to the car dealership. There, a mechanic began a little speech no one wants to hear: “You know, if you get caught tampering ...”

A man called Tank

That happened long before we met Tank, who came into our lives the day the battery in Chauney’s old Ford truck died in the woods. Tank would never make a speech like that, no siree.

One look at him and even years later it’s easy to recall his nickname, and everyone calls him that. This gentle barrel-chested Mr. Fix It with a heart as big as an engine block has helped many an outdoorsman out of car trouble, and now it was our turn.

I don’t recall who told us about Tank, but I do remember Chauney walking off toward the Cherry Springs to Wharton Road, along which the man was said to live.

Which house was Tank's was easily deciphered once Chauney saw a dozen or so old F150s parked beside and to the rear of a nicely kept rancher.

The next time I saw my buddy, 3 or 4 hours later, he was getting out of a strange vehicle in our yard, a battery in his hands. Nodding good-bye to the driver, Chauney told me the battery was a loaner from his new friend, given on a handshake. That's the kind of guy Tank is.

For the record, Pittsburgh-area native Ralph Halfhill, a.k.a. Tank, is on hiatus from his job as a gas well tender. Fortunately, there are 13 trucks right outside his door in need of immediate attention, yes siree!

Aw, the trailer lights ain't workin'

You might think of a good auto mechanic as someone more adept with wrenches than words, but sometimes they can fool you.

On the eve of a fishing trip to Canada with Chauney I discovered the boat trailer lights were kaput, probably from too many saltwater dunkings. In desperation, I turned to Dave Brightbill, who ordinarily sticks to fixing cars at M & S Auto, the garage in Hummelstown that he runs with his incurably upbeat and savvy sidekick, Max Herniak.

Dave has earned quite a following, not only among his customers, but also with fellow repairmen whom he's helped to guide through automotive adventures at competing shops. More than once while waiting for an oil change, I've seen Max wink, put someone on hold and announce over the intercom, "Call on Dave's Tech Line."

Well, I wasn't using the help line, I simply needed my friends to get me off the hook and on my way to Ontario to catch some bass. For no extra charge and while kneeling beside the trailer, a screwdriver in one hand and his pliers in the other, Dave threw in this theory on the possible gender of electricity:

"You know, Doug, electricity is a lot like a woman: We don't know exactly how she works, but we all enjoy the benefits of her."

Thus illumined, Chauney and I rode north before sunrise.

Our longest walk

One of the shortest stories ever heard around our camp table is about the longest walk Chauney or I ever took while spring turkey hunting. One of Us had located a gobbler just a few hundred yards off a dirt road as dark fell, and next morning led the Other to the spot. With a heavy frost and a full moon, the woods were as bright as midday; the bird sensed our presence and disappeared like the star in a Harry Houdini magic show. We opted to return to our vehicle and hunt elsewhere.

We probably hadn't walked 200 yards into the woods and were now exiting alongside a stand of rhododendron. One of Us, mindful that he hadn't walked through any of those leathery-leaved plants the night before or this morning, motioned for the

Other to join him in skirting the patch to the right where uphill our vehicle was plainly visible. For some reason, that didn't happen, as One of Us watched the Other disappear into the dense rhododendron plantation.

Checking the time back at the vehicle (6:09 a.m.), One of Us waited and waited and waited. And then waited some more.

The car was parked along a finger of the 30,000-acre Hammersley Wild Area, Pennsylvania's largest roadless tract and part of the 265,000-acre Susquehannock State Forest. Anyone who gets lost in the Hammersley's northern reaches (where we were) and tries to walk south following a stream out is facing up to a 26-mile hoof to Cross Fork. And he'll still be in Potter County.

Finally, right at noon, a stranger pulled up in a red pickup. The Other stepped out from the passenger side, waved to the departing driver and silently rejoined One of Us. No matter what One of Us asked the Other about that morning's walk, the answer was always the same: "16 miles by the odometer, 16 miles."

Can turkeys tell time?

Sometimes a lunchtime story involving a turkey technically isn't a hunting tale because of where or when the bird shows up – or both.

One especially hot May morning I'd quit hunting a little early and stopped at a roadside spring to refresh while returning to camp. Rounding a curve, I slowed as a handsome gobbler descended the mountain on my left, waltzed (I could almost hear strains of Strauss's "On the Beautiful Blue Danube") across the macadam five paces in front of where I'd halted, ducked under the guardrail, marched a few yards downhill and stood still. I shifted into park, put on the four-way flashers and glanced at the clock: 11:55 a.m.

As far as that gobbler was concerned, I was invisible and so was the truck; not even the flashing lights rated a glance uphill. Powerful toes feverishly raked the duff, and his eyes seemed as busy as those feet, constantly peering here, there and everywhere – except in my direction. His head never dipped to the ground, so he wasn't feeding. It was as though he had lost something and wasn't leaving without it.

At precisely noon – quitting time for early-spring turkey hunters – the bird reappeared at the guardrail, calmly passed beneath it, re-crossed the street and proceeded up the hill he'd left minutes ago. Ten steps in, he let go a thunderous gobble and disappeared on the shady incline.

Back on the road and still shaking my head, I rounded a bend and within 200 yards passed the Blue Ribbon hunting camp, which had several autos parked in the yard and three pairs of feet resting on the porch rail, their owners no doubt discussing the day's hunt. Three hands waved, but I didn't stop. The trio couldn't have heard the gobbler – there was too much mountain in the way – and besides, who'd believe a story like that?

Wild turkeys show up at the unlikeliest of times and places. These two toms were caught crossing a suburban street in Ross Twp., Allegheny County. Photo by Andrew S. Edris.

We don't shoot strangers

When it comes to shooting turkeys, our gang usually gets to know them first. Gobblers whose habits become familiar generally are the ones providing the action. Sometimes we get so well acquainted with the bird and/or his territory that one or the other earns a lasting nickname – with or without a killing shot for punctuation.

The first place we nicknamed was the Golden Triangle. This intersection of two muddy woods roads was anything but golden on the spring day we arrived to hunt the area in 1972. Rain fell nonstop into the next day.

We learned the first morning that the boss gobbler of this hill was a stay-at-home type. Though he did a good job of disguising it, we managed to pick up his *modus operandi:*

From the top, he would gobble downhill a few times, wait patiently, then disappear for half an hour or so before returning. We determined that when leaving he'd go straight away from us, as his last calls would be successively fainter. On his return, the first gobble we'd hear also was fragile. Mystery solved – he must be visiting the other side of the mountaintop to give a repeat performance.

Near quitting time the second day we were perched on a hill opposite the one the bird was working. We took note that he never came back to the same spot twice, always just a little to the left or right. Our plan was to wait until the gobbling decreased in volume – signaling he was off for the other side – then hightail it downhill and climb toward the spot to which we guessed he'd head upon returning.

On the third day – the first dry one – we became separated during the long down-and-up stalk. Of paramount importance, of course, is to take a position out of the other guy's shooting range before any trigger is pulled and, with sunrise minutes away, that's what we did. At least, we thought so.

One gobble, one yelp with my mouth call in answer, and the bird was standing 30 yards away on the edge of the mountaintop staring at me. One step forward and he was airborne. I opened up with my new 12-gauge Ithaca, the pellets slamming into a large tree.

I didn't know it, but Chauney was on the other side of that tree and, luckily for both of us, he stayed put. As he would say later, "With Dohne doing the shootin' there were bound to be three shots."

And he was right – it did take two more shots to drop the turkey.

Truly it was a golden day for me and my partner. Sunshine returned, what could have been an awful accident was averted, and I bagged my first gobbler.

As for the Golden Triangle, that name didn't surface until later, after traffic smoothed its ruts, the sun dried the dirt, and its yellowish color reappeared. To us, rain or shine, it's been the Golden Triangle ever since.

Father and sons show off the Golden Triangle gobbler. Photo by Marie Correa.

John Martin and daughter Laurie & son Brian
with Chauney's first spring gobbler, 1969.

Finding Ditchmo

This bird came to our attention when, after being thoroughly chagrined by another gobbler at least a mile away, we were just about back to our vehicle.

As it was past legal shooting time, our weapons were empty. Our energy level was running on E, too, but the voice of the wild turkey rescued our sagging spirits. Words were unnecessary; we'd be back in the morning.

Later, hashing over happenings of the day, we struggled to find common ground on that second bird. He'd been nearby, we agreed, but exactly where was he? When it comes to the five W's – who, what, when, where and why – often in hunting the fourth is first in priority.

Chauney summed it up:

"You knew by his gobble he was close – maybe 200 yards, I'd put it – but in what direction? There are so many hills and points in that area."

This was a locale in which we often parked but never really hunted, thinking it too accessible. Why risk someone else walking in on your hunt? We came here to commune with nature, not collide with man. Well – just this once, we promised each other – we'd park as usual but hunt nearby.

From that point almost any direction of travel leads downhill – probably another reason we normally chose the mountaintop and hunted away from it. The descent opened our eyes to a hillside contoured by perhaps a dozen small ravines that seemed to cover every square inch of hillside.

It was now clear that yesterday's nearby gobbling had been rendered indistinct by the convoluted range of the turkey. For this fellow, life was a ditch.

Further complicating the job of finding Ditchmo, as he'd now been dubbed, was that three mountains converged in his territory. There were so many places that bird might be you couldn't even count 'em. Ah, but once we heard him!

Chauney was so turned off by the topography that he declined to return, but his younger son, Brian, came along. Our first crack at Ditchmo turned into an electrifying experience when my gun barrel contacted a wire installed by foresters to repel deer. Yes, it works on people, too. *Lucky you didn't touch it with a wet nose like a deer!*

We got close but never lucky. Once in a while a bit of scratching was spotted in the duff alongside the scat of a tom, presumably the one Chauney and I had heard, and once he came to the call but got hung up behind a huge black cherry tree and on the wrong side (for us) of a stream that apparently marked his territorial boundary. Four days after I first heard him, Ditchmo was still on the loose, and Brian and I were homebound.

King of the Road

Just over the hill from Ditchmo's domain lived a bird with a habit that certainly could have proved fatal. Just the opposite of Ditchmo, he showed himself the first day we walked into his territory. Nor was there any mystery about this fella's regular route.

Chauney and Brian were hunting in a hollow adjacent to the one where Brad and I stood listening to the gobbler hold forth. We'd been caught on a fairly open hillside marked sparsely by dead trees about half a foot thick, some of which had lost their tops to wind and now roughly resembled large fence posts.

As normal practice, I wouldn't recommend hiding right out in the open, but that's what we were forced to do when the gobbler turned and headed our way. He was sounding off about 100 yards downhill from where we stood, each with a hand on the other's shoulder and his shotgun resting on the ground – barrel up and, hopefully, resembling a sapling. We, of course, had become just two more fence posts.

We got away with it as the bird worked into a position barely beyond shotgun range below us. He shot a glance our way and let loose a gobble that challenged our ability to stay still.

We passed that test only to watch the turkey work away to our left, his calls diminishing and finally ceasing after he topped the hill and kept going. *Definitely a traveler, and you know how much ground they can cover.*

We moved downhill and found our boy had taken an old logging path. Just as we often choose the path of least resistance, wild turkeys do, too. Trailing the gobbler put us on a similar path of the same vintage as the first and bordering another clear-cut.

To thoughtful humans, a clear-cut is an eyesore, a reminder of how much modern loggers waste. To wildlife, such spots are welcome refuge. Turkeys are ground nesters, and the relative impassability of a clear-cut attracts hens wary of the fox, raccoon, coyote and bear out to feed on them and/or their eggs.

The list of turkey predators, of course, includes people, four of whom had reassembled in the logging road and were peering into the maze of fungus-encrusted stumps, twisted logs and branches beneath a sparse green canopy that defines a regenerating woods.

All that gobbling had not gone undetected by Chauney and Brian, who showed up about the time we reached the spot where the bird had topped the hill.

“Wow, look at all that turkey sign!” said Brian, pointing with the toe of his boot to droppings in the roadway.

Just a few feet away were more brown-and-white calling cards of the wild turkey; the freshest were fishhook shaped, left by a gobbler. A brief reconnaissance revealed more of the same elsewhere along the path. Obviously the gobbler was using this roadway regularly, so somewhere along its edge within shotgun range was the ideal place to set up.

It turned out there was one crucial difference between Ditchmo and the King of the Road: Whereas we’d had most of a week to focus on the former, we met the latter on our final day in camp that trip. He got lucky because we were out of time.

Pincushion Knob

Sometimes other hunters show up at the most inconvenient of times.

Despite getting into the woods extra early one morning, we heard a gobbler already sounding off uphill from us. No, make that two gobblers. As it was still too dark to pick a proper setup spot, our only option was to plop down by a tree to avoid busting the birds.

We were hunting during a drought, and Chauney detected a gobbler while scouting near water the previous night. We had the location part figured out, but getting pinned down on the approach was a bad start. And it was about to get worse.

Someone with a shotgun slung over his shoulder stopped the bicycle he was pedaling up the logging road and played his box call. Obviously the intruder was unaware of our presence and probably hadn't heard the birds. Nor did he get an answer from either gobbler, but he sure got one from Chauney.

"Hey, whatcha doin' calling from a bike in the middle of the road! You should stop and listen before you call. Now you've messed up our hunt!"

The guy apologized, sort of, after admitting he hadn't heard the gobbling. He said he was a telecommuter and could sneak in a hunt whenever he wanted.

Mr. Two Wheels shoved off before sunrise and so did we, opting to approach from a different angle. But our change in tactics didn't pan out because we never heard either bird again that morning.

The next day, over the hill, I was reminded that other hunters aren't the only pains in the butt one encounters in these woods. Once again forced to set up in the dark within earshot of an active (and too close) gobbler, I felt something jabbing my backside.

With morning's first light came a chance to check out the source of my discomfort.

Standing up would risk spooking the turkey, but I did it anyhow. Quick inspection revealed that the spot where I'd been sitting was laced with porcupine quills, a trio of which needed to be removed. Ouch! Ouch! Ouch! Tom, of course, didn't stick around for the extraction ceremony.

A short climb from that spot brought me to the remains of a red fox, dozens of porky quills protruding like oversized whiskers from its snout. Nearby lay the carcass of a porcupine that was missing lots of quills, especially from the rear end.

The porky faces away from its challenger, quills directed at foe. I rubbed my sore behind and shuddered at the thought of how terrible the combat must have been for both animals.

Back at the truck, another problem awaited discovery: The car key we'd cached beneath a nearby log was missing, apparently stolen. We hid the key so either of us could use it if necessary during the hunt. By now my tender butt was no longer such a big deal.

Big Boy, Part I

The biggest gobbler I've ever encountered in the wild approached within 15 steps one sunny May morn in 1979.

That spring was so damp we wore hip boots to hunt. So relentless was the rain that we were in denial, reminding each other there'd really only been two showers. The first was underway the day we came and lasted till the next morning; then the storm that started that night and was still going, or coming, if you prefer. We were also pretty well into our beer supply.

We've never had a telephone or TV at camp; heck, we didn't even have indoor plumbing. There's a radio, but reception is limited and unreliable. We were never much into tape decks, but CDs eventually helped brighten camp life, as did the advent of Gert.

This wholly imagined girl of the forest was strictly the kind of luxury we could afford in our early days. Through the years she has emerged in our collective eye as more tomboy than beauty, someone less apt to entertain under roof than from afar. A typical "sighting":

"Spotted Gert today over on the East Fork. She was with some guy I've never seen before, and they were sitting on opposite sides of a big ol' hemlock smoking corncob pipes."

Sometimes she's right there in the yard when someone's throwing out the dishwater and says – loud enough to be heard indoors – "Oh, I'm sorry. Didn't see you there, girl! Ya gotta speak up, Gert!"

This particular week we were mostly into reading books and playing cards. And we spent hours at the dartboard. Chauney was better at it – good enough to compete in a league back home – so I had to make do with what I had. The winner got a quarter, but the loser got to call the next game.

The board-maker's name, Champion, appeared at the top, and when things were hopelessly out of control, I might go with: "See the 'i' in Champion? Any dart in the 'i' scores a point, but any dart in the wall takes it away. Batter up!"

We played baseball style – each player shooting three darts per inning. If the score was tied after nine – a likely scenario in this game – it went into extra innings. This sometimes disrupted the norm – him winning, me losing – to the extent that I might even get back one of my quarters.

When that didn't work out, my resourcefulness might be informed by the weather. If it was thundering out there, why not in here, too – frying pans falling to the floor with your opponent just about to shoot, for instance.

Naturally, that didn't go over well with Chauney, but fortunately this tactic's effectiveness didn't require constant reinforcement. Apparently, after one experiences raining metal objects at critical moments its recurrence becomes a psychological certainty, not just a forecast. Turnabout is fair play, of course, so any reprieve was temporary.

By midweek, weary of darts, books and cards, we were ready for a change, any change. Which made sunrise the next day quite special because Ol' Sol really was up.

I chose a hill adjacent to a clear-cut, and my climb paid off in the distant but unmistakable serenade of a gobbler. A run of yelps on the call Red and I designed triggered a throaty reply.

However, I was caught in a poor calling position, violating one of Roscoe's rules. It was too open for concealment from piercing turkey eyes and, judging by his deepening voice, tom was getting close.

I hit the ground on my stomach, elbows on the edge of the hill, toes downhill. As the rain runoff continued, some of it entered my boots, reaching roughly ankle level by the time the gobbler arrived.

Turkey encounters are always exciting, colored as they are by the knowledge that their outcome is anything but certain. It's all about expecting the unexpected. One thing you can count on is that these magnificent creatures, once up close, will captivate you in a way that is disarming.

Around camp yours truly is known as the fella most likely to empty his shotgun at any gobbler lucky enough to come within range. And lucky is the right word because the overwhelming majority of those gobblers – three in a row, one spring – have gotten away without losing so much as one of their black-tipped breast feathers. I've been advised by, um, friends to carry a camera in the woods and buy my drumsticks at market.

It can be difficult to judge sizes and distances while prone in a forest, but right away I knew the gobbler in front of me was a big boy. The long red neck was craning, the blue head bobbing this way then that, his white wattles glistening. I felt like saluting!

Three white birch stumps, each about 4 feet high, were clumped approximately 15 yards away. One of them got 6 inches shorter with the first of my three true-to-form errant shots at Big Boy.

Once again I'd gotten caught sight-seeing instead of seeing the bird in my gunsights. Emotion had granted yet another stay of execution, and mentally I was berating myself – this time in rhyme:

Get your cheek down on the stock,
or you'll miss the whole darned flock.

My vexation deepened when a young driver pulled over just as I reached the road at the bottom of the hill. He offered me a lift to my car, and on the way I couldn't help but notice the vehicle's faux fur interior; it was purple.

If the décor was modern, our conversation was as old as the hills. In a matter of seconds the time-honored question whenever hunters meet in the woods hung in the air:

"See any?"

"I just missed the biggest gobbler I've ever laid eyes on."

Ordinarily I wouldn't share such information with a stranger; just wasn't done making mistakes that morning, I guess.

"Saw him back in March; he was twice the size of the next biggest bird in the flock. There were 12 of them – right on the other side of the hill you just came down."

Into each life some rain must fall

Moon Valley Lodge is a perfect setting to soak up the wisdom of Henry Wadsworth Longfellow's poem, "The Rainy Day," which contains the seven words immediately preceding this sentence.

Just as in the lowlands, water is a central theme in mountain life, and many lessons flow from it. A spring deep in the woods is a magnet for thirsty animals – man included – so the careful hunter will be extra vigilant in its vicinity.

The spring's cousin is the seep, a quieter, less showy version of water surfacing in which it unceremoniously oozes from the earth. South-facing seeps are the wintertime saviors of the wild turkey and other birds, offering grit, food and water in one stop.

Rain allows for quiet walking; its companion, reduced visibility, cuts the turkey's eyesight advantage. But a wet hillside is a tumble just waiting to be taken.

During one especially wet week in the Seventies we learned something about munitions and moisture. Chauney had located a gobbler near a slate quarry and gotten familiar enough with the bird's habits to guess where he'd pass the next morning.

Close by were the remains of a huge stump, conveniently hollowed out by fire enough that he could crouch within it, reaping the twin advantages of camouflage and shelter.

Squirreled away in his wooden lair before daybreak, Chauney was hoping to see the rain go away and the gobbler approach. Maybe he should have been wishing instead that he wasn't so cramped up in there. When tom did come to the call, the shot was awkward – and a clear miss.

Chauney is the dead-eye of our camp. I've watched him bring down crows and pheasants at 60 yards or more with his Model 12 Winchester.

But not this morning. And he had plenty of time for a second shot, too, but none rang out: The paper shell, swollen by dampness, had jammed in the chamber – the gun was inoperable. To this day we use plastic shotgun shells, never paper.

We'd been able to hunt only two mornings of the first five that week, and cabin fever set in. The topic of discussion was food.

"Somebody was telling me that leeks grow wild up here," One of Us said.

"OK, I'll bite, what's a leek?" asked the Other.

"That's a spring onion that grows in the hollows. He said the locals cook 'em up with ham."

Scalloped potatoes and ham had served themselves up in the conversation earlier, and that might have laid the groundwork for what was about to occur.

Before the Other could even ask what the heck a leek plant looked like, One of Us was out the door and scouring the back yard, shovel in hand. He returned, dripping wet, carrying a bright red bulb nearly as big as a pingpong ball.

The Other was leery, but One of Us insisted it had to be a leek and ate it without further comment.

Experience is an effective teacher, though cruel in method: First the test, then the lesson.

Something obviously was wrong because within minutes a scarlet ring appeared around the mouth of One of Us. At first the Other guessed it was blood, but closer inspection suggested it was an allergic reaction to whatever One of Us had ingested.

The spring closest to camp was tainted by rain runoff, rendering us temporarily out of drinking water. Suddenly thirsty, One of Us settled for a beer. Whatever it was stayed down, only to take its revenge later in the privy.

The wild leek revisited

Much later we learned, we two,
which was leek and which was not,
that yon red-stemmed version
ranked just a wee bit too hot.

Wild leek, garlic, onion, ramp –
they're the Allium genus,
herbs of hill that to ID
nowadays takes no genius.

Five decades of friendship dear
owes a nod for its flavor
to the broad- and smooth-leaved leek
that we still seek and savor.

.

You can spot its light green arms
clustered tightly in the sun
when some tom's call to mate has
Nimrod reaching for his gun.

A land of deer, bear and trout
this well may be, but in spring
ham-and-leeks, not venison,
is the oh-so-scrumptious thing.

P.S.: In time, we became so enamored of the wild leek that, in e-mail, he signed as Big Leek to my Li'l.

Inside, leek lovers (L to R) John, Brad,
Brian and Shane Martin are ready for lunch.

Outside, a healthy leek plantation sprawls
across Potter County hillside on May 1, 2016.

Doing Hobo Suppers like an Indian

Chauney and I usually arrive a day or so before the spring gobbler hunt to open camp for the season. That includes clearing the grounds of fallen branches and, the late April weather permitting, building a fire in the backyard pit.

All of which sets the stage for a Hobo Supper, the classic American meal with which almost everyone is familiar: veggies sliced thick and packed with hamburger in an aluminum foil pouch.

You can cook this poor man's pot roast in a kitchen oven, over a gas grill or charcoal, but an open wood fire adds distinctive flavor. Some 19th century sage observed that while the white man builds a big fire and stands back, the Indian makes a small one and stays close.

So, think like an Indian: Better to build a small fire and let supper cook a little longer than risk charring a delicious dinner. No need to time anything; the sizzling means the meal's cooking. Let your nose decide when it's done.

The only elk steak I was ever lucky enough to set my teeth into was cooked hobo style, and it was marvelous. Beefsteak or an extra thick pork chop can substitute for the hamburger, and practically any vegetable combo will work. My favorites are potato, carrot, sweet onion, summer squash, snow peas and tomato. Last thing before sealing the pouch, add a tablespoon or two of water and a pat of butter or dribble with olive oil. *Bon appetit!*

Sawyer's Rest and Big Boy, Part II

The woods can be slow to surrender their secrets. I never again caught up with Big Boy, but years later I met someone who might have.

Our chance meeting came in a large grape tangle, a magnet for turkeys and other birds and animals, man included. On a vine-shrouded knob was a double-stemmed oak whose trunk formed a V starting just above ground. Long ago a two-man saw was left, its teeth pointed skyward, in the tree crotch, and subsequent growth now hid most of the blade. I call it Sawyer's Rest.

Close by a turkey was gobbling downhill from my position, so I set up a hen decoy and tried to call him up for a shot. With one end of a piece of fishing line tied around the decoy's neck and the other secured to my left foot, I hoped to bring realistic movement to the fake bird. It all seemed to be working fine – until the gobbler apparently caught my foot in motion and skedaddled.

Moments later I wasn't so sure what had spooked him because a tall, elderly man in blue jeans was walking the side hill below me where the turkey had been. Looking up, he headed my way.

This fellow said he learned growing up on a turkey farm how to talk their language – without using any artificial call. He was a retired lumberman from Latrobe, PA, with hands as big as ham steaks and a small cabin at the bottom of the hill. He invited me down to see what he called his "state-record" gobbler mount.

I declined to visit but listened to his story:

The bird fell to his rifle in autumn 1980 on a 30-yard shot taken not far from a cabin at the juncture of two streams. By his description, I knew the camp was due east half a mile from the site of my encounter with Big Boy. The time frame was about right, and two dominant toms coexisting in one area was unlikely. Was it the same bird? That's a good possibility.

Lou Hoffman Memorial Highway

The only other turkey hunter I remember in blue jeans and calling with just the voice God gave him was Lou Hoffman. When I met Lou in the Sixties, he was a high school biology teacher, one of Chauney's deputies.

He had an uncle who owned a camp in Conrad, Potter County, and some of Lou's turkey haunts coincided with ours. His favorite was Jamison Hollow, which he preferred to hunt from the top down.

While scouting early one spring in the Seventies near the Jamison, he saw a huge turkey track in melting snow. Lou's plan to hunt the big gobbler was scuttled by his duties as publisher of the Pennsylvania Sportsman magazine, but he told Chauney about it and gave these directions to the spot:

"Heading toward Cherry Springs from Conrad you just make four right turns in a row, the first being onto Horton Run Road."

It was raining when we pulled into camp the eve of the hunt, and clearly it had been a wet week. The dirt roads had turned muddy, and the clay made for slip-and-slide driving in the station wagon. Oh, those ruts were driving me nuts!

It was still dripping as we left camp in early morning darkness. The first three rights were routine; the fourth was anything but. It was a two-track heading into the woods and then took a quick sharp left and led downhill.

Despite the absence of ruts, hinting that this was a new road, I blithely drove on. In a matter of seconds there were ruts – ours. The farther downhill we went, the deeper the wheels sank into mud. With the car resting on its frame, our decision was easy: Hey, we're here, it's time to hunt, let's go after the turkey Lou told us about.

The storm persisted all morning with neither of us hearing a gobble, just the sound of pounding precipitation. It was letting up by the time we rendezvoused at our mud-mobile, but any sense of relief was brief. On the windshield was a note:

"This road is solely for use in harvesting forest products. Remove your vehicle within 24 hours ..." The scribbler was a district forester.

Obviously a bad situation had just gotten worse. Not only was the car stuck in muck, stranding us miles from the cabin, but now we also were in trouble with woods officialdom. Insult was added to injury as the rain picked up again.

His vehicle's tracks showed the note writer had come within a few yards of our roadblock and then backed out. He had 4-wheel drive for sure, and likely packed a tow chain as well. If he had other chores to do, he could have written that he'd return later to help us out and clear the road. But Mr. Nice Guy he wasn't.

Getting along in the woods requires self-reliance, so we didn't dwell on it, but this guy sure missed a chance to show some compassion. Just a little cooperation might have resulted in the reopening of Lou Hoffman Memorial Highway within hours of its closing that Saturday. Instead it stayed shut till Thursday.

I don't remember the passerby who must have given us a lift back to camp, but I do recall the next person to come to our aid: Ed Clark, a fellow game protector and friend of Chauney's, who lived in Austin, about 20 miles away. He and his gracious wife, Eleanor, opened their door to us one spring hunt when we needed a place to bunk. Right now what we needed was a tow.

It was a sunny day when the wrecker hauled my blue Volvo up over the mountain and we were once again mobile. Never was a steering wheel so welcome to the hands. By week's end, however, the joy of overcoming deprivation would turn into a hollow victory.

Without a car, we'd been unable to pursue the bird Lou put us on, so we hunted the hills nearest to camp. The only turkey we got even close to was hanging out by the solitary hemlock on the hill facing the cabin, judging by all the fresh turkey scratching. All our calls went unanswered.

The ground was still so soggy on getaway day that I'd only been able to pull halfway up the driveway. We were just finishing the back-and-forth parade to load up. I'm pretty sure we hadn't heard a gobble all week, but just then we did.

Turkeys will holler reflexively at thunder or any loud sound they perceive as a possible challenge. In this case, all it took was one of us slamming the car door. The turkey was on the mountain in front of the cabin. Chauney and I exchanged glances, shook our heads and climbed aboard. There was no reaching for hunting jackets or shotguns. Silently we headed home.

Lou Hoffman died in middle age and, so far as I know, never took a drive down the roadway we named for him.

Chang Hollow

A place that beckoned the first time I saw its wooden sign was Chang Hollow, situated on an edge of the Hammersley. Hunting was the excuse but exploration was the essence of that initial visit.

Physically I was on vacation, but I was still thinking like a copy editor: *Some Chinaman must've met a terrible fate here: a mountain lion? He lost his life but this hollow found a name – yeah, something like that. Hey, wait, maybe it's just a typo in which shang, a nickname for ginseng, became chang. Hmmmmmmm.*

No such explanation turns up in the record, but if it was a chang-for-shang mixup this hollow is probably where two of my relatives spent a "wonderful" summer vacation a century ago.

It turns out that not only was there an earlier newspaperman in our family, but he also was drawn to the wilds of northern Pennsylvania. Warren L. Loope (1871-1964), one of my mother's uncles, owned, edited and published a small newspaper in Millerton, NY. He, too, was a hunter of sorts.

Appearing in his mimeographed memoir, "SOME PLEASANT MEMORIES (And a few others)," is this account of "The Shang Hunt":

It was during the early nineteen hundreds (1902) that my brother, William, and I had a wonderful vacation trip into rather wild territory in northern Pennsylvania – and, unusually enough, found it financially profitable.

About that time many people in the Cortland-Homer-Little York area who had plenty of garden space near their homes, indulged in the raising of ginseng, not for home consumption but for ultimate sale of the dried roots to be exported to China. The Chinese at that time considered ginseng roots very valuable, and perhaps they still do.

Growers built shade for their ginseng beds and planted the small, young wild roots only a few inches apart. For shade they used 4-inch-wide boards set upright, about 2 inches apart, and overhead a roof of similar material and construction.

The demand for plants was such that wild roots, too small for profitable marketing in dried form, could be sold to growers at 6 cents per root, if alive.

Somehow we heard that this herb was a very common plant in the "barrens" of northern Pennsylvania – areas which had been lumbered some years ago and now grown up to weeds and bushes – which was the usual condition of woodlands south of Elmira, Wellsville and Olean, and as we had a few summer weeks to dispose of we decided to go down there and ramble.

Before going into the wilds we consulted some local businessmen in the area. We were warned at the start that rattlesnakes also thrived in the barrens and were inclined to be hostile to all two-legged invaders. We also were informed that a certain merchant, still in business at Emporium, I think it was, had in former years bought and shipped large quantities of ginseng.

So we went to see him and found that he still dealt in the roots but on a much smaller scale than in former years. He said he had shipped the dried roots in lots as large as five to 10 barrels in the old days, and told us in what areas it was most likely to be found somewhat abundantly. He also suggested that we ought to have a guide, if we hoped to get back, and suggested a few men he could recommend and whom he thought might be willing to serve as such.

The first one we contacted was available and seemed to be interested, so we engaged him for a few weeks, got together the necessary supplies and hired a livery stable operator to take us as far toward our objective as roads were available, and to meet us there on the date we hoped to return to civilization.

On getting into the wilds our guide located a ginseng plant before we had gone far on foot, and we sort of memorized its appearance from various angles before we dug up the root and sank it into a small sack of damp woodland soil to keep it alive.

While in camp we found and sacked about 2,000 ginseng roots. Our guide also offered to do some shang hunting on his own and ship the roots to us if we would pay him one cent per root plus express charges. We agreed to pay that price if he would ship not fewer than 500 roots. And sometime after we got back to Cortland we received a shipment of 1,000 roots from him.

So we sent him ten bucks and sold the roots to the same grower who had bought what we brought back, at six cents per root. And so William and I felt that the total of $120 for what we brought home and a gain of $50 on the thousand we bought, made our summer vacation trip rather a success, as $170 in those days had some purchasing power.

Not exactly like striking it rich in the Klondike, but not bad.
For the record, nowadays it is illegal to harvest wild ginseng on public land for sale outside of Pennsylvania without a vulnerable plant license. Harvest season is September through November, while the fruit is bright red, and the seeds collected

must be planted in the immediate vicinity to help sustain the colony.

My two granduncles certainly were lucky: After its early mention, the word rattlesnake never again reared its ugly head.

Emporium, the Cameron County seat, is about 20 miles on a straight line from Chang Hollow, which I believe is where Warren and Richard Loope conducted "The Shang Hunt."

Mother told me that Warren was an avid trout fisherman and introduced her to sweet flag (a.k.a. calamus), a perennial marsh herb with long leaves and a pungent rootstock.

"It isn't sweet at all, but the face I made only made him laugh the harder," she said, adding that this prankster was also a lawyer.

W.P. Dohne with a young wild turkey gobbler taken in Alabama.

Mr. and Mrs. William P. Dohne, Doug's parents.

Lonely Boy

Encountered during another soggy spring in the Seventies, this gobbler was coming off a winter in which, locals told us, snow piled up man-high in the woods.

Springtime is always an adventure in Potter County, especially the weather. Chauney and I wore plenty of wool and saw a lot of snow on those early hunts. It was not unusual to have to skirt hollows that were still choked with snow several feet deep.

At times we found deer carcasses – half a dozen or more – along creeks at the bottom of those hollows. Swollen by snowmelt, the rushing streams seemed to shout a message of revival. It was a sad study in contrasts, Mother Nature's beauty vs. her cruelty. The creeks and the sun were on the rise, as if to rescue weary white-tails, but these deer were down to stay.

A wild turkey can lose about 30 percent of its bodyweight and survive for several weeks if snow dictates staying put in a tree. Often the problem is a lack of grit. Even with a full crop, our avian friends will starve when ice or deep snow deprives them of the tiny stones they need to grind food.

The endurance test takes place on a branch: Will the turkey run out of food, grit and/or moisture before receding snow permits it to descend safely, refuel and return, or will winter's grip prevail? Besides man, turkey predators include the coyote and bobcat, which might be lurking close by, hoping for a poultry snack.

It was just that kind of spring when I got to know Lonely Boy. Chauney and I, discouraged after hearing not one gobble five days into the hunt, knew the turkeys had been walloped by winter. We wondered if the flock had been sufficiently decimated to make this our last hunt.

Then came a single gobble from uphill behind camp, immediately and dramatically rescuing me from the imagined demise of the wild turkey hereabouts. Talk about an upper! But listening patiently for another gobble didn't mean it was coming.

One gobble is all? Spooked by another hunter? Nah, haven't seen anyone else in these woods all week. We seem to be the only ones left with any hope. No, more likely he's moved away from the side hill; probably just pulled back on top and out of earshot.

The hillside, slippery with snowmelt and still white in spots, was a hard hike with no further gobbling to show for it. I took a seat on a fallen tree and peeled a hardboiled egg, then an orange. I hoped breakfast would be followed – if not interrupted – by turkey talk, but it wasn't. The only birdsong was from much smaller species, whose intensity seemed born of the belief it could hasten spring's arrival. That wasn't happening either.

Two hours later, descending the hill, I somehow spotted turkey scat in the snow and glary sunshine. The find, near one of the few big hemlocks on that hill, raised my spirits but some questions as well.

I'd heard the bird from below, but he couldn't have been higher on the hill than this tree. In other words, he was on that hill the whole time. But I'd caught just a solitary gobble early in the morning when tom should have been sounding off regularly.

Except for his own, this guy isn't hearing many turkey voices this spring. Maybe his sparse calling is simply a natural defense mechanism: Fewer gobbles mean fewer reminders that he's alone. Sure, that's it – he's just a lonely boy.

We ran into each other at that huge hemlock bright and early the next morning. I spotted him about 30 yards uphill from the tree, and just then he came a step closer and flushed – straight at me but smack into the hemlock! As gobbler getaways go, this one was off to a poor start.

It was raining hemlock needles and twigs as wings beat branches. But where, exactly, was the bird? Oh, there he goes, back out the same side he came in! No gobbling had heralded his coming, and no shooting marked his exit. At least for once this spring, Lonely Boy was content to be alone.

I was happy the way it turned out, too. After all, few enough turkeys had made it through the winter. It was no time for killing; this was healing season.

Wild turkey flock visits an old orchard on a snowy day in Venango County, PA. Photo by Pamela Taylor.

Favorite Son

Miles away, near the town of Austin, the recovery was more advanced. A gobbler was singing his heart out on a nearby hill, and we went to check it out, running into a traffic jam on the mountaintop.

Drivers got off the dirt road as best they could, but it was evident some of them were uninitiated in such maneuvers on narrow dirt roads – non-hunters, in other words.

It was a free concert, of course, but you had to stay in your seat – the one you rode in on – for the entire show. Slamming car doors might be interpreted by the soloist as something other than applause. This didn't seem to matter to most of his fans because they'd already seen him – close up, in fact – that winter.

The gobbler belonged to a flock that was forced from the forest by heavy snow and just showed up in town one day. They were taken under the wing of villagers, who provided that essential grit and kernels of corn in the wake of the town snowplow.

As drivers slowed down and stayed vigilant, the newcomers learned to depend on it. When they needed to get away from it all the turkeys simply headed for the drainage pipes under Main Street.

In this manner the flock survived winter and returned to the woods in spring. They hadn't gone far – just up the hill behind town, lingering like exiting dinner guests at the door. The boss gobbler, by now the favorite son of Austin's flock, was giving a farewell concert, trumpeting triumph over adversity and hope for the future. The locals loved it and so did we.

The game of itsy bitsy

We were tipped off about Favorite Son during a card game hosted by the Clarks.

Among those coming to their poker table in the Seventies was another game protector, Pat Neeley, whose visits had increased now that he was retired. When it was his deal, the old man loved to call itsy bitsy, in which one wins by taking no tricks. Essentially, you bet that yours is the lousiest hand at the table and someone else's will beat it every time.

Neeley would chuckle quietly as the rest of us took trick after trick, then rake in the pot.

Meanwhile, wildlife biologists were starting to play their own version of itsy bitsy – in the game of turkey management – and Neeley had a hand in that, too.

When raised in captivity, the turkey often fares poorly in the wild. Susceptible to predation and harsh weather, such birds also can carry diseases capable of wiping out any wild flocks they join. And they simply aren't anywhere near the hunting challenge that their wild cousins present. After all, they've been conditioned to gather at the feed trough when humans show up – not run and hide.

The Game Commission began to hedge its bet on pen-raised birds by giving a boost to the other players in the game, the wild ones, in an effort to expand Pennsylvania's forest flocks. In Potter County, the last pen-raised birds were released in 1952, and Pat Neeley was the guy who did it.

Elsewhere in the Keystone State the practice of pen-raising turkeys to be turned loose in the wild hung on. Hatched in 1930, the program produced 200,000 birds, the last of which went to the woods in 1980.

Two decades before that a new tactic had begun – capturing wild birds in prime habitat and freeing them in areas lacking established flocks. Trap-and-transfer, as it became known, eventually encompassed 39 counties but – in contrast to pen raising – involved just 2,800 turkeys.

More importantly, this approach jumpstarted an amazing comeback by the wild turkey. Hunters took just under 15,000 turkeys in the fall of 1960, when trap-and-transfer began in Pennsylvania. Seven seasons later the kill was 23,000, and the inaugural spring gobbler hunt was staged the next year.

There were setbacks along the way but, generally, the wild turkey population took off, as reflected in the hunting harvest.

The turkey's high-water mark came In 2001, at least in terms of the hunters' total take (97,000), which included 49,000 gobblers in the spring and another 48,000 birds (of either sex) that fall. It was the first time the spring harvest topped autumn's – the pattern ever since.

Boosted by trap-and-transfer, habitat improvements and fall hunting restrictions, Pennsylvania's wild turkey flock swelled to 280,000 early in this century, then nosedived to under 200,000 within a few years. This state held an estimated 215,000 turkeys in 2015.

A typical turkey hunt

For readers willing to endure detail to savor the flavor, here's a peek at my diary account of our spring 2008 hunt. (The meals are listed mainly because yours truly was the evening cook. Chauney and Brad handle breakfast and lunch.)

April 25: The day before the season opens, hear a gobbler on the hill behind camp at 5:50 a.m. See 3 more elsewhere – 2 have hens traveling along – a bobcat and 2 deer, one of which is way pregnant. Run into retired special-ed teacher Dick Reber on Game Refuge Trail; he tells of seeing a doe give birth last spring: "It wasn't on the ground 10 seconds before a coyote dashed in from out of nowhere, grabbed a hind leg and dragged it off." We quietly agree that cruelty is a recurring theme here. It seems whenever I see coyote scat in these woods it always contains deer remains. Drive 10 miles to a phone, ask Brad to bring along insect repellent and his Shop-Vac. Back at MVL, press on through Hemingway's boomerang *ménage a trois*, "The Garden of Eden." Slice spuds for home fries as clouds reappear.

April 26: Opening day is always a Saturday and that means, other hunters. Try the trees at Patterson State Park, but some Jersey boys are in there early. Bust a pair of foraging hens along a deer trail; they fly west into the long hollow. Head south toward the smaller of 2 clear-cuts. Yes! There is a gobbler, but at great distance. It will be a steep descent to begin, through the residue of last summer's huge blackberry thickets – as is often the case adjacent to lumbering operations, then up a slippery slope (springs flowing and lots of shale). Finally, 55 minutes later and just a few more briar scratches to go, it's time to pause, catch a breath and collect my thoughts. Bam! That's probably one of the Jersey boys shooting, about 150 yards away. Then powerful wingbeats end the newscast of this particular encounter between hunter and hunted. *It's gonna be a burger kind of supper tonight, Chauney.*

April 27: Stay busy on Sunday just lickin' our wounds, some of us anyhow. "Well howdy, Bradley," so fresh and full of youthful energy. "Welcome to the party," as would be Roscoe. Were he here, Roscoe, in the time-worn tradition of the aged, would be content just stoking the campfire. So far he's a no-show for this hunt. Brad and I get 2 gallons of ladybugs on the first of several harvests inside camp with the Shop-Vac. Now it's a whole lot easier to relax and sleep! Chauney has a problem: His right knee has grown considerably larger than the left, and he needs to ice it. "There's a bird in Wild Boy," he informs everyone at the dinner table but no one in particular. He got hurt in a fall. Just now I've had my fill of turkeys and the stories that hunting them spawns, but still hunger for Hemingway. Papa inebriates my intellect with "A Farewell to Arms." For the body we have a decent cabernet sauvignon, for the soul the simple solitude of nature. Hey, this is a complete experience. Ham and mashed all around.

April 28: The 70s are gone – the temps, I mean – and that's refreshing. The gnats, knocked down by a near-freeze overnight, are being finished off as an annoyance to hunters by a morning drizzle. *Thank You, Jesus, for this merciful and timely shower.*

Brad, DD hear one wind-withered gobble on a hill east of an old clear-cut near Cherry Springs. A hen's clucking (a real hen, right?) steals the old boy's attention, and with it our only chance today. After separating from Brad, I spot a lone hen turkey in the beech; she is quickly past my position and on her way. The sleet lays thick enough on this mountain right now that footing is treacherous, even over the level. Forced into an early retreat to camp, on the way we are treated to the rare passage of 6 helicopters running just above treetop along the Wharton to Cherry Springs Road (dirt until 2 years ago). Coincidentally the choppers herald the arrival of Brian, who appears at camp within the hour. He has driven 12 hours from North Carolina for this special reunion in the woods. We mark the occasion by cutting half a truckload of firewood from fallen limbs in the neighborhood. Following Steaks For Real Men (1.75 inches thick, from Pronio's Market, Hershey), Brian wins at darts.

April 29: Young fellas challenge the vocalist of Wild Boy Hollow. Brian, our least seasoned member but nevertheless a veteran, hears the gobbler but cannot stop or get him to answer his box call. "He's a traveler," Brian offers in terse description of their encounter.

Sounds like he's trying to discourage anyone else from taking up pursuit.

Duly noted, young fella. Brad never heard the bird at all.

He should have pros check his hearing ASAP.

Meanwhile, in the huge Jamison, I'm slipping on a wet and, in spots, icy hillside while ascending to the crest that last fall held a large turkey flock during a deep drought. But Chauney has it harder still, being ousted from the parking spot he chose on privately owned land. No real harm is done, it appears, as the only things passing between intruder and owner are words. Still, his hunt is disrupted for much of the morn. And then there is the complicated pickup of his partner (me), unaware of the run-in with an angry landowner. As one consequence of last year's drought, tonight there is but a solitary peeper announcing a willingness to participate in his kind's essential spring ritual along the little creek out front. The peepers' music to mate by has summoned me to slumber so many times, yet I had taken it (and them) for granted. I recall a comment Mother's father made in his 90s after I'd noticed his toe tapping to a tune on Dick Clark's "American Bandstand." Yes, Doc said, he knew the song, but "in its original version." Peering over his newspaper, he added: "You have no idea how lonely it is being the last leaf on the tree." Or the last peeper on the stream.

April 30: Boys are skunked again by the Moveable Feast (a tip of the hunting cap to Papa) that is the Wild Boy Hollow gobbler. Brian notices a large black bird that's smaller than a turkey. It jumps from the ground into a tree and hisses at the intruder; definitely not turkey behavior. The boys' father and I, meanwhile, are in the Cherry Springs bowl. He encounters 2 deer while I have 4. A gobbler's sounding off for the third time in 5 days on yet a different part of that hill. He is wary and I am weary, and the sun is reaching the noon position. Sausage and cabbage. PM: Brad, DD explore grassy pipeline over Chipmunk Trail and he, partly as a price of my miscalculation, is way late coming out of the woods. There is no moon, and his tardy exit means an hour walking in pitch black woods. He's still talking to me, but barely; in the morning he prefers his brother's company to mine. Can't say I blame him. This afternoon Brian and I repair an 8-inch hole punched through the cabin floor by a porcupine. Consulting several books on bird identification, we decide it was a turkey vulture that he ran into this morning.

May 1: It's 28 degrees this morning on our little patch of Eden. The bird I've worked for 3 days now is busy with another hunter, who has preceded me into the forest. So I'm back at Pat Park, minus the Jersey boys, and admiring what I think is new territory. Oh, silly me! Over the mountain and across the stream I find a leg of the always well-marked 80-mile Susquehanna Trail System, a figure-8 loop. A 400-yard-or-so hoof brings me to Sunken Branch Road and then to the Billy Lewis. We've killed at least 1 gobbler in Sunken Branch, but I never would have thought I was anywhere near there today. Lewis was a colorful PA politician of the Twenties and Thirties, and it is said of the gravel road bearing his name that if a cabin were built along it the rainwater from one eve would fall into the Susquehanna River Basin while that from the other side would flow into the mighty Ohio. Haven't been over here in 12-15 hunts. Exiting the hollow, I pass a cabin half the size of ours at the base of a hill. Before re-crossing the creek, I note the side-by-side tracks of a bear and a turkey in sandy soil. They are 18 inches apart and lead in the same direction, but were left at different times, obviously. Back up the hill I slog, pausing to observe a trillium couple, one red and the other white, growing close enough that their blossoms are bumping in the breeze. They are the only flowers of their kind on the hill that I can see. Back at MVL, we're having fish tonight. "Shrimp, boys, come and git it!"

May 2: Now it's 41 degrees and cloudy. The boys' report of yesterday's doings has stirred my turkey hunting instincts like a glimpse of the neighbor girl, the pretty one. They told of heavy T sign, and I'm hearing 2 widely separated gobblers in the same area this morning. Halfway uphill there's an old railroad bed, its metal missing – courtesy of wartime scavengers? Pausing to shed some clothes, I get caught in the open with my eyeglasses and turkey calls tucked away in buttoned-down pockets when a gobbler sounds off 100 yards uphill. Gobblers call for various reasons, of course. Right now, this bird has detected a visitor and is calling out for some ID. This is the sergeant-at-arms call. What he wants to hear is a demure putt, chirp or purr, perhaps a cluck or maybe even a short series of yelps, signaling a hen ready and willing to mate. I can offer none of these, darn it, so I exercise my only option: Drop to the ground and gripe in silence about the resurging gnats. My only hope is, he just slowly passes by above. By the time I get my camo duds back on and the diaphragm call in my mouth, the bird is out of earshot. I give a soft 3-yelp call anyhow. Whoa! That gobbling is coming from the opposite direction! There are two gobblers on this hill!

Yup, and No. 2's gonna pass just below me by the sound of it. I let out the softest of putts. Anxious minutes crawl by like caterpillars on a cold morning. First one hen, then two more feed by, then there's a gobble but no gobbler in view. Presto! There he is, standing with his hens. Sciatica is knifing my right leg, and my left arm (yes, the one I need to hoist the Ithaca) has fallen asleep because I've been too long prone. Regardless, it's time to make a move. Two hens take wing and another legs it as my 12-gauge booms, harmlessly. The gobbler stays put, just 22 yards downhill from a gun quite capable (in the right hands) of killing at 60 yards. He's behind a huge cherry tree, tail feathers sticking out on one side, head now and then jutting out a few inches the other way. I opt for a shot, but he pulls back his head in time. Another miss. Now the show goes airborne – the bird moving left to right, my favorite shot, oh boy – and I time my last blast as he reaches an opening at about 45 yards. My No. 4s slam into his right wing and drive the gobbler (even at that distance his beard sticks out noticeably) in a counterclockwise downward spiral in which he makes 2 complete turns. The thud of his landing is followed by the beating of at least one wing in leaves, and then the sound softens as I charge downhill. Not a feather in sight, nothing to signal any drama at the base of the hill – until I glance up the railroad bed and see the gobbler hightailing it a football field or more away, carrying his right wing a little lower than the left. Double drat! Too tired to cook tonight. Gimme a cold one, Chauney, and gimme room.

May 3: In truth, this hunt is over for me; anything else figures to be anticlimactic. But I'm fighting against letting that thought sink in. Our junior members have dispersed, probably not to reappear (at least in camp) until autumn. One of the best things about turkey hunting is that the next season is never more than 6 months off. I like to dwell on that particularly on the last day of whichever season is winding up. Chauney declares himself out of this, the last day of our 41st spring hunt, and no amount of cajoling can take his mind off that once-again swollen right knee. Ow! Revisiting yesterday's battlefield (remember, the first bird passed without incident) is a no-brainer but, alas, unproductive. Topping the hill, which I didn't do yesterday, proves fruitless – until I cross it and take a seat on a log to monitor birdsong from the opposite hill. There are 2 distinctly different turkey voices in the chasm!

Chances are, this would be the same pair I encountered yesterday. It was amazing that they were operating in such close proximity; one even had hens along. Mature toms simply do not tolerate competition for a hen, yet these two were still together. OK, this hunt truly has come to an end. Oh, you can hang around on Double or Nothing Hill (see how these things get started) long enough to dry out that pair of sweat-soaked camo hankies in your back pocket, but this is over.

The selection of a walking stick from a pile of downed timber equips me for the walk to camp. Turkey hunting certainly has its ups and downs: After losing out on a mountaintop you descend to camp to receive your comeuppance at the hands of hunting buddies only too happy to oblige. It's a beautiful day to be homeward bound from deep within the woods. As Robert Louis Stevenson put it:

Home is the sailor,
home from the sea.
And the hunter,
home from the hill.

When it comes to shooting

Roscoe was so upset by my wounding of the turkey that the next time I saw him he immediately launched into a do-it-this-way lecture:

"Stick to 40 yards as the maximum for shooting when you're in the woods, period. Sometimes it's hard to judge distances, so when you're setting up just pick out a tree here or there that you think is about maximum range. If a bird passes on the other side of the tree, come back and try tomorrow."

"Yes," I managed to reply, "but didn't this ever happen to you? Don't you ever miss?"

In five decades of turkey hunting, Roscoe said, he could recall just two such occasions, adding: "I miss some because I aim for the head – just one or two pellets will do the trick."

He was in his 90s when a gobbler "came back to life" behind the seat during the drive home from camp. What began with a shotgun in the woods was finished with a hammer in the garage.

Still in all, Roscoe maintained, it is the challenge and not the killing that is this sport's main allure; the latter simply results from accepting the former.

Here's how he expressed it:

"You have to be lucky, but you also have to know where to go and when to be there. I like when it rains and then gets sunny. I'd bet my last tooth that I'll see turkeys on a day like that. You must get close enough. People ask me if ego is part of it. You are the only one who knows that, deep down inside. All I can say is, I try to live every day to the fullest."

An earlier brother of the brush, Spanish philosopher, essayist and politician Jose Ortega y Gasset (1883-1955) wrote in his "Meditations on Hunting":

"One does not hunt in order to kill; on the contrary, one kills in order to have hunted. If one were to present the sportsman with the death of the animal as a gift he would refuse it. What he is after is having to win it, to conquer the surly brute through his own effort and skill with all the extras that this carries with it: the immersion in the countryside, the healthfulness of the exercise, the distraction from his job."

Bullets vs. hooks

At the end of Nimrod's day
no catch-and-release has he
to take back the perfect shot
and thus let his prey go free.

As a footnote to the somber side of hunting, I would add only this: Primarily out of respect for life taken in the woods, there are no turkey heads, fans or beards on my walls. The same goes for camp; the only turkey on display there is a gobbler shot in full strut by a photographer who had perfect timing.

Eventually you wind up on Blue Dot

A fool learns from experience; a wise man learns from the experience of others.

– Otto Von Bismarck

Well, the Iron Chancellor never walked the trail we know as the Blue Dot, and we two fools never followed his words of wisdom – at least re: turkey hunting. Our only defense is that what's learned in the woods through personal experience somehow seems to outlast the other kind.

For a turkey hunter, the lessons sometimes loom as large as the mountains on which they are taught. A young man studies the topography and its wildlife, then gets to know the lay of the land and the ways of the wild. By middle age his knowledge and woods skills are honed and well tested by the hunt. He has taken turkey and trout; he relishes the leek. And if he's lucky he's acquired some humility, too, because there's nothing like a mountain he's climbed more often than he can remember to let him know that now, in old age, he'd better forget it.

At any age, the tricky part of spring turkey hunting is to find a gobbler you can work on exclusively. Even in the seemingly endless Susquehannock Forest, interference is often inevitable.

Bad weather can boost your chances of going solo with tom – provided it's not prohibitive, i.e., lightning or high wind – by keeping others at home. Your odds of enjoying solitude shrink when weekenders swell hunter ranks.

Of the many factors affecting human turnout in the woods, you can control only two – when and where you choose to hunt. If you've taken a week off from work, the when part already has been determined. It's been expressed this way at camp:

"We know who, what, when, why and how," (OK, maybe we're still struggling with that last part) "but where are we going to hunt this morning?"

The answer to that question has taken us down many difficult paths over the years. In our early outings we insisted on getting "back in" away from any roads. We'd pick our way a mile or more through the woods following deer trails, if available. The hunt didn't start in earnest until we sensed seclusion; if that was shattered we simply rounded a hill and moved on.

Most often that approach failed to produce a one-on-one audience with a gobbler, but at least it satisfied our desire to try. It would go down as a successful hunt, or at least a step in that direction. Those days were filled with the high hopes that propel the young.

Fast-forward nearly half a century and the answer to the question of where to hunt is colored by age. Potter's highest hills are a risky playground for the elderly.

Compromise is the first – and last – resort of senior woodsmen. We can't seem to go anywhere without it. So, nowadays we stick to the mountaintops and skip the sides; flat is in and steep is out.

One place whose topographical test senior turkey hunters can pass is Blue Dot, so named for the manner in which some hiking club long ago marked the path. This is a nearly level walk through woods in places thick enough to hold grouse and elsewhere sufficiently open to put a feeding turkey flock at ease. Its intersection with a natural gas line offers hunters ideal setup and listening spots.

The downside of BD is some of the hunters it attracts. The straight, wide open pipeline appeals to those who are afraid of getting lost. When plagued by boredom, they tend to select inappropriate targets and too often overplay their turkey and owl calls.

Despite all that, my first impression – that it was a good choice for aging nimrods – makes more sense now than ever.

The white-haired gentleman from Galeton I ran into that on my first visit was standing right where Blue Dot ends and the open forest begins. I was an uninitiated twentysomething in need of a break after hours of trekking through the trees, and stopped to chat.

He carried a double-barreled 12-gauge, a pronounced patina encircling the trigger area testifying to a history of regular use. He was overdressed, probably because of declining circulation, and a seat cushion dangled from his belt. His go-find-it stage of hunting was over; now it was wait-and-see, which wasn't sitting well.

"Bet that old Rem pulled down a pheasant or two in its day," I guessed, letting him know that at least this young buck could recognize the make of his weapon.

"Practically raised two kids on pheasants, rabbits and grouse with old Boomer here," he confirmed, patting the patinaed part and looking me in the eye for the first time. Then he glanced at his wristwatch and scowled. "She'll be here anytime now."

"She," of course, was his wife, but he wasn't complaining about the person he called "a good woman." His main agitation seemed to be that his only living hunting buddy was too sick to come along. Delivering a one-word assessment, "Sad," he turned toward the road and was gone.

Happily, Chauney is still with me in the woods, but mostly for the same reasons that have brought us to the Blue Dot, the only species other than turkey that's still on my hunting calendar is the pheasant. The rowdy ring-neck favors habitat that's tolerable to hunters hobbled by arthritis, and for a chance to stay in the hunt I'm indebted to Steve Smith, younger son of my venerable 96-year-old next-door neighbor, Quentin. Steve's new English springer spaniel won or took second in 10 of the 11 AKC trials he competed in as a puppy. Gunner's future looks bright.

Nightlife in the woods

No, I'm not talking about doin' my sportin' at the hotel bar in Wharton, as its sign suggests.

In the pre-cellphone era, we drove to Wharton or sometimes the state park at Cherry Springs to make a call. Poor attendance led to a decision early this century to close the park. Well, the bureaucrats who called that shot obviously didn't know what was going on in their park at night.

News of the closure plan sparked an immediate protest – from Manhattanites. Huh? Remote Cherry

Springs State Park, it turned out, was the ideal spot for Big Apple astronomers to view the nighttime sky.

Far from artificial light sources, the park was adjacent to a little used airfield whose operator for years had rented state land. During an event attracting hundreds of stargazers, some of them spilled onto the airfield, igniting a confrontation.

Today the former airfield is equipped with permanent outdoor seating and telescope pads: Cherry Springs is home to Pennsylvania's only dark-sky state park.

Tyler got his first glimpse of Saturn through a telescope at Cherry Springs, and so did I. Education and entertainment teamed up to give us a clear view of the separation among its famous rings and the planet's body. "Look, Pap, it's moving!"

That night both of us got to see the sixth planet from the sun, second largest in our solar system, in a new light.

There was no need for a telescope or even binoculars to observe Halley's Comet in 1986 while Chauney and I were lodging along Sinnemahoning Creek, just downstream from Wharton where East Fork Creek joins it.

While staying in a trailer – dubbed Camp Mahon after the widow who owned it, Mildred Mahon – we saw what was first mentioned in the historical record, by the Chinese, in 240 BC. Faithfully reappearing every 75-76 years, Halley's is the most famous periodic comet simply because it's visible on Earth to the naked eye, and we got an eyeful right there on a little front porch.

Because of its visibility and reliable return (next show, 2061), Halley's Comet has become identified with various historic events and may even have been targeted for excommunication by an early pope.

Returning to camp from hunting the day after our first glimpse of Halley's, there was a note from Mildred – my mother-in-law had died. Now I knew just how an event could become identified with Halley's, and I wished I didn't.

A light in the forest, a fisher on the run

My lone experience with swamp (or marsh) gas came as dark fell while I was scouting during a spring turkey hunt. This is methane, formed when organic matter decays in the absence of air. Mother Nature can really get a guy blinking when she fires up the gas lights just as his eyes are adjusting to the dark. But when an animal I couldn't identify ran out a few paces in front of me, I really began to wonder what was going on.

Later it became clear that the mystery animal was a fisher *(Martis pennanti),* a species larger than two of its relatives, the weasel and mink, but smaller than a third, the marten. According to the dictionary, the fisher is a:

large dark brown, somewhat vulpine, arboreal, carnivorous mammal native to much of forested North America

Further back in the big book, vulpine is described as:

akin to the jackal, fox or wildcat; exhibiting, slyness or predatoriness; crafty

Everything seemed to fall into place the night Brad and I heard what later was confirmed as the voice of a fisher – a series of catlike screams, nasty enough that instantly I believed the dictionary's description.

And when I found out that fishers climb evergreens to prey on any porcupines or turkeys they find up there, well, they sure had my attention.

Turkeys take to the boughs for a safe night's rest, while the porkies climb to munch on the bark. While nowadays the fisher is on the prowl for both of them, it wasn't always so.

Nineteenth century America's hunger for lumber nearly took the fisher down with the trees. The state Game Commission had just one single fisher sighting – in Mifflin County – on record for 1923.

Seventy-one years later the agency teamed up with Penn State University to reintroduce the species. By 2010, the population was judged sufficiently restored to support limited trapping. A harvest of 443 fishers was reported by 6,637 permit holders trapping over much of southwestern, central and northern PA in 2014.

Champion chewer

Hands down, that would be the porcupine, especially when it comes to gnawing on plywood – and so much the better when Big Lumber is buying dinner.

A case in point was the large sign erected one spring in a section of forest not far from the dark-sky park. Identifying the area as Rockin Ridge, it related the story of the woods starting in the 1800s.

The succession of various tree species was listed, explaining why they appeared in that order, the dates of fires, how often the timber was harvested, etc. This was obviously the work of someone with ties to forestry interests, possibly a student or a Scout.

The plywood sign's creator clearly had a firm grasp of silva culture, but just as obviously was unfamiliar with at least one animal species on Rockin Ridge. Anyone who knows what a board foot is also should know that porcupines have a penchant for plywood.

Porkies love to run their long, protruding teeth over plywood – yes, even sheets employed for lofty purpose will do – to reach the glue that binds one layer to the next. Those teeth methodically march through layer after layer, pausing only briefly for porky to savor the flavor of the mucilage before resuming the attack.

What had taken much research, thought and effort to build, the porky nearly destroyed. Apparently erected early that spring, its remains were unrecognizable as a sign when I returned in the fall.

Porkies have a taste for camp

The day its builders drove home the last nail our one-room camp became an outpost in need of protection from porcupines.

Not only have these members of the *Hystricognathi* branch of the vast Rodentia order savaged our cabin's wooden undersides, but they've also attacked its aluminum siding. The white exterior coating apparently contains a bonding agent that porkies find irresistible. So relentlessly have they put tooth to siding that the corners of the outhouse have been shredded into pieces that wave like silver threads in the wind.

Over the years we've repaired or replaced lots of plywood flooring, sometimes driving nails through to discourage chew-crazy porkies. Wire that once caged in chickens now blocks out porcupines.

About the time I thought we had the camp all porky proof, Tyler's sister, Claudiea-Mai, paid her first visit. She was about 10 and undaunted by the privy. She picked wildflowers out back and caught trout in the stream out front. And she made me proud with the .22.

"What's that little light over in the corner, Pap?" she asked early one sunny morning just after we'd gotten up. She was pointing to the cabin's east end.

Well, "that little light" was the sun peering through a hole the size of a nickel made by porkies and heretofore overlooked by everyone else. Impressed by her power of observation, I worried that the discovery might somehow deflate her sense of security. Claudiea's next comment set me straight:

"How are we going to fix that?"

Oh, that was the easy part. Soon we were examining the cabin's puncture-by-porky wound, then dressing it with a piece of dowel and adding a bandage of metal sheeting.

"Now can we please shoot the rifle again, Pap?"

And with that, everything that needed to be fixed, was.

Porcupines are most active at our camp around 3:30 a.m. You can almost set your watch by it. But after a day of hunting and fishing, a fella is about as happy to wake up to the scraping sounds of the pesky porky as he is to the pitter patter of yet another rainy day. Things are really bad when he has to deal with both at once.

An assault by porky is announced by the grating rhythm of enemy teeth on plywood floorboards, a call to action you can't ignore even when fast asleep.

If you're lucky, it's someone else's turn to rise to the occasion. Either way, there will be no more sleep for anyone until the foe is vanquished or simply leaves. Ignoring the intruder only leads to mounting aggravation with each trip of porky's teeth.

So someone gets up, grabs the flashlight and, once outside, picks up the long stick we keep handy for jabbing porkies to send them on their way. Usually they get only as far as the neighbor's cabin before that awful grating sound resumes. Now, mercifully, the munching is barely audible, and you can get back to sleep.

But that's a best-case scenario; sometimes when the lights go on the porkies retreat into the darkness and wait for you to give up. And they can be very patient! About the time you're easing back into bed those teeth are re-running their route. No, better to stay out there and get the job done.

If the sky is clear, the Milky Way may brighten your wait – at times it can even cast a distinct shadow. If not, maybe a shooting star or an owl call will help fill the intermission between porky performances.

One night a pair of great horneds was calling nearby, as if perched on the cabin roof. Their song – 3 to 8 deep hoots, with the second and third sometimes running together – sounds like "You awake! Me too!" These two were as close as the one I long ago mistook for a pheasant.

The monogamous great horned is this continent's most widespread owl species and maybe its most powerful. It often attacks animals larger than itself – including the porky. I stood still, hoping to see a demonstration of that very thing, but porky was a no-show. He must know that song, too.

Wily and wary

Once porky patrol was disrupted by the nearby bark of a coyote. From atop a distant ridge came an answer so similar it could've been an echo, but it wasn't. Though far apart, these two were staying in touch while pursuing their common purpose.

There was sufficient starlight to make out the form of a four-legged hunter on the dirt road in front of our cabin. He stopped, evidently sensing the presence of possible prey, and let loose a series of six shrieks, each more robust than its predecessor. The hair went up on the back of my neck and I broke into a cold sweat. *That's it, this must be how coyotes hunt: With that ferocious vocal attack they try to scare their prey into involuntary movement. Then it's on with the chase!*

Coyotes kill to live, and while it's tempting to say that their main predator is motivated by the challenge and, increasingly, the contest prize money, in general that's just not true.

Pennsylvania's estimated 40,000-a-year coyote kill – very likely tops in the nation – has little to do with the lack of limits on harvest or weaponry that makes every day coyote season. Nor do this state's approximately 20 annual hunting contests, whose prizes are worth thousands but result in coyote deaths totaling only a few hundred.

Most coyote casualties in the Keystone State are a byproduct of fox trapping and deer hunting – unintentional in the case of the former, opportunistic in the latter.

Taking a coyote under any circumstances is no small feat because he is a hard hombre to outsmart. He also is resourceful and resilient – simply one super survivalist.

This is the second time around in Pennsylvania for *Canis latrans,* which was exterminated within our borders in the last century. On his return – from the Western U.S. – the coyote interbred with the wolf in Minnesota before re-establishing itself in New England then pushing south.

There is photographic evidence from as early as the 1930s of what now more accurately could be called the coywolf in Pennsylvania, but its population didn't really begin to explode until the 1980s. The southern half of the state continues to see more coyotes as this highly intelligent species adapts to farm and even urban habitat. The coyote resides in all 67 Pennsylvania counties – yup, Philadelphia, too.

The Game Commission in part bases its coyote kill guess on May hunter surveys, meaning spring gobbler chasers.

Well, if I'm ever surveyed – and so far, in 48 years as a spring turkey hunter that's never happened – the data will be scant. Of perhaps 10 coyote sightings, all but two fall in the "just a glimpse of a rapidly disappearing tail" category.

The only coyote I ever got a good look at in the wild showed up at midday during a long ago fall turkey hunt. Chauney was wading through a hillside thick with man-high beech sapling; I was slightly ahead and in the open. Judging by the noise he was making, my partner was about to pop into view.

Instead the next thing I saw was a flushing grouse, followed immediately by a coyote that must have been stalking it. Then a red fox darted out, spotted its archenemy, instantly executed an about-face and dove back into the thicket.

I had the better part of a minute to study the coyote, which was mostly black with a spot or streak of brown here and there, and had bounded into the open much like a deer. Sure-footed and easy moving, he could have passed in appearance for a German shepherd.

I'm guessing it was hunger that kept him hanging around in the open, barely out of shotgun range, glancing back at the brush from which he had just bolted. In one fluid movement the coyote seemed to shrink in size and slink out of view.

Maybe two seconds later Chauney stepped into sight and said:

"Oh there you are! See anything?"

My buddy hadn't even gotten a fleeting peek at the coyote's tail.

The coyote rivals Pennsylvania's largest predator, the black bear, in feeding on fawns; together they account for two-thirds of such activity.

Still going up

Ursus americanus has maintained a steadily increasing presence in Pennsylvania for at least 100 years. Game Commission data show that only four times from 1915 to 2015 has bear season been closed, and the four-figure harvest that began in 1983 continues to this day.

The 2014 season attracted a record 173,000 hunters, who tagged 3,371 bruins. While eight of the 10 greatest kills have come in the last 10 years, perhaps even more telling of overall bruin health is their size: 68 of those taken in 2015 topped 500 pounds, up from 41 the year before.

Except during hibernation, the bear is almost constantly in search of something to eat. His sheer size calls for calories that can be hard to find in the woods. As bruin's population has expanded, his stomach and territorial nature inevitably have put him on a collision course with other bears – and us.

A sharp-spurred old gobbler that fell to my shotgun in May 2005 refused penetration by the fork even after spending nine hours on the stove. It was like he was having the last laugh on me for even trying. (We resorted to stovetop cooking after mice invaded the oven and the smell when we fired it up was unbearable.)

Anyway, the aroma of cooking turkey attracted four visitors whose presence was announced by a quiet metallic tap-tap-tapping. *Must be the wind rattling those empty ginger ale cans someone left on the porch.*

It was dusk when I opened the door and looked into the eyes of a full-grown black bear, her hind feet on our little back porch. A soda can, evidently caught on a tooth and protruding at a weird angle, came loose and fell just as I slammed the door shut.

Mama was not alone, and soon her cub trio was putting on a performance whose price of admission, plainly they hoped, would be a turkey snack. The sow sat off to one side watching, as if inviting us to do the same while her young raced round and round the yard, nipping at one another, huffing, tumbling, tackling and generally cutting up like kids on spring break.

This obviously was not their first time onstage, and their exuberance and enthusiasm hinted that earlier audiences had treated them kindly. The bears came for the turkey, but in the end settled for a few drops of leftover ginger ale.

Man feeding bear is foolish behavior for both species, but unfortunately too many of us – and them – don't get it. Taking handouts can dull bruin's natural instincts and inflict cruelty when man isn't around. Sometimes the tables are turned and people pay the price.

Besides, the black bear does just fine when left to his own devices. He has an excellent sense of smell and, lacking any dietary hang-ups, will put away just about anything that his incredible resourcefulness can snare.

Food also was at the forefront of an encounter Brian had with this same bruin quartet the previous spring. Climbing the hill behind our cabin, he paused to rest and spotted mama bear and her first-year cubs on a bench below.

This was a dry spring and woods walking was anything but quiet. As already noted, bears are hungry all the time, and this sow was showing her charges how to handle the situation. Brian's account:

"When I first saw the bears, they were moving single file as though in some sort of follow-the-leader play. Mama would stop and look back, and the first cub would copy her move, then the next and finally the little guy. Each stopped and glanced back. It was kind of comical, especially when the last one did it.

"They were close enough that I should have been hearing them, but I wasn't – because they weren't making any noise.

“Now they were walking on the trunks of fallen trees, and it hit me that this was no game: They were hunting.

"The sow was teaching her cubs how to stay stealthy in a dry woods. When she stopped to look to the rear, it wasn't to check on her cubs. She was hoping to spot prey that, once they passed by, might've relaxed enough to make the mistake of moving."

While that didn't happen, at least on Brian's watch, a partial deer haunch found elsewhere in the hollow indicated the bears weren't exactly starving. And nearby lay the residue of dessert – a mass of rock-hard, compressed grape skins and seeds shaped like a section of pipe. Two inches in diameter and about a foot long, it definitely was a product of the bear, um, pipeline.

A big ol' boy

The biggest bruin I've ever seen in the woods was flat-out drunk.

"You guys wanna see a really big bear?"

The question was posed at camp one October day in 2011 by Roscoe's son, Frank, and after lunch he guided Brad and me to a nearby hilltop. We weren't hunting, just sightseeing.

Huge black cherry stands had produced a bumper crop of fruit. Not only were the cherries plentiful but they also were extra plump, presaging a record Potter County bear kill (327) and driving a new statewide mark (4,350) as well.

For the animals, of course, it was a feast. And there was ample evidence that the black bear was making the most of this fruity windfall. There were so many bear plops under cherry trees that you literally had to watch your step.

One reason bruin favors steep-sided hills is that we don't. Man predictably takes the top or bottom of a hill because it's easier walking. Thus, for a bear, steeper is safer – and that's right where Frank was leading us.

An enormous black bear was sprawled just below us on the slope, its head atop outstretched forepaws. He wasn't asleep, but he wasn't exactly awake either.

The bear's ears twitched occasionally, and he was making mild groaning sounds every so often.

Several times he half lifted his head, then put it right back down. Occasionally he licked a forepaw just like a dog. I guessed his tongue at about the size of my forearm.

What we really wanted to see, naturally, was the bear on his feet, so we could get a better idea of his size. What happened next shouldn't have, but boys will be boys ...

First one, then another stone rolling downhill in his general direction was all if took to put bruin on all fours. That was rather startling because our stupid stone trick now had this absolutely immense individual looking our way. And he was on the move!

But he didn't get far because – as we all could plainly see – the bear was so inebriated from ingesting fermented cherries that he couldn't walk a straight line.

This fella was about as big a threat to us as a wartime sailor on shore leave is to the enemy when returning to ship from a night in the bars. Bruin stopped to steady himself against just about every tree in his path, and before going 15 yards he collapsed mightily into a prone position, head once more resting on forepaws.

That empty feeling

OK, that's a peek at the black bear in fat times. What when he has to go without? Does his stomach roll like yours and mine? The answer to that came in loud and clear one shiny day.

Half of what once had been an 8-point deer rack was protruding through beech leaves on a little knob in the Cherry Springs vicinity. I admired its overall heft and the spread of its points, imagining the animal whose head it had decorated as a magnificent specimen bounding through the forest just a few months ago.

A short walk from there, I left the path for a nearby hemlock stand and sought out the small but reliable spring it shaded. The boss hemlock of the hill stood close by, as if guarding the cool, precious liquid.

Laying the shotgun aside and doffing my cap so it wouldn't wind up in the drink, I knelt for a sip. Refreshed and back on my feet, I caught a flash of black in bright sunlight 15 yards away in a stand of shoulder-high hemlock saplings.

Black is a turkey color and this was spring gobbler season, so I was envisioning ol' tom as I stood under the big hemlock, my Ithaca back in hand. So it came as a surprise when an adult black bear emerged, loping downhill away from me. An even greater surprise was the about-face bruin executed seemingly in mid-stride.

I don't know what the bear did next because I was too busy getting out of the way, which somehow I managed to do without spooking it. From a point about 30 yards uphill of the spring, I watched the bear go right to it and drink.

Just then came the distant barking of dogs. Bruin immediately glanced up at the branches and, moving close to its trunk, reared, put his forepaws to the bark and began to climb.

My broadside view of the bear was unobstructed. From ground to perhaps 20 feet above took him 50 seconds by my watch to reach, achieved in three mighty bursts with heavy breathing in between, groaning and lots of flying bark. *Talk about a tough climb!*

Once secure in the boughs, he stayed still as stone and just as quiet. I guessed he was listening for more barking, but none came. As he rested in the tree and I stood on the hill, we both heard the growling of an empty stomach, and it wasn't mine. *Hunger is a bear's constant companion, right, fella?*

Quietly I climbed the hill and headed for camp and a warm meal. *God is great, God is good, let us thank Him for our …*

Oh, just humor me

Rarely do bear/man encounters make the 6 o'clock news. Most often nothing more than a good laugh results.

Someone staying in a neighboring camp found a midnight visit by bruin particularly captivating – because he was caught in the outhouse for the whole 20-minute show. Another time he photographed a bear with its nose pressed to the window of the cabin between his and ours. He said the bear's behavior reminded him of a kid at a candy counter.

One evening as we returned from turkey scouting, our headlights shone on a small bear beside Camp Mahon. Bordering the property were several evergreens and, as we passed, the animal faced us, rose on hind feet and stepped behind one of them.

Mildred had trimmed the lower branches to enable mowing around the trees, whose trunks couldn't have been more than 4 or 5 inches in diameter.

We stopped and, backing up, sure enough the bear returned to view, his forepaws now extended and grasping a tree trunk, as if to hold it in place and block our view. When we moved a little, forward or back, he'd shift accordingly to stay "hidden."

This was a laugh-out-loud stunt – and we did – but there are times when a bear can almost make you cry.

Chauney and I drove past a juvenile bear sitting (just as a human would) on a camp stoop near Conrad early one fall afternoon. It was as if he was waiting for someone, but it certainly wasn't us because he rolled off the step and slipped around the corner and out of sight.

We pulled away a short distance, stopped and waited. In 20 seconds there he was back on the stoop. We agreed that most likely this guy had eaten here previously and was back for more.

And very likely the someone he was waiting for was that favorite individual in any youngster's life, especially at mealtime – mom. He was about the right age to be sent away by the sow so she could mate and begin the life cycle all over again. Bears reproduce every other year.

Another pitiful sight that same autumn but miles away was the little fella – maybe 50 pounds – that I nearly ran over as he lay in the middle of state Route 44 just uphill from Carter Camp. He kept eyeing us – Tyler was along – while scrambling out of the way, as if to ask if we'd seen mom. This one and the bear on the stoop were like a set of sad-sack bookends with not one mother between them.

Lost!

Among other predators afoot in the forest at night is man. But if you're not out there on porky patrol or after foxes or raccoons, maybe you're just plain lost. Like I was one gorgeous spring evening in Cameron County.

I was scouting for turkey at dusk but what I was seeing was this continent's largest rodent – the beaver. There were two of them, about 15 yards away, and they were taking turns preening each other on a large, nearly flat rock that rose just inches above the roiling surface of a small creek. Behind the beaver I could see a fair-sized pond and knew their dam had to be nearby.

They were chatting away as they worked and, one a bit bigger than the other, their bond was unmistakable. *They're just so much like little people!* In proportion to the rest of the body, the tail of *Castor canadensis* is huge – and flat like a shovel, excellent for dam building.

This peaceful scene was suddenly shattered by what resembled small-caliber gunfire as the beavers slapped their tails on the water and dove into the security of the stream. I'd been spotted and the show was over. The only thing I could see now was moonlight on creek water.

Even in the company of Flower Moon – the Algonquian nickname for when it's full in May – to stumble around in sticks at night is to dance with danger. I sat down on a log to think. *You were headed downhill when you saw the creek and then the beaver to the left. That means the way back to the truck is away from the creek.*

During this pause for review Flower Moon burst into complete bloom. As each trunk and branch returned to view, picking a path was easy, and an idea fell into place: *The trick to getting out of here is being able to maintain a straight line of travel. You need a compass …*

Looking around, I realized that in effect I had a compass right there in the woods. It being early spring and the trees still leafless, their trunks were casting shadows – all in the same direction, naturally.

In my mind's eye these pointing shadows coalesced into the arrow on a giant compass, only on this model the needle was pointing west, not north. With that in mind, I set my direction of travel accordingly and took off.

It worked perfectly, and in 20 minutes or so I broke out of the trees and headed downhill to the huge fallow farm field along whose edge I'd parked. *Thank you, Flower Moon, for pointing the way out of the woods.* With that, her wink on the windshield led me precisely to the truck.

One day not long after that or far away, I spotted a large steel leg trap that had been anchored in a natural rock stairway over which a small stream tumbled. The contraption was cocked open – set to spring. Even in daylight I nearly tripped it. This illegal device looked big enough to fit a bear's ankle, and its jaws crushed a 2-inch-thick branch inserted to test it.

Woods walking on a moonless night without artificial light means feeling your way. You can see with a stick, so to speak. A straight branch a little longer than you are tall works fine. Keeping it upright in front helps to avoid walking into tree branches, sort of like a blind man (which at night, in effect, you are) using his cane. Maybe such a stick would have set off that big trap and spared me certain agony, but I'm glad I never had to find out.

Deerly beloved

On the sprawling stage of the Allegheny Mountains, Pennsylvania's big stars are the white-tailed deer, the black bear and the wild turkey. The deer dominate by sheer numbers.

A staggering 16 million of them were taken in hunts from 1915 to 2015, as recorded by the state Game Commission. Seven million wore antlers, 9 million did not.

That compares among the other primary big-game species for the same period with 2.7 million turkeys in the bag, and 109,000 bears on the lodge pole.

Our largest game animal, the elk, numbers only in the hundreds and is subject to closely controlled hunts with harvests in the dozens. As a fundraiser, though, *Cervus canadensis* is impressive: Someone bid $85,000 for a special PA license to hunt elk in autumn 2016.

The Roaring Twenties were exactly that for Pennsylvania's deer herd. From a whitetail harvest of 3,300 at the outset of the decade, the number had jumped eightfold by its end.

As the deer flourished game managers experimented with allowing doe hunting, which was banned in the first eight seasons and would be closed in 13 hunts yet to come.

The 1938 season was for antlerless deer only, and 171,000 were taken – this state's first recorded six-figure harvest. Does joined the bucks as legal targets in the next two hunts, which saw the total harvest fall to 63,000 in 1939, then rebound to 186,000 in 1940.

Not until after World War II did Pennsylvania hunters record another six-figure deer harvest. Occurring only twice in the Fifties, that has been the rule since 1971.

But the deer were only getting started. The whitetail harvest hit 300,000 in 1986 and, just four years later, topped 415,000.

As deer numbers rocketed, the state Game Commission in 1999 tapped its veteran bear management chief, Gary Alt, for guidance on the whitetail. While it seemed like common sense – balancing herd with habitat – his approach nevertheless upset a lot of folks.

Alt was at the helm in 2002 when the whitetail harvest made its first – and so far only – leap above the half-million mark (517,000). From its zenith, the estimated deer kill declined steadily to 303,000 in the 2014-15 season.

The stress of managing the thinning of the deer herd took a personal toll, and Alt resigned the last day of 2004. His somewhat ironic legacy is the collection of exceptional whitetail trophies being racked up these days by Pennsylvania hunters, some of whom doubtless complained about the antler restrictions Alt imposed years ago.

Rest of the story

For the most part, the deer saga plays out in the forest and on the farm, but they also die by the tens of thousands on concrete and macadam, where the danger is the motor vehicle, not the rifle or bow in the trunk.

Just how large is our deer herd, and how many wind up as road-kill or victims of poachers, predators (primarily black bear, coyote and bobcat), disease, or are removed because of farm crop damage?

Here's some insight from Chris Rosenberry, the Game Commission's chief of deer and elk management:

An estimated harvest by hunters of 315,000 deer in the 2015-16 season means the state herd is 1.26 million strong – four times the kill. Only half of the fawns live past six months, and 70 percent of those survivors eventually fall to two-legged hunters.

Total annual deer mortality is roughly one-third of the herd or about 420,000 individuals, with 8 percent (35,000 or nearly 100 a day) occurring on roadways. Accounting for the remaining 70,000 deer deaths are the other causes listed above. Notice that winter mortality is missing from the lineup – and by its absence, more evidence of our changing climate.

THE DEER THING

Here's what to do if you're a non-hunter in Pennsylvania (Thanksgiving, 2001)

It was homecoming in heaven for three college men, as St. Peter quizzed the first one about his alma mater.

"Yale, Class of '43. I'm a medical doctor," came the reply.

Pointing to the newcomer's right, the man dressed all in white said, "Through that door, please."

"UCLA," self-started the second man, "Class of '52. I have an MBA and an IQ of 167."

"Hmmmm. You belong in there," said the man in charge, motioning to a door directly to his rear.

"Penn State, class of..." erupted No. 3, only to be cut off with: "Did ya get your deer yet?"

Truly, Pennsylvania is widely identified with deer. This year's season, launched by the archers in early October, continued last week with the first mini-hunt for elk in 70 years. The hunt shifts to a much louder and larger phase on Monday when the rifle contingent goes forth for antlered deer.

Deer hunting is anchored in our culture, riveted into our heritage. It's about kin, old and dear friends, perhaps a place in the woods.

But besides the million-plus hunters, the state Game Commission's 130 district game protectors and their 600 deputies whose job it is to police the hunters, and those who sell the guns and allied hunting equipment, cut up and wrap the venison, that's about it. The deer thing doesn't have much effect on the 90 percent of Pennsylvanians who are nonhunters, right?

Wrong! When it comes to *Odocoileus virginianus,* you can hunt 'em or not, but it's everybody's deer herd to deal with, bucko. Consider:

Construction work usually slows down this time of year anyway, but with the arrival of deer season all of the builder's wheels seem to grind to a halt in unison. If that new addition on the house isn't finished by now, you can forget it for a while. In the secret code used by sportsmen, "contractor" means "deer hunter." And if my experience is indicative, "drywaller" is code for "serious deer hunter."

Your crew most likely is off deer hunting. Chances are they will eat breakfast on Monday at one of the myriad churches and fire companies that traditionally host predawn opening-day pancake breakfasts.

If you live in a rural area, odds are the schools will be closed on Deer Day. All the kids, teachers and administrators will be off, hunters and nonhunters alike. Regardless of where you live, the hunt could result in a delayed medical, dental or legal appointment, if your health pro is also a nimrod. Or maybe deer season means you'll have a little extra to do at work, to help take up the slack for those who are off hunting.

For tens of thousands of nonhunting Pennsylvanians, the impact of the deer herd is a more direct thing. Tens of thousands of white-tailed deer are mowed down by motorists every year. It happens everywhere -- yes, even Philadelphia. In 1982, the road-kill was 26,180. In '87 it hit 37,239. By 1992 we were whacking 40,000 a year, and the Keystone State was paying $8 million to haul 'em away ...

Some drivers pick up the carcasses and have them butchered. It's their right under the law. The former practice of serving road-kill in county homes and hospitals has been outlawed. Some is utilized in cooperative trout nursery programs where meat is ground for use as feed. Landfills take very few road-killed deer these days. Some make it to the rendering plant, but often the carcasses end up in pits along state lands wasting away under a blanket of lime and earth.

Sometimes, of course, it's the drivers who get carried off. In 1989, auto collisions with animals -- many of them deer -- took 132 human lives and caused untold injuries nationwide. Enter the coroners, doctors, nurses, lab technicians, pharmacists and ambulance crews. And the police, firefighters, insurance adjusters, maybe a lawyer or two. And lots and lots of auto body repairmen.

The deer is a survivor, having been around for about 10 million years. Some variation of the animal we call deer exists from Ecuador and Colombia, where full grown they weigh under 20 pounds (too much coca-leaf munching?) north to Alaska, where a bull moose can tiptoe toward a ton.

One step down in size is the elk, about 60 of which have been struck and killed by cars or trains in this state since 1991. The average elk stands about 5 feet tall at the shoulder and 7 feet long. A bull elk averages 700 pounds, but some top half a ton.

Road-kill remedies have included underpasses and overpasses for the deer (costly, therefore rare); more careful planning on where roads are built; re-examination of the grasses and shrubs planted along roads; dispensing with salt as a way of ridding roads of ice, since deer like salt; more of those artful yellow-and-black warning signs; fences (almost prohibitively expensive); wildlife warning reflectors (much cheaper); and whistles attached to vehicles to frighten deer by emitting high-pitched sounds (inexpensive, somewhat successful, notably in Texas).

Most of the roadway deer kill occurs from October through January. That's the deer mating season, meaning they are running. Once in the rut, deer are oblivious to danger, hunger and just about everything else that's not directly connected to the drive to reproduce. They run in such strange places and at such odd times that the most attentive driver can be caught unaware. Even if you spot them in time and slow down or stop, often they will dash smack into the side of the vehicle.

Old-timers know that the simple honk of a car horn often will do the trick, but they also know better than to count on it.

If the need arises to have a deer carcass removed from the roadway, call PennDOT at (800) 349-7623 and ask for your local county maintenance office's number. Nowadays it's part of their job.

A clutch shot with Chauney's F-150

It was a dreary, damp afternoon in October as we motored along a twisting mountain road toward camp. It was foggy and daylight was fading.

Taking my turn driving Chauney's Ford, I slowed to well under the 45 mph speed limit, and was scanning the shoulders of the road for any feeding deer. But the whitetail in your path is the danger, not the one on the berm …

What I'd failed to do when taking the wheel was to move the seat up enough that I could fully depress the clutch. So, as I simultaneously hit the brake and clutch pedals when metal struck fur, the F-150 kept on rolling!

When I realized what was wrong and managed to tramp the clutch pedal all the way, the hapless critter we'd been pushing along suddenly shot straight out front, a virtual venison cannonball. The animal skittered headfirst over wet leaves along the shoulder and parallel to the road, somehow missing several large stones and coming to rest about 25 yards from where we stopped.

Jumping up spritely, the deer glanced our way and shook its ears as if they were fingers and I was being admonished to pay closer attention. With that the animal wandered off into the woods.

Yes, Mother Nature's creatures are amazingly durable, sometimes even when we run into them on the road. In the Eighties and into the Nineties the deer were as much a nuisance in the woods as on the highway.

There were so many of them that they interfered with our turkey hunting. If deer weren't blocking our path to a spot where we could set up to call a gobbler, they were winding us once we were working the bird. Then they crashed off through the woods and tom would fall silent and flush or simply disappear.

Late last century we often saw deer by the dozens, occasionally even a herd of 100. The largest whitetail gathering I ever witnessed came drifting by one fall day late in the Nineties. It resembled a cattle drive without cowboys, each animal trailing closely the one ahead. They were near enough for me to count noses, of which there were 157.

A very chilly hunting trip

When it comes to weather conditions, deer hunting in PA can mean anything from the better-wear-sunblock days of early archery season, to the insulate-don't-hibernate challenge of late January.

A snowy 4-hour drive brought stepson Jason Hoffman and yours truly to camp midway through the 2005 rifle season.

"Hey, Kevin has what looks like a nice 8-point hanging out back – see it?"

Getting no response, I glanced over at Tyler and Claudiea's father. The wide eyes said it all: Jase was jacked up.

We'd stopped along the way and bought candles, in case of a power outage, but what we should have picked up was a Phillips (Tyler calls it a "plus") screwdriver. Who knew?

With snow filling the hilltops – and maybe driving the deer down – the next day's prospects seemed good. Mindful that the camp turkey alarm clock gobbles – ready or not – at 4 a.m., we turned in early.

We detected no deer on the mountain out front, not even a track the next morning. Nor was it any livelier on the other side of the hill. The only thing moving was the snowflakes, of which a few inches had piled up. Ham steaks helped but couldn't completely overcome, if you get my drift.

The post-pancake part of Day 2 began auspiciously enough with a snowy owl gliding silently about 15 feet overhead as we invaded the pines behind camp. Its pronounced dusky frontal barring marked the bird as a female.

Buck rubs near where she took off and turkey tracks bordering an old railroad bed below at least lent this area a lived-in look. The rising sounds of a coyote pack on the hunt coincided with fading daylight as we exited the woods.

After demolishing a couple of steaks and lamenting the storm's theft of starlight, we stoked the woodstove with oak. It was 25 degrees outside and 50 in here as we tucked in. Almost immediately, over in Jason's corner, increasingly sonorous snoring rose to challenge the wailing wind. It was no contest, really.

Jase's old F-150 had seen better days and, while the 4WD still worked, it was a gas hog, needed new springs and was on its first and likely last trip to camp. It was top of the line when new, power windows and all, but years of farm work had taken a toll.

We were barely on our way home when it happened. As we hit the second bump in the lane, the driver-side window jumped off its track and fell inside the door. And we had no toolbox aboard.

Twenty-five degrees isn't too bad for early December in the mountains, but the wind-chill inside that old truck made for one wickedly cold ride home, all 167 miles of it. After downing a cup of coffee, Jason had the window back on track in under 10 minutes. All it took was a Phillips.

LAST-CHANCE BUCK // A father, his sons & the wily whitetail

(Monday, November 27, 2000)

Twenty-one deer hunts later, the season of '79 still stands out. I guess for our family, it always will.

It was the year of the nuclear nightmare at Three Mile Island, which struck in early spring a mile or so from our farm in Newberry Twp., York County.

Like thousands of other midstaters, my wife fled with our three boys from that horrendous hydrogen bubble. Unlike many others, we had dogs, cats, chickens, pigs, cattle and a goat. I stayed behind, with friends in New Cumberland, to tend the animals.

For a family living so close to the soil, the summer that followed was an unsettling time. No one was quite sure about such things as radioactive fallout and possible tainting of farm wells. I remember that the five of us seemed to have more worries than answers during that agony-of-the-atom era.

Nature's orderliness and its predictable patterns had appealed to me even as a boy, well before I was old enough to grasp why. Much later I would understand, with help from such folks as Ralph Waldo Emerson, that in the woods, man returns to reason and faith.

Slowly, and in spots erratically, our family resumed the routine of farm life. That is to say, we returned to our collective reason.

At summer's end, our oldest, David, was off to Penn State's Mont Alto campus. The old forestry school, with its woodsy setting and nearby trout streams, quickly became his new home. That he wanted his younger brother, Dan, and me to join him there for a deer hunt that fall told us all we needed to know about how he regarded his new neighborhood. Little brother Dennis, too young to hunt, would miss the outing.

For those so inclined, time together in the deer woods is perfect pairing for children and their parents. The natural dependence of youth on its elders for direction and instruction -- a useful imbalance easily upset by such things as the telephone, TV and computer – is restored, if only temporarily. Thus reconnected, the two generations can go forward as one into a classroom that existed before there were students.

Danny got a lesson in patience and a sense of what it means to be a team member on that hunt, even before we hit the woods. "Everybody's taking off from school tomorrow -- even the teachers -- to go deer hunting. Why can't we, Dad?" Because of my job and your brother's college studies, the anxious 15-year-old was reminded.

The first Saturday of the antlered deer season – the sixth day of the hunt -- arrived during a bitter cold snap. I mused that it was so frigid it just couldn't snow.

Dan and I had made all but 10 miles or so of the trip to Mont Alto when a light snow began to fall.

After an early-morning reunion with Dave, over scrambled eggs and home-cured bacon, we were into the woods, walking in two inches of fine, gritty snow.

Dave chose a spot on a knoll along a natural gas pipeline. Dan climbed a tree on the edge of a pine plantation bordering an expansive thicket. I took a hillside stand somewhere in between, confident I was close enough to hear either son shoot.

An hour passed. I never heard the shot – a mystery that endures to this day – and, following a plan worked out with Dave, I began a quiet drive through the narrow strip of woods where he was on stand.

The unmistakable sounds of spooked game gave rise to the hope that, though unseen by me, a nice buck would be passing No. 1 son's position soon. Instead, tracks in the snow revealed, the noisemakers had been turkeys, a flock about a dozen strong.

"Dad," Dave said excitedly, "they nearly ran me over! I never knew wild turkeys got that big," this last rendered with a hand held waist high. "Lucky I was behind that big stump."

We quickly agreed that chocolate and/or soup warmed on the Coleman stove back at our station wagon seemed in order.

The snow had intensified, slicing visibility and letting a feeling of isolation slip in.

Back at our vehicle we found a dancing, prancing Daniel nearby. No one spoke, Dave and I seeing Dan's movement as just an effort to keep warm. Then Dave spotted the partially snow-covered four-point buck, hanging from a small oak next to the Subaru.

"Got him through the heart, Dad." His delivery was in a low and measured, respectful tone. We had tried to instill in our kids a sanctity for all life, and I was inwardly grateful for Dan's reflection of reverence.

Then, just as though someone had pushed a switch, he turned back into the excited teen I knew at that moment he had to be. The discovery, again David's, that Dan's rifle was missing was a hint as to just how excited.

"I hid it under some leaves," he blurted, that revelation momentarily detracting from his accomplishment, "and I couldn't find it in the snow."

Revisiting the scene, we had Dan re-climb the tree and direct us to where the deer had stood.

"To your left, Dave, by that little pine tree. Over there, yeah, that's the spot!" Dan shouted, emotion returning to his voice. It was 47 paces from the point where we recovered the stubby
.30-30 Marlin to the base of Dan's tree.

It was his first deer, and his brother and I were there to share in the savoring. It was the kind of experience one instantly hopes will be repeated, but that was not to be: Tragically, the youngest member of our hunting party that day would not live to see another deer season.

Which underscores, in one last final way, why anytime is a good time to take your children hunting.

The Wild Boy and Old SOB

One of Chauney's and my earliest turkey haunts acquired its colorful name long before we arrived; the other we came up with ourselves. And believe me, that hulking, many-hollowed monster of a mountain deserved to be called the Old SOB.

On the moonlit, frosty spring mornings of our early years in the woods we'd strip down to our underwear and, clothes and gear in hand, charge up that hill in

20 minutes flat. It was a rite of spring, something to anticipate. Sure, now and then there was a fall and a scratch or bruise blossomed.

"Aha," One of Us would inquire, pointing to such a wound on the Other, "Springtime snowboarding again with no board, no snow?"

Occasionally there were disapproving witnesses to our frisky hill climbs. A deer would snort, an owl hoot, or a bear crash off through the timber. Once I ran into a pack of raccoons – well, actually it was the other way around. The crafty critters were chattering constantly as they hurried downhill – on a beeline for my position. Ducking behind a tree, I saw six as they blurred by me single file. *Probably hoping for a meal of crawfish from Wild Boy Run.*

Chauney and I cut our teeth as turkey hunters on the Old SOB and adjacent Wild Boy Mountain; the former was "his" hill, the latter "mine." Often we heard gobblers on each other's mountain and came over to get in on the action.

This happened so regularly that each expected the other to show up right near the bird. "See you at the bird" was a typical parting shot as we split up at the outset of a hunt. His explanation for this phenomenon is simply, "We think alike in the woods," and if that's not it I don't know what is.

Wild Boy Run was named for the young settler who built a crude hut on the East Fork in 1842. Living a solitary life 6 miles from his nearest neighbor, the hermit became known to locals as the Wild Boy. It was years before they learned his real name.

According to W.W. Thompson, who founded The Potter Enterprise in 1874, the Wild Boy was Lewis Stevens, born in Toms River, NJ, in 1825. The son of drunken parents, Lewis left home at 11 to tramp the countryside, learning tinsmithing along the way.

He was 17 when he wandered into Cameron County and up the Sinnemahoning Creek, noticing how sparsely the area was settled and deciding to stay. Lewis built a dwelling of logs, mud and moss, and ate wild game, fish, berries and nuts.

Periodically he would step back into the world, once tinkering all the way to Connecticut. He joined the Army in 1845, fought in the Mexican-American War (1846-48) and returned to action in 1861, with the 46th Regiment of Pennsylvania Volunteers.

With the Civil War still raging when Stevens came home, neighbors thought him a deserter, probably upset over having to salute the officers. No evidence of the sort ever surfaced.

Thick hemlock stands populate the Wild Boy area, so dense in spots that even on a cheerfully bright day there are places the sun doesn't penetrate. They remind me of the dark side of Lewis Stevens, who spent too much of his childhood and all of adulthood grappling with the demons of his dysfunctional family.

Wild Boy Run flows through Conrad on its way to the East Fork. The village got its start a year before the Civil War ground to a halt, but it didn't get a permanent name until 1887. Founder Samuel Hull's settlement bore his name until the Post Office Department objected. His wife chose her father's first name as an alternate, and Conrad it's been ever since.

The Baltimore and Ohio Railroad arrived during the Hull era, bringing hunters and anglers into the East Fork valley, customers for his hotel. Between the railroad and the post office, this budding mecca for outdoorsmen gained a dual identity: Travelers got on and off the train at Hull Station, but those in need of lodging had addressed their letters making the necessary arrangements to residents of Conrad. The railroad whistle was heard there for the last time in 1942 when a storm ruined much of the track.

A mile away lived another hermit

Not far upstream from Conrad, little Horton Run empties into the East Fork. Horton Hollow also was once home to a hermit, this fellow an American Indian whose given name was Gilbert Vergusson. Like the Wild Boy, he was a soldier and had been wounded in battle.

To receive his Army pension, Vergusson walked about a mile to the Conrad P.O. There he picked up not only his checks but also a nickname, Gilly, and found a friend in Bert Walker. In time, Gilly relaxed enough from the solitary lifestyle of his mountainside lair – still known by locals as Gilly's Nose – to make a weekly visit to town.

Conrad thrived in the heyday of wood, whose great enemy was fire. Hull and Walker were among a group of men who, one after another, erected five hotels on or near the same site, four of which fell to flames. When the barrel-stave plant that once was the backbone of a community 300 strong burned in 1912, it was more like an exclamation point to an era than a calamity. Most of the villagers already had moved on – the epic harvest of the forest was over.

One of the camps in modern day Conrad is owned by Raymond Dean Miller, whose father belonged to the Dover Rod and Gun Club and brought his boy along to hunt. Ray, later a co-worker of mine at the newspaper and now well into his 80s, says that when his boyhood thoughts drifted from hunting, usually it was because he'd rather have been prowling Gilly's Nose.

"There were remnants of a wooden shanty in the hollow," Ray told me during a visit to his camp in 2011, "but it was no longer in use. Where we picked up Gilly's trail was right on the hillside. Apparently he often relocated from spot to spot – probably setting up his teepee based on the sun's movements."

The Indian camped over natural depressions in the earth, Ray said, likely lining the bottom with leaves and grass as bedding. Physical discomfort surely resulted from such a lifestyle, no doubt exacerbating that old war wound. For relief, Gilly resorted to Vicks VapoRub.

"We found several of those little blue Vicks bottles in places where it was plain Gilly had camped," Ray reported. "No wonder! He must have had aches and pains from the dampness and cold. That's a tough way to live."

Indeed, so tough that Bert Walker built a shanty just across the road from his hotel so Gilly could escape harsh weather.

If Walker had a good heart, his construction skills were suspect: He died of blood poisoning after being bitten by a rat that evidently had entered through a crack in the wall of his bunkhouse.

Gilly passed of natural causes in 1955. Long gone, too, is that humble wooden monument to compassion and friendship.

Ray introduced me to Conrad's unofficial historian, Doris Ianson, the refreshingly no-nonsense, straight-forward sort of soul you sometimes find among mountain folk. In her 70s, Doris is among just a handful of year-round residents of the village. In Gilly's day she was a girl living along its dusty, stony road when he came to town.

"He was tall and wore a big hat, like Abe Lincoln," she remembered. "He'd walk straight down the street, arms clasped behind him, head down. I was a little girl and so scared that I'd just scoot out of his way."

The flood within

As she spoke something washed through me. Those inner tears we know as heartbreak flowed with the realization I'd been in her home once before, long ago. Doris Ianson likely was home on that sunny first Saturday in May 1980, but we never met.

Chauney and I had separated to hunt near Gilly's Nose. It was opening day for spring gobblers, but it was the voice of a man and not a turkey that I heard. The words were loud but garbled. Someone was using a bullhorn. Moving closer, I made out "... Martin hunting party ...."

Climbing the hill, I spotted a vehicle, the red light on its roof flashing. Other than asking for ID and calmly ordering me into his cruiser, the handsome young state trooper was tight-lipped as he drove downhill – and straight to Doris Ianson's house. Receiving permission at the door, he escorted me inside to a rotary telephone, then dialed, handed me the receiver and left.

The mother of my children sounded steady but tired – no, weary.

"Doug, sit down and get a grip on yourself. I have some bad news: We found Dan last night in the barn. He's dead, Doug. We've lost Dan."

I vaguely recall the phone slipping from my hand and clanging to the floor, then the cruiser door closing. As the officer drove, my mind and heart struggled to put the brakes on this nightmare, but it would not stop.

As we pulled up at camp, I rallied enough to say thanks, get out and go inside. Tears hit the floor and knees buckled as Chauney waded right in, a true friend to the rescue.

He simply walked over and pulled me into the biggest bear hug he could muster. No words passed between us, and our mutually chosen refuge of silence lasted all the way home.

Dan was hanged in an improbable accident when baling twine formed the noose that did the deed, then snapped, depositing his lifeless body on the barn floor. His mother approved organ donation and chose cremation.

Dogged by closure issues, I was dismayed to discover that carrying an organ donor card could not stem those inner tears. As our once close family agonized through a period of readjustment, the marriage foundered.

In a perfect prescription for the divorce that followed, I took lengthy walks in the woods, while she pushed deeper into the real estate business. Meanwhile, even though one's in Hawaii and the other in Pennsylvania, David and Dennis have done a much better job of sticking together.

Chapter 3 - *Splash!*

Why we fish

If it was stomach empty
that first drove us to attack,
now we're hooked on challenge sheer
and just can't help coming back.

MAN DOUBTLESS WAS guided to the water's edge by hunger.

In a practice known as trout binning, hammering on rocks in a stream stunned nearby fish long enough to allow their capture by hand – caveman style fishing.

Primitive fishermen along the sea didn't bother with picking up hammers, just their feet. Their technique, still in practice, relies on the sole of the foot to pin a flounder to the bottom until it can be grabbed by hand. The Grande Internationale World Flounder Tramping Championships are held each August in tiny Palnackie, Scotland.

To handfish, according to Webster, is "to catch with the hands, sometimes with bait as a lure," and to guddle is to capture them "with the hands ... by groping in their lurking places." Trout tickling, a method that relies solely on having the right touch, is mentioned in several of Shakespeare's plays.

The ancients also employed spear and net, and fashioned crude hooks from fish bones. The arrival of the angle in fishing lent it an alternate name.

Sometimes the drive to fish springs not from the stomach, but rather the heart, mind or pure instinct. The following column was an attempt to identify some of angling's other-than-hunger motives.

The author, streamside in Clinton County, PA. Don Sarvey snapped this 1990 photo and caught half of the fish.

Catch of the day: Trout pans out as gift of the gods
(Wednesday, April 10, 2002)

Ever go fishing just to get out of the house?

Sure, me, too, but just as often I'm on my way because I want fresh fish to eat – not some I've bought, but some I've caught.

My favorite fish is wild trout, and my preferred spot to eat it is right along the stream while seated on a log.

Fresh-caught wild trout is a gift of the gods, a springtime feast for body and soul. The flesh is typically more succulent, flavorful and brilliant in color than that of its hatchery-raised cousins.

My custom, once they are thoroughly cleaned, is to place the fish in a tinfoil pouch with a little spring water, butter, salt and a sprinkle of dried parsley, then plop them atop the coals of a small campfire, beside an already baking potato. Wild leeks, pulled from the hillside (if this is an early spring outing), are steamed as a side dish. Dessert is a small handful of holdover teaberries (just enough to freshen the breath), gleaned from a patch spotted earlier along the stream.

Now it's time to kick back, find my place in Hemingway – by the light of a candle lantern, if necessary – and get my taste buds set for fresh trout. It'll be ready quicker than Papa can land whatever fish it is he's battling in print just then.

OK, millions of Americans go fishing, but is everyone out there after supper?

It seems to me there are two main reasons to fish, both represented above: You go because something's pushing you (i.e., an unpleasant situation at home or work) or pulling you (a desire for fresh fish). Reduced to its essence, fishing is a push me/pull me kind of thing.

The getaway reasons for fishing include the deadline – as in: April 15 is coming, better get those figures in order for the tax man. Wrong! Mid-April is trout time, so I'd better get my gear ready. Or, the wedding is only three weeks away, and you need a tux. Nah, what I really need is an afternoon on the river waltzing with the walleyes.

Frustration, failure, embarrassment, anger, the death of a loved one or anything that shreds one's self-respect can bring on a fishing trip.

Ditto for the soured business deal, the promotion that never seems to come through or just the job in general. This group of reasons to fish even has its own bumper sticker: "A bad day fishing beats a good day at the office."

Trouble in a relationship can send a wounded party to the water's edge, fishing gear in hand, faster than a wild trout can spot a fake fly. Whole books have been written on how the push to end a failing marriage can gradually turn into a pull toward new beginnings.

In his poem, "Our Biggest Fish," Eugene Field (1850-1895) poked fun at the fishing fraternity's storied propensity for truth-stretching, thereby hinting at one of angling's mightiest lures, the competition:

It never was a little fish
– yes, I am free to say,
it always was the biggest fish
I caught that got away.

Fish for the sheer sport of it, revel in the chase, view it as a contest between those with fins and those with feet? Count me in.

Fish are worthy adversaries, and seeing them glide into view is always truly mesmerizing. It's as if there is something spiritual in their swimming. Maybe it's all those fins working in unison – as if pulled by strings from above – that lends such grace and ease to their movement. Certain species have survived for millions of years, against all comers and every change in habitat. To compete against such creatures with hook and line ranks as an honor and first-rate challenge.

And then there's the element of human competition. Herbert Hoover observed that "all men are equal before fish." But oh how we fishermen love to believe otherwise! A phone call from a fishing buddy is always welcome, even if the invitation is posed without polish, as in:

"Hey, let's hit the crick this afternoon. My neighbor says they're bitin' like crazy!"

Who will land the first fish? The biggest? The most? The one that tail-walks farthest?

In contrast, others fish for the sheer joy of it. A high school chum of brother Steve's chose an ocean fishing trip for blues to mark the occasion of his graduation, inviting us to come along. We landed so many of those ferocious fighters that ever since it's been known as Blue Monday. This lark just as easily could have occurred at an amusement park or on the boardwalk, but someone wanted to go fishing.

Tradition often plays a part: It's opening day and you always go to the same stream with the same companion(s). Or, it's your birthday, or a friend's, and you always fish together on those days – been going since you were kids and played hooky to do it. Or, suddenly, it's closing day: You want one more shot at the big, wary denizen of the deep you've been stalking all season. By now, you might even have nicknamed him.

I'd like to believe that most of us fish in answer to the call of the wild, glorying in the gurgle, refreshed by the rush of the stream where it whitens, whipping through a narrow, rocky turn on its awesome advance. The truth is, fishing means different things to those who partake.

In the case of some sturgeon aficionados, they leave their hooks at home. Watermen for centuries have thrilled to the big fish's curious habit of vaulting in erect posture, falling on its sides and causing thunderous percussions that sometimes carry for miles.

Many fish jump, some dramatically, and the speedsters of the sea come to mind – the billfish, tuna and tarpon. The sturgeon is a cellar dweller, a whiskery relic of dinosaur days, and why it leaps is one of the great mysteries of the fish world. Someday, perhaps on New York's famed Hudson River or Wisconsin's Lake Winnebago, I'll be lucky enough to witness the in-air antics of this ancient mariner. That will be a self-given present of a peek at the past.

Then there's the adventure aspect of fishing, the challenge of the unknown. Sometimes if we knew what was going to happen we'd probably stay home. A candidate for this category is described in my diary entries for Aug. 6-12, 2011, labeled:

A memorable fishing trip

At first, the fishing gods seem to be smiling. I'm able to pick up everything on my list at Ducky's Boats near Middletown for our annual August bass fishing trip to Canada. Yes, they have the right 12-volt battery for my boat motor, and the boat-trailer replacement rollers I ordered have arrived. Hey, all right!

Then a hitch develops when the outboard motor won't start. I'm nowhere near the mechanic that brother Steve is, but good enough to figure out it's an ignition problem. The fix is as simple as changing a sparkplug, but that realization is slow to come. I should be seeing this as a harbinger of hell week, but I don't. I'm in a fishing frame of mind, blind to everything else. Soon I will be reunited with Chauney as once again we drive up I-81 to the Land of the Bass, one of our favorite homes away from home.

Well, the travel part is uneventful, and by 3 p.m. we make it to fishing camp near Erinsville, Ontario, about an hour or so above the border. We are warmly greeted by hosts Anita and Wendell Embury, and the vine-ripened tomatoes we brought along make her light up like a Christmas candle.

The trouble starts 4 miles away at White Lake. Before launching the 17-foot Grumman I somehow neglect to insert the boat plug. Overanxious, I guess. The plug is designed to be removed after the vessel is hauled out of the water so any that found its way in while the boat was afloat can discharge. It must be reinserted prior to the next launch because water rushes in where fools fail to plug.

As the bow gently rises I realize my error and scramble into the lake to insert the plug. Then, using an oak board that luckily I brought along we are able to half lift, half slide the boat to shore.

Removing the plug to let out the water, I notice the trailer has been left somewhat askew by the brief encounter with its heavyweight cargo: Viewed from the rear, the trailer is sagging 5 inches to port.

Later I realize that the stabilizing bar for the motor – used during long-distance hauling – apparently was dropped earlier in the weeds and forgotten during the boat-plug fiasco. Now it's missing; someone must have picked it up.

Nevertheless, a-fishin' we do go that first night, landing a few small ones and inhaling and eyeballing the beauty that is Canada. Next we learn the tilt/trim motor is kaput. This little electric motor plays a big role: It raises and lowers the outboard engine that powers the boat, thus allowing safe navigation and maneuvering close to shore.

Chins bounce on chest like deep-diving fish lures on a rocky lake bottom as we contemplate how this week's angling will be restricted by the T/T's loss. This dismal discovery is followed by rain.

A quiet overnight soaking yields to a cloudy but fishable morning, with Chauney landing a nice smallmouth. Lots of fish – about 50/50 largemouth and smallmouth – come into the boat, and no more raindrops.

As sunshine reappears and I don sunglasses – self-customized with pieces of white plastic to protect the nose after Mohs surgery last winter – Chauney lets fly a little levity: "Hey, too early for Halloween!"

After lunch I finish a magazine devoted to "Mark Twain: In His Own Words," and pick up a decrepit little black book on Buffalo Bill Cody. Later, on the lake, it's a repeat performance: loads of little guys, no keepers and more rain.

Monday morning we catch a bunch on the Crippled Minnow. That word, crippled, keeps resurfacing in my mind. *Now just what else will come along to further complicate matters?*

Don't have long to wonder about that: The bilge pump's not working. With the motor ramrod straight up-and-down and no way to pump water from beneath the boat's floorboards, we're in trouble deep if we get caught in a downpour. The worst-case scenario: We'd be unable to pull the boat out of the lake, it'd be too heavy – and/or the motor, shoved down by the weight, might catch bottom as we try to pull out.

On we fish, keeping a wary eye on those clouds. Chauney boats a feisty largemouth, a fat 18½-incher in the 4-lb. range.

No fishin' tonight as those ubiquitous clouds and a suddenly pesky breeze hold forth. Read and read until finally Buffalo Bill rides off into the literary sunset (only one available just now) and then pick up Kipling's "Kim." Anything to avoid thinking about those darned clouds …

Next morning we have three keepers – another great meal – and then it's gloriously sunny. A break in our luck, maybe? Remembering the trailer rollers, I drive to the lake and get to work removing the old worn out ones. Well, I get the removal part done, or at least three-quarters of it.

Unable to get the fourth roller off, I'm confronted by this: The new $38 rollers don't fit over the spindles on which the originals turned. Also, the end caps that held the old rollers on the spindles have been ruined during removal. (Nearly destroyed my left index finger with a hammer in the roller removal process, too, but never mind that.)

Forced to reinstall the dilapidated rollers, I resort to a trio of Vise-Grips from the toolbox to latch onto the spindles in substitute for the destroyed end caps, taping the handles closed and fastening them to the trailer frame. Jerry-rigging at its finest – Rube Goldberg reincarnated.

A steady wind comes up, but not enough for us to shrink from our evening rounds on the lake. We venture out until, surrounded by white caps, we are doubly daunted. The lures on both our fishing lines snarl about 50 feet apart in a large weed bed.

I respond to this revolting development with yet another *faux pas*: Instead of cutting my line and losing one lure to focus on retrieving Chauney's, I let out extra line, put my rod down and steer toward his line. Buffeted by wind and blinded by a setting sun and its wild lake-top reflections, we get off course.

Jerked by the invisible hand of a fish god, my rod suddenly springs out of the boat and into White Lake. Translation: I've run out of line and the movement of the boat yanks the rod away.

What comes next should never happen to two guys who've seen a combined 145 fishing seasons between them, but it does anyhow.

Leaving my wallet behind (very good) but not my watch (you dope) I dive for the missing rod and reel. (While the rod, a 6-foot Ugly Stik by Shakespeare, is nothing special, the big Daiwa reel certainly is. Valued in three figures, it's a long-ago gift from four dear friends at work, among them the former owner of the boat out of which I just jumped.)

"Hey," I holler over the wind to Chauney, "kill the engine before you run me over!"

Now there is no sound save that of the wind, and sanity is making a comeback. I'm in water over my head, my energy ebbing because of a stupid mistake, and I'll be lucky to make it back into the boat. With that accomplished, we take off, disgusted and disbelieving of events to this point.

Here comes Thursday and – even though I have backup fishing equipment along – all I can think about is losing that reel last night. So back over the weed bed we troll, dragging the bottom with a makeshift grappling hook, trying to snag my rod.

Half an hour later we give up and get back to fishing. Immediately my spare rod and reel – yeah, I know, it's almost psychic that I had 'em along – are the hot combo, outfitted at the business end once again with the Crippled Killer, yellow phase. The bass are taking it near shore on an all-of-a-sudden sunny morning.

Later, in one of those inexplicabilities that alternately bless and baffle anglers, the fish are gang-tackling yet another of my lures, a little dark deep-diving number. Feeling bad for Chauney, fishless this morning, I pass the rod to him. But, alas, the fish gods are having none of it, and the action abruptly ends. Soon he hands it back and we quit for lunch.

Then, without warning, as we pull up to our mooring tree – hey, this is Canada, there are no docks with handy slips and neon Bud Lite signs – a new word splashes into the North American Bass Fishermen's International Dictionary (unabridged edition):

"Slewfoot," meaning (according to Chauney, whose 38 years as a PA wildlife conservation officer and lifetime of relentless reading qualify him as a wordsmith) "someone who has repressed so much anger that when he tries to kick a tackle box over the lake, he just discombobulates the closing clamp." Translation: I inadvertently dumped the contents of his tackle box into a many-hooked mess in the boat.

Following a verbal free-for-all between us, heavy clouds ambush the sunshine and a light rain commences. Recognizing that an overnight downpour literally could sink our crippled boat, we reluctantly decide to yank it and head home a day early.

Now out of the water, the motor's propeller helps unravel yet another yarn: Judging by the wad of monofilament encrusting it, my line must have been caught and "eaten" by the prop, which pulled rod and reel into the lake when the line ran out. We must have pulled the rig quite a distance behind the boat before the line finally tore. All of which means that trying to snag it by dragging the next morning was doomed; rod and reel were nowhere near that weed bed.

With the boat properly seated and secured to the trailer, the latter is attached to the truck, we think. Off we go, one last time, headed for camp and an early bedtime before the trip home. That vision ends noisily as Chauney, at the wheel, hits the brakes at the sound of metal on macadam.

The trailer, despite being padlocked to the hitch, has come free and, as we slow down, boat rams into truck and destroys tailgate. It's a freak accident, a mechanical mystery, but somehow we're able to rejoin trailer to hitch in proper fashion. And those Vise-Grips are still holding fast.

The only other excitement during the trip interrupts my daydreaming as we pass the Scranton exit. I'm mentally changing the name of my boat from the original black-lettered Free Floating to the now more apropos Moby Debt – red letters, of course – when suddenly a dashboard light blinks to life, signaling: "Transmission trouble." We stop to eat and never see the light again.

At home and relaxing in the shower, I smile inwardly at the memory of having cut a square foot or so for use as a washcloth from the only bath towel I'd brought along – a sacrifice softened by the fact we also had no dishcloth, and so it served double duty.

Toweling off, I find a tick attached to my ribcage and instantly suspect its source as my last woodsy walk with bass entrails to the camp fish pit. I came home from the spring wild turkey hunt with a tick, and now this. It's barely through the skin and easily ejected. My wife says I'm getting to be something of a tick magnet. Ha! Hey, die laughing or drown in your tears.

Then reality settles in like a low-pressure system over Ontario, and I know the boat, motor and trailer have made their last trip. Repairs are cost prohibitive, period. I am lucky to find a buyer, even at the bargain price of under $500. The best I can say is that Moby Debt reeked of fish when last we parted.

Turns out the truck also has made its last run to Ontario. Remember that tranny light? Well, over at M&S Auto, Dave's translation is: $3,500. With the old green Ford's bluebook value at $1,350, I'm out looking for new wheels. As our Canadian friends might say, maybe something smaller but still big enough to drag a boat, eh?

Chauney Martin checks his hook.

John Martin displays an Ontario smallmouth bass.

Doug waits out an Ontario rain, 2011.

The author takes a daybreak swim to retrieve his boat, which slipped its moorings in a storm overnight.

Why we fish often dictates where

Ask 10 anglers about their favorite fishing spots, and most likely you'll get a few stony stares, a quizzical look or two, at least one smirk and three or four terse replies – reticence in full flood. As for those who do answer, let's just say that only a fool would believe them.

Seriously, it always strikes me as an odd question because, before deciding where to fish, I have to consider what's in season, whether I'll be alone or with others, etc. Is this a catch-and-release outing, or do I (we) want fish to eat? Are we going to wade or fish from a bank or out of a boat?

Suppose it's Christmas morning 2001, your company won't be arriving for several hours, and your stepson says he'd like to go fishing. That scenario – played out at our house in Hummelstown – dictated that we fish somewhere close by.

So Jason and I grab our tackle, lawn chairs and a jug of coffee and drive a fraction of a mile to the empty-as-can-be parking lot at Hoss's Steak and Sea House in the west end of town along U.S. Route 322. We park and approach the Swatara Creek nearby. It's a crunch-crunch-crunch walk because the ground, having frozen then thawed, is refreezing. Edged in white, the stream testifies to winter's return overnight.

The Swatara – Swattie, to locals – is a tributary of the Susquehanna River. This creek is not a trout stream and, even if it were, late December is hardly primetime for fly-fishing. This is a warm water stream, heavily influenced by runoff. The pool we are fishing, just upstream from Indian Echo Caverns, likely is holding rock bass, perhaps a smallmouth or two and sunfish for sure.

While popular with local anglers, especially the young, it's not a great fishing spot. What it is – especially today – is handy. So we position our lawn chairs on the bank and get to it, trying an assortment of surefire artificial lures – all of which misfire. Between us we manage one weak strike on a silver minnow. At least the coffee's hot. This abbreviated outing is the 36th and final fishing entry in my diary for the year.

Sometimes I favor a spot just downstream from that one when it's raining, or threatening, because the bridge over 322 serves as shelter. And the fade in, fade out hum of traffic adds rhythm to the sounds of the storm, entertaining its small but appreciative audience.

By now you're probably wondering, what is this guy, some kind of troll who comes out to fish under his bridge on rainy days and holidays? Not really, though admittedly on occasion I have been accused of going a little overboard on the fishing thing. As it says on the mat at our front door, "A fisherman and a normal person live here." The mat, by the way, was given to us by a couple of normal people.

From a land of lakes to the riverside

Raised in a family attuned to relaxing by lakes, I was slow to embrace the riverside. I went to the creeks of my boyhood, like the one that flowed under Main

Street in Cortland, NY, right past Doc Loope's garage, to skip stones and catch frogs, not to fish.

I was 29 before all that began to change in 1972 when we moved 20 miles from small York New Salem to even smaller Cly, to be nearer my work in Harrisburg.

The village of Cly, along the Susquehanna River in northeastern York County, and nearby Shelley Island owe their names to an early merchant, Clymer Shelley, who set up shop during the stagecoach era on the river's west bank across from present day Three Mile Island.

Cly has had a front row seat for two dramatic moments in American history. Union loyalists, retreating from the bridge burning in 1863 at Wrightsville during the Civil War, visited the village hotel to eat and toast their accomplishment, which spared Lancaster from the advancing Confederate forces who took control of York.

A century and 16 years later, the villagers found themselves much closer to the action – just the river's width away from a scary hydrogen bubble at TMI that many feared would explode, triggering a meltdown at the nuclear power plant.

The hero that day was scientist Harold Denton, whose calm manner as he led President Carter inside the disabled plant helped soothe the public psyche. If you're old enough, maybe you remember the news photo of Denton and Carter walking into the plant, their shoes covered by little white booties.

The rhythm of the river

When your front yard is a river you grow accustomed to a rhythm of change. The water rises, the water falls; the surface freezes and then it thaws. The geese fly south as winter nears, north as it leaves.

True, the drama and damage of flooding are facts of life, but so are the interludes of sunshine reflecting off water and filled with waterfowl hunting, fishing and catching turtles. Mmmm, snapper soup.

During my slow immersion into the water-dominated world of Cly, I found a delightful resource and plenty of dry humor in my nearest neighbor. Late in his 80s, Roy Hoover lived across the street in an old house that reflected an owner stubbornly resistant to change.

He was without running water or central heat, and no car was parked out back. There was a hand pump in the kitchen to draw from a well, and he had electricity, barely. A bald lightbulb protruding from the ceiling and a small radio (diehard Phillies fan) plugged into the only wall receptacle in sight made me envy his monthly power bill, if not his lifestyle.

Occasionally we could entice Mr. Hoover over for supper (homemade apple pie would usually do it). On his first visit to our table, he told us that as a young man, long before retiring from the now-defunct paper mill at nearby York Haven, he'd captained a dredging boat in the heyday of coal.

Living near a dam

Thanks to inefficient mining methods, small pieces of coal lost upstream rode the river currents to York Haven, site of the first hydroelectric dam on the lower Susquehanna. This distinguishing feature of our new neighborhood was 5,000 feet long and touched parts of Dauphin, Lancaster and York counties. The low-head diversion dam was the world's third-largest when built in 1904.

The dam and its headrace straddle natural rock formations where the Susquehanna's level drops 19 feet in ¼ mile (officially, Conewago Falls). This all adds up to a turbulent flow – one that in Roy Hoover's day brought coal bits bouncing along the bottom and piling up in the reservoir behind the dam. And the job of Captain Hoover's crew "was to bring as much of that coal into our boat as possible," he said.

To young ears at the dinner table, this was startling news; to older ones it was history come to life. The idea of finding lost coal resonated with the boys, I think, because they often went along to local farm fields to pick up ears of corn left by the hit-or-miss harvesting machinery of the day. Largely through gleaning we fed the livestock on our little farm.

One of our boys – I think it was little Dennis – asked our neighbor how much coal might come aboard in a day. The answer – "Tons!" – so impressed his three grade-school listeners that in time they elevated him to "Captain Hoovy" whenever he came up in conversation.

At a Dohne boys reunion in Syracuse (L to R)
Dan, Den, Grampa (the host), Doug and Dave.

Teatime in Cly

It got to be a regular thing that when I came home from work and stopped at the mailbox, Mr. Hoover was on his porch swing reading or listening to the Phillies game, but never both at once.

"Care for some tea?"

This was his coded invitation to come over for a glass of homemade elderberry wine, clearly intended to mislead any eavesdroppers. But his closest neighbor was a sweet old widow who kept to herself, so there really was nobody around to overhear anything.

Once during, um, teatime I heard this story of a young man from the neighborhood about to head off to fight in World War I:

"'Before I go,' this fella told us, 'I want to eat one of those swans.'*

"Now, his family was poor, but one of them had a single-shot 12-gauge, and a friend had a canoe. Someone brewed a batch of beer – they kept it cool right over there in that spring (pointing across the street to my property).

"Is it still running?"

Assured by his guest that the spring was indeed flowing freely, he picked up the story:

"This boy didn't have too long to wait. One morning he spotted a few swans off the tip of Shelley (Island) and took off for the canoe, which he kept upstream, figuring he could ride the current along the edge of the island right into the flock.

"That part worked out – he got close enough to shoot a swan. But the canoe upset and he lost the shotgun in the river.

"Well, they cleaned up that big ol' bird and roasted it on a spit over an open fire. Most of the beer was gone before it was time to eat, and everyone was good and hungry.

"Things went downhill when that young man put the fork to the bird. It was so tough no one could eat it!"

So whatever happened to the swan-slaying doughboy of Newberry Twp.?

"We heard he wound up fighting over there in France, but he never made it home."

**Likely a tundra swan, most common of the three migrating species using the Atlantic flyway*

Getting upset

Overturned boats are not unusual on the Susquehanna. Like the unfortunate soldier, I, too, once overturned a boat while waterfowl hunting. The difference was, I didn't get wet. Huh?

It happened on a solo outing for geese on a cloudy, breezy day with snow expected, and the hunting wasn't going well. I was using an old 14-foot Sears aluminum johnboat, but the few honkers encountering my edge-of-an-island position showed no interest in the six decoys.

I was a novice waterfowler, having been given the boat by occasional hunting partner Bill Burkett, an investigative reporter who decided somewhat abruptly to quit the newspaper and work as an AFL-CIO organizer in Florida. He was a seasoned duck-and-goose chaser and had taught me enough that I now suspected a flawed setup was probably to blame for my lack of action.

Suddenly it was sleeting and I remembered Bill preaching that bad weather often made for good waterfowling. *OK, now the huntin' begins! Get ready!*

Instead of waterfowl, the rising wind delivered only more sleet, now slapping my face in earnest. *Can't leave now – home is directly into the wind, and this little 3-hp Johnson* (a loaner from a neighbor) *won't cut it. You're stuck!*

The only thing left to do was pull the boat up on shore, flip it and get underneath. Not a bad turn of events: With the boat bottom now a roof, I gathered the seat cushion, my raincoat and the decoy tote bag for bedding and lay there experiencing the rat-a-tat-tat symphony of sleet, a percussive masterpiece in the key of C. *Doug, you dummy! Should've taken the motor off. Bet it won't start up again after this …*

An hour later the sleet was melting into a bad memory and the boat was once again afloat, the little motor propelling me homeward. *And no shotgun was lost nor any waterfowl killed. RIP, Newberry doughboy.*

A flourishing fishery

The Susquehanna River at that time was home to a thriving smallmouth bass fishery that had rebounded from pollution so severe a century earlier that a dam was built at Harrisburg to stifle the river's summertime stench. Let's be clear: The purpose of the low-head Dock Street Dam was to hold the river's level high enough to cover pipes discharging raw effluent and other wastes from the city. The August smell must have been abominable.

The comeback of the bass – indeed, the resurgence of the entire river – was powered by a citizenry sufficiently enlightened to outlaw pollution, finance and build sewage treatment plants, etc. Then Agnes blew into town.

Downgraded to tropical storm status before slamming into Pennsylvania late in June 1972, Hurricane Agnes killed more than 100 Americans and caused damage topping $2 billion. For the Susquehanna and many other rivers, this was the so-called 100-year flood. Four and a half decades later, Agnes remains the reference point against which all other floods are measured.

Our family was moving into a hillside home at Cly just as Agnes was leaving town. During a break from all the lifting, carrying and putting down, I recall thinking how out of place that week's brilliant sunshine seemed for such a darkly destructive time. Many people had lost their homes, some even their lives.

From our porch we saw whole trees, telephone poles, roofs, boats, docks and even some truck trailers – yes, the big ones you see on the highway – all floating down the river. At one point half a dozen Holstein cattle drifted by in a gruesome last roundup. Relentlessly the swollen Susquehanna drove its debris to the York Haven dam, where an incessant thunder testified to the awful bashing and tearing.

In spots a mile wide, the river is normally shallow and placid, its bed a prime spot for heavy metals and other dangerous pollutants to collect. Agnes gave the floor of the Susquehanna a good sweeping – a huge environmental upgrade for all of the river's life-forms, the smallmouth bass included.

What followed were fat times for bass fishermen and their guides, outfitters and lure makers. Ditto for boat and motor retailers. In short, the timing of my arrival was perfect.

Night of the cereus

One of my favorite floats for smallies in the Seventies began at Goldsboro and ended at the dock in Cly. How long it took depended on river currents and the wind – the trip was shorter when both were headed the same way – and how often I dropped anchor.

When the fishing was good, sometimes I lost track of time. That's what occurred one night when so many bass came into the boat on my Jitterbug that I quit counting at 50. But it was catching a glimpse of our cactus in bloom that made this night truly special.

It was well past midnight when the johnboat glided ashore at Cly and one very tired fisherman trudged home. After a snack, I grabbed a flashlight and went out to check on that night-blooming cereus.

This plant was several years old, but we'd never seen it in flower – a once-a-year occurrence. Well, tonight was showtime. It was intriguing how the blooms seemed to seep right out from the edges of the leaves as though they were bleeding.

All the fish had been released back into the river, soon to be forgotten, but the image of that cereus in flower remains locked firmly in memory.

Two different kinds of fishing

River angling and the lake kind are distinctly dissimilar. You can sit in a boat on a lake and – if the wind is absent or at least light – leisurely yet thoroughly fish one spot, then move on to another. Grabbing a few winks while they're not biting – yeah, you might get away with that on a lake. Try it on a river and you're pushing your luck.

Well, I wasn't snoozing, but on one of my early outings for smallmouth on the Susquehanna let's just say I wasn't very vigilant. I was afloat alone in the (this time motorless) johnboat, watching my lure bob along with the current, focused on fishing and definitely not on navigating. Fortunately my ears were standing guard. *What's all that noise?*

The dam! I was headed for the York Haven hydroelectric dam – way too close and way too fast …

Splash! That's the anchor going overboard as I catch my breath and make sure the oars are at the ready. The Susquehanna is flowing, and so is my adrenalin. *Father, please deliver this fool and his boat from danger. Now!*

Bending to the task, I weigh anchor and start rowing in a single frantic motion. Soon sweat is getting into my eyes and everywhere else, and clothes are sticking to skin like moths on flypaper. The struggle to escape the grip of Conewago Falls calls forth every ounce of energy – just to progress in increments of inches.

Once out of danger, I drop anchor, rest and reflect. *Thank You, Lord, for bringing me safely through. I'll try hard not to bother you again too soon. Promise!*

The perils of hook and bullet

Regarding the dangers of fishing vs. those of hunting, once I thought the latter was the riskier pursuit. *The reason you have fewer hunting partners than fishing pals is because hunting is more dangerous. You have to be very careful around rifles and shotguns – better pick your hunting companions with care.*

While the logic is strong, experience really doesn't bear it out. With the exception of my shot at a turkey flying past a concealed (and fortunately, protected)

Chauney, my challenges in the woods pale alongside those on water. Besides the boyhood foolishness that resulted in an owl's death, the worst that ever happened was getting lost a few times – and never overnight.

Fishing has been quite a different matter. For openers, I've had to remove fishhooks from both of my hands and one of Chauney's. The latter procedure was done over saltwater as we headed out from Wachapreague, VA, after flounder.

The culprit that late spring day was a so-called circle hook, more than an inch long. It was the biggest – and deepest – human hooking I've had to undo so far. The point had pierced the palm and resurfaced about half an inch away, exposing the barb.

As we rode the tide, awaiting sunrise and better light, we weighed the options: pinch the barb shut and back the hook out, or cut the line and push it through. The patient gambled on the latter tactic as the least painful, but you can bet your best fishing lure it hurt plenty. He made no sound throughout the ordeal, nor did I. *Chauney, I know you can be a quiet guy, but right now your silence is thundering!*

Tiny hook, huge hurt

It was a little hook that caused the worst pain of any I've had to extract from my own hide. Fly-fishing a tributary of Lycoming County's Little Pine Creek on a breezy spring day, I snagged a No. 18 Royal Coachman on my right earlobe.

Most often the small needle-nose pliers in my fishing vest is used to secure flies that require repair while in use. That day it became a surgical instrument in a procedure complicated by the fact that the, um, doctor couldn't see what he was doing. His other problem was that the little barb was completely buried in flesh – and doing a fine job of holding fast, thank you. *The longer this goes on the more I'm going to suffer. Lord, with your hand over mine on the pliers I know everything will work out OK. One, two, three …*

Rather than further discomfort, the yank brought a burst of blood; I had no idea so much could flow from an earlobe. My emergency stash of toilet paper got used for something other than its intended purpose, and so did a big red (and fortunately, still clean) hanky. About a yard square, those hankies alternately have served as hand towels, tourniquets and scarves. And waving one of them can be a real attention getter for, say, an approaching hunter who hasn't yet spotted you.

A regular patient

My early medical fieldwork was a family thing, thanks to Dennis, the clear leader among the Dohne boys in run-of-the-mill accidents outdoors. At about age 10, he fell from a grapevine into a rocky, shallow streambed, gashing his head. Driving him to the doctor's office took both hands – one on the steering wheel and the other poking at the patient to keep him conscious.

On a 1982 visit to Gatlinburg, TN, Dennis needed more stitches to his noggin, this time due to a river-diving accident. My biggest role that day was using a motel bed sheet to slow his bleeding during the trip to the only medical clinic in town, which was about to close. We lucked out: The doctor was just getting into his car as we pulled up.

A winged one

Instead of fingers, fishhooks sometimes wind up in feathers, such as the time Brad snagged a seagull. Besides me, there were two other witnesses to this fowl deed, Shane and Chauney. It was Shane's first foray for flounder. Once again we were afloat in May on Atlantic coastal waters.

Seagulls are opportunistic by nature, as any beachgoer who has ever tried to eat french fries while relaxing on a blanket knows. Gulls are smart, too. I've seen them drop clams onto rocks to break open the shells. And persistent: They swoop down after each drop to see whether it's time to eat or take shell in beak and try again. With their excellent eyesight, seagulls seldom miss a trick. But it does happen.

It was a breezy day, but when you've trailered your boat 250 miles to the shore, you go fishing. We were using a sea anchor, which by design slows the drift and reduces rocking but does not hold the boat stationary. Maybe it screws up seagulls, too, but who really knows.

One sure thing is that gulls love to surveil fishing boats as they move with the wind and tide. You could have a flock in attendance, or maybe just a few. Sometimes the bait – a live minnow and/or strip of squid – will come off the hook if a cast is less than smooth or too hard into the wind. Bingo! That's just what your winged companions are waiting for: time to dive and dine. If this occurs regularly, your fowl following is sure to swell.

This particular day we attracted a solitary seagull, a rather large individual that was getting very few chances to swoop and scoop. *You're gonna be gone any minute now. It's costing you way too much energy to stick around. Give it up, gull, it's a bad bet.*

Brad's next cast had the bird on a dive even before bait struck water. Vigilant, opportunistic, perseverant – so far, all normal seagull behavior. But the bird flunked its eye exam because there were two hooks and two minnows, and it went for the minny still on the hook.

Snagged by the wing, the startled seagull quickly lifted off. Once again overhead, it enlisted the wind in the battle to break its monofilament bond with Brad. Somehow the line held and the exhausted gull at last was reeled into the boat. So ill at ease was our visitor that someone had to clamp the fishing net over him before surgery could begin.

With that unpleasantness over, it was time to lift the net and discharge the patient. Regaining its feet, the bird glanced around, hopped up on the gunwale and was off. The right wing seemed to beat a little slower than the left, but soon the gull was gone from view, if not from memory. *Watch out for those fishhooks, big fella!*

Ray, ray, ray your boat

Especially for flounder fishermen, there are lots of other fish species to hook up with while testing the waters off Virginia's coast. Skates and ocean rays, for instance.

Like the sharks to which they are closely related, these two flat fishes have skeletons of soft, pliable cartilage, not bone. Skates scour the seafloor, burrowing and hiding in the sand, attacking any passing prey – the same *modus operandi* as the flounder.

So, when fishing for flounder your hook easily could wind up in the mouth of a skate. If so, prepare for battle as one with, say, a 2-foot wingspan, is a powerful creature. They have teeth and often escape by biting off the line.

With luck and a pair of pliers that you DO NOT drop overboard in the process, it's fairly easy to let a skate off the hook, but watch out for those teeth.

Occasionally you just have to cut the line and lose the rig – two hooks, a sinker and three swivel connectors. In any event, where you catch one skate, it's axiomatic: There are more. So it's time to relocate, captain.

Of course, it could always be worse – which it was, the time we tangled with a big ray during one of my early saltwater outings with Chauney.

We set out in a borrowed or rented boat, I can't remember which, to try the waters off Wachapreague. Known as the Mother of Presidents because more of them (eight) were born here than in any other state, Virginia probably has more barrier islands (if you count at low tide) than there are voting members of Congress (535).

Our encounter with the ray began just off one of those islands, a place we call White Stick, because of its myriad markers warning boaters of shallow water. There are so many white sticks visible along the Atlantic's edges in spots that, at low tide and from a distance, they resemble snowbanks. So don't look for White Stick Island on any map.

Chauney picked up the ray – really, it was the other way around – as we rode the outgoing tide in deep water on the ocean side of White Stick. Suddenly the boat was headed in the opposite direction.

This turn of events meant two things: First, we were bound for shallower, slower moving water; second, we were heading toward a slew of small vessels, some at anchor, others adrift – like we wished we were.

Fishing over a shoal, our neighbors were catching flounder at a good clip, so our intrusion was unwelcome and marked by griping as we passed the first few boats. It wasn't like we were deliberately steering that little 14-foot aluminum craft too close, snagging and pulling their lines along the way. Nope, our engine was off, but we were on a trip just the same.

“Fish on!” we hollered in warning during our approach as the complaints grew angrier in tone. Briefly I caught a whiff or two of alcohol.

“Just cut the damn line, man!” one fellow demanded.

If Chauney had done that, he’d never have gotten a glimpse of the ocean ray that hauled us at least a mile. And he might’ve surrendered too much line in the process to continue fishing. We were about halfway into the trip when Chauney saw what he thought were the pectoral fins.

Some rays are bottom feeders, rooting for crustaceans and mollusks buried in sand, while others are filter feeders, using a sieve-like body part to strain plankton from water. Regardless of whether it deliberately took Chauney’s squid-dressed baitfish or was a filter feeder and somehow got foul-hooked, we continued in its tow.

The voyage was made in four or five successively shorter segments, each time the animal waiting a little longer to return to task. Finally, our boat halted and Chauney began to crank in his line. The fish fought back, forcing its foe to reduce the drag and listen to the reel sing its song of a ray on the run.

This time the boat stayed put because the fish fled not away from it but downward. On went the fight: up and down, down and up, until Chauney decided he’d won back all the line he was going to get. A swirl, strong enough to rock the boat, followed the cutting of the line. Two words sufficed as we locked eyes and Chauney spread his hands far apart: “Big ray!”

Sometimes it’s where you get hung up …

Errant casts sometimes embed fishhooks in places where at first they cause no pain.

I was in Canada bass fishing with office buddy Bill Shearer, and between us we had a huge stock of spinner-bait lures. But on that trip unless your lure had the hue of bubblegum, the smallies just turned up their noses at it.

We were fresh out of that color, but we did have a friend in a neighboring trailer who had some. The bad news: He’d all but exhausted his supply while fishing the week before.

We bought his last four pink spinner baits and began to catch fish. But it just wasn’t the same old wide open approach to which we were accustomed. Our style was being cramped by the defensive tactics we were forced to employ.

In a normal week we’d leave a few fishing lures dangling in out-of-reach tree branches, while others were lost when the line broke or was bitten off by a pike or muskie. So we stayed away from trees, far away, and steered clear of the acres of lily pads that in the past visits had produced so many big bass.

Despite our efforts to avoid it, three days into the week we were down to one bubblegum spinner bait apiece. Then mine got snagged on a submerged log in open water, and risk-taking season was upon us.

Ontario's lakes and rivers are so pristine that if I were a fish, that's where I'd want to live. Water clarity is such that you can see to amazing depths.

Peering down, we could spot the pink lure hugging the side of the log. It was my lure and my job to get it back. Submerging the rod and my arm up to the armpit, I couldn't quite reach the lure – the plan being to knock it free with the rod tip.

With Bill grasping my belt I went headfirst into the water about to my waist but again came up empty. The third time was the charm, but by then he had me by the ankles.

The whole stupid stunt was dangerous and unnecessary. I should have handed the rod to him, dived in, followed line to lure and released it by hand. Why take such a foolish chance? I can explain that about as well as I can guess why the bass were taking only bubblegum-colored spinner baits that week.

… and sometimes it's how

Fishermen get hung up on plenty of things besides logs, of course, and sometimes there's no hook to blame. A rocky bottom at low tide can quickly become a very effective anchor when an inboard/outboard motor propeller descends on it.

That was our predicament during a Gulf outing led by brother Carl. We'd put in near Homasassa, FL, aboard his 21-foot Pro-Line. Joined by his son, Scott, we were fishing for spot. And we had chosen a bad time and poor place to do it.

Features of the cuddy cabin caught my eye as we drifted with a gentle southwest breeze, then Mother Nature abruptly shifted us into park. Everything came to a halt – the fishing, the conversation and, most noticeably, the boat. We were at the mercy of the tides, facing a lengthy wait and perhaps a propeller and drive shaft too damaged to operate.

It's never been a mystery to me that young men fall in love with the sea, forsaking life on land to be with her. Confronting the unknown out there, on the other hand, calls for courage. Like, for instance, that moment when an unidentified ship pops up on the horizon. Is she friend or foe?

"Hey, you guys need a pull off the rocks?"

Now that voice could be coming only from a friendly vessel, definitely friendly. My reverie had been interrupted by the surprise arrival of a fellow fisherman. Though smaller than ours, his boat and motor nevertheless are powerful enough to undo our awkward anchorage.

Refusing any payment with a shake of the head, our rescuer snaps a salute as he slowly backs away.

"Thank you, good man!"

Back on land the bent prop is repaired, and that's the extent of the damage. Our love affair with the sea is on again, at least for now.

Carl, left, and Steve Dohne sail the Susquehanna River on July 5, 1976, in a boat the latter built.

Know your knots, sailor

Steve is also a boater and even built one. And like us, he, too, got upset by things that happened out there on the water.

Steve was in his 20s when he bought a boat-frame kit and went to work in the basement of the rented home he shared with two other young men. After 500 hours of labor – yes, he kept track because that's what mechanical engineers always do – his 14-foot sailboat was ready for its maiden voyage. But first, there was a bill to pay.

"I had to build a trough to soak the exterior boat boards in warm water so they could be bowed into shape. The trough was fairly long, to accommodate the 16-foot lumber. We had an oil-fired furnace, which warmed the water," he recalled years later.

"One day we came home to find that the hot-water spigot was running cold. We were out of oil! I'd emptied that whole 275-gallon tank (a detail guy down to the last drop) in the middle of summer with my boat project."

And how did his roommates react?

"Well, they didn't really seem too upset by it. Heating oil back then was (wait for it, wait for it) 30 cents a gallon."

All went so smoothly
when builder and boat
on friendly water
that first time did float.

Buoyed by the construction project and his early success in operating the craft it produced, Steve invited a young lady to go sailing on the Chesapeake Bay, and she packed a special picnic lunch for the occasion.

He met Lynn Watson on the ski slopes of Vermont, and now he and this vivacious redhead were going out in his boat. Would they someday set sail on the sea of matrimony?

"It seemed like a fine day for sailing to us (a novice couple, aqua-wise), so we crossed the bay and tacked around to Cara Cove," Steve remembered. "Then the wind picked up and the waves grew, and then some more.

“Next we noticed that we were alone – all the other boats had left – and we knew we were in for a test. We had to get back across the bay, and in the rising wind I was losing control of the boat.

“We struggled, but the boat capsized and we were in very cold (43-degree) water.”

Potential tragedy was thwarted by a power-boater watching from shore who now charged to the rescue.

“Forget the sailboat, we need a blanket!” blurted Steve, once he and Lynn had climbed safely aboard their lifesaver’s craft. It turned out the hero of the hour had both blanket and towline along, so the sailboat was hauled to shore as its former occupants recovered from their ordeal.

Steve lost more than lunch that day; he also lost contact with Lynn for quite a while. Eventually they did wind up braving not-so-choppy marital seas – a voyage now in its fifth decade and complete, when all hands are on deck, with two daughters as lovely as mermaids and a grand little girl who sparkles like sunshine on seawater.

Near Davy Jones’ locker

Most harrowing of all was the time Chauney and I were caught in the crosshairs of an ocean storm bearing down on our little boat several miles off the Virginia coast. We were flounder fishing with dozens of companion boats at first, but only one in the end. That made all the difference.

Even with land in sight the ocean can be a lonely place, but usually not for long. Company always seems to be just around the corner.

Once I encountered hundreds of dolphins cavorting back and forth between two small coastal islands a few miles offshore. Apparently they were migrating and had pulled into this protected spot to rest.

Another time I ran into a school of skates so large it made fishing a fool's choice. They swarmed the boat like seagulls after a careless kid with an ice cream cone. One summer we were visited repeatedly by a seal that had taken up residence in the harbor and was after our bait minnows. And there was a turtle whose brownish-yellow head reminded me of Mother's bathing cap, but its head was larger than (and not nearly so pretty) as hers.

As for human visitors, all any angler has to do is start catching fish and they'll come. Truthfully, Chauney and I were anything but lonely that day as the talkative Roscoe Stiles was aboard.

We rented a boat after the one we brought along developed engine trouble. In our regular boat we typically had a 5-gallon fuel tank and a full backup the same size. Probably because the owner of this one didn't want us venturing too far, he supplied just a 3-gallon can. Hey, smaller boat and motor equals smaller gas tank. It looked right, but it wasn't.

A funny thing about fishing is that when they're coming in over the gunwales like traffic at rush-hour it's as though the fish drive everything else out of your mind. What sunburned lips and cheeks, hunger, thirst and fatigue? The no-see-ums and other pesky biting insects that only moments ago held your rapt attention now don't even rate a swat. Ditto for that all-but-empty gas tank, but no one knew because no one checked.

That's what was going on in our boat when others started showing up. Soon they, too, were boating flatties – and proving me wrong about being unable to focus on anything but the fish we were landing. We were griping about this one or that one getting a little too close, disturbing our fishing.

"That red boat's so close he's gonna cut our lines with the prop!"

"Wow! Check out the yellow bikini in the big blue Whaler!"

For a few marvelous minutes it seemed like every hook in the water held a flounder. Then it all changed quicker than you can remove a tattered hook and put on a new one.

The wind shifted, bright sunshine paled, and all eyes were trained on an ominous dark cloud that had bloomed and was now booming far out at sea. Within seconds motors were humming as fishermen fled for shore.

But our motor wouldn't start, and when Chauney hefted the gas can it was so light it nearly clipped his chin. We were out of gas!

The ranks were thinning fast, and no one heard our calls for help. *Maybe they overheard our grousing earlier and took offense …*

Suddenly remembering the little whistle in my tackle box, I sounded the alarm. Heads in one boat – but only one – turned in our direction, and help was on the way.

Our rescuers were caught in circumstances close to ours: They were low on gas, very low. That ruled out towing us in, but the Tanytown, MD, trio agreed to give Chauney a lift to summon help.

Wind was whipping up whitecaps as my friend stepped from our boat into that of strangers, leaving me and Roscoe drifting toward a small island that was about to disappear from view under the surging storm.

We closed on the island quickly. *Lord, please be present in our boat and bring us through this storm.* My gaze fixed on Roscoe, then well into his 80s. The tales of long ago turkey hunts that he'd been retelling nonstop had worn thin and he'd fallen silent.

Suddenly straightening up in his seat, Roscoe – in a bass voice like a big brother to his normal tenor – gave this brilliant command:

"Drive the oars into the sand on either side of the boat, deep as you can, and lash them together with the anchor rope."

By the time that was done the storm was upon us in full fury. No longer were we straining to hear or see a rescue boat. We were frantically pushing down on those oars, clinging to an island that seemed to be submerging like a submarine.

The Coast Guard rescue vessel came so close – and straight for us – that I nearly dropped an oar, fearing a run-over. But whoever was at the wheel simply shifted into reverse and gunned his engine – the equivalent of braking in a boat – as a wind-burned officer threw us a towline.

Quickly we were shore-bound, and Roscoe once again was talking turkey in his usual voice.

Thank You, Lord, for placing the raging sea at our back. That was your voice out there, wasn't it? Thank You for speaking up!

The danger below

The drama that day was above water and plain for all to see, but you never know what's going on below. It was on an earlier Atlantic flounder outing that I heard a far different kind of Coast Guard story.

This time Jason and I were guests in the boat that Bill Shearer hadn't yet sold to me, and its owner was feeling some pressure. Far from shore, we'd neglected to bring along a bucket for emergency use as a latrine. In line with his sensitive nature, Bill elected to, well, go overboard while Jason and I continued to fish.

Just as Bill was climbing back into the boat, Jason had a violent strike. Part way into his retrieve the line went limp, and all that was left on his hook was the head of what once had been perhaps a 2-foot flounder. Was the clean, rainbow-shaped cut the mark of a shark?

Sharking

Not surprisingly, that incident touched off a lively conversation about our fellow swimmers at the beach. Though he never said so, Bill clearly believed a shark was to blame. Psychologically – though mercifully, not physically – an impression had been made on him by the flounder's demise. Soon we were listening to a shark story from Bill's Coast Guard days.

While such missions as search and rescue and drug interdiction may afford some excitement, boredom is not entirely unknown in the Coast Guard. Let's just say that ocean mapping and weather data gathering had ganged up to rob Bill's crewmates of their focus – temporarily, of course. It all began with a petty officer's mealtime complaint, "This chicken crap's not fit for shark bait."

Never let it be said that this was a crew to shrink from challenge. Bill's account:

"A day or so later, a big stainless steel hook – gosh, it was nearly a foot long – just sort of showed up. Next thing we knew there was a bunch of chicken breasts hanging from that hook, which was bolted to the underside of a board and now trailing the ship on a cable. We were fishin'!"

The petty officer was proved wrong on the second day of this impromptu and illicit shark season.

"I guess the guys were so intent on getting a shark – any shark – to bite that they never thought about the rest of it," Bill continued. "Well, when you hook a fish you reel it in, right? The retrieval part was easy because the cable was on a winch. But once they got it on deck nothing was easy.

"We never did figure out what kind it was, but it had to be 16 feet long. And man was it ever powerful! It sprang around that deck like it was on drugs! Someone got tomahawked on the shin so bad he was carried into sick bay on a stretcher.

"That did it: Once the officers wised up, the order to 'Clear the decks!' rang out. The cable was cut and that shark was back in the ocean in a heartbeat."

Another finned opportunist

The theme of big fish going after smaller ones is as prevalent in freshwater as it is in salt. Predation nearly robbed me of a dandy smallmouth one evening on the Swattie.

Neighbor Dale Anglemeyer was along in the johnboat that August day. We were drift fishing, rowing only when necessary. A steady upstream breeze slowed our progress as dusk fell – now we had to man the oars fulltime. Wait! It was time to land a fish that was vigorously trying to shed the Crippled Minnow it had just inhaled.

This was a nice bass, one to be admired up close and then released. Dale was in the stern, net in hand, as the weary smallie came alongside. In failing light I couldn't make out the fish, but I did see my friend preparing to land it. Then he pulled back, let out a gasp and blurted:

"Wow! Did you see that monster?!"

Before I could respond he had the net in the water and the bass in the boat. Sadly, the fish was so enmeshed in treble hooks and taxed by its struggle that it didn't survive.

But what had my partner seen?

"Doug, I didn't know there were fish that big in this little creek! It was twice the size of your bass (19 inches) and then some. You should have seen the head – it was huge! This guy was after your fish, but I think I spooked him."

From his further description it likely was a muskellunge. Shoot, the only muskie ever known to visit my boat and I never even got a peek. *Who knows, maybe that bass was just plain scared to death.*

Dale Anglemeyer with Doug and a Swattie smallie.

The bass are always up for a snack

If fish played football, the acrobatic trout would catch and run with it while the big (up to 5 feet long and 100 pounds) Asian carp battled up front and the smallmouth bass laid on the licks at linebacker. At any post-game smorgasbord, I think the bass would steal the show.

Compared with the finicky salmonoids – the first thing a fly-fisherman learns is the importance of presentation – and the always hungry bass, the invasive and voracious silver, black, bighead and grass carp will outeat just about all comers. Indeed, with no natural predators, these rascals are a threat to supplant native species in the Great Lakes.

But watching this invading force eat would be boring: They are filter feeders, thriving on plankton, so there's little to see. Nah, for the sheer show of it, the curious, athletic and aggressive smallmouth is the most entertaining of the lot.

When considering a change in tactics or sometimes just to straighten the back, my habit is to put the rod aside for a few moments, usually in a position spanning the gunwales with the lure hanging just above the water's surface. Should another boat pass and cause ours to rock, the plug might slap the water a time or two.

The first few bass that hooked themselves by striking my briefly unattended plugs caught me by surprise, as did those that attacked on the backswing. But really, I should have expected it. The smallmouth is the quintessential predator with a well-honed chase mechanism. It doesn't matter what causes the prey to move; when it does – bam, game on.

Grampa Dohne was playing pinochle on his New York cottage porch one night when he hooked a respectable smallmouth. He'd been out on the lake for bass earlier and left the rod – with his favorite Crazy Crawler still on the line – upright in the boat. When the fish struck, the rod slammed against the boat and the dock where it was moored. Somehow Grampa got there in time to reel in a 13-incher.

The best performance by a leaping smallmouth that I've been privileged to witness occurred in Ontario. Chauney and I were working the shoreline of White Lake about dusk.

The idea was to cast the plug close enough to branches overhanging the water that, to a fish, the lure would seem to have descended from a tree. I'm not sure which one of us had rod in hand when his line, sporting a yellow Jitterbug, got wound around a branch.

Up to this point, we'd seen it all before: With the lure suspended 3 or 4 feet above water, your partner maneuvers the boat toward it as you slowly take up the slack line. Soon you're reaching for the plug and – wow! – this time something beats you to the punch.

A foot-long smallie, its attack mode triggered by the Jitterbug's dance as you tried to yank it free, breaks water right below its target. A few seconds later it's back with an even greater leap, though still falling short of the mark.

In the end, we got the plug back, the fish got rave reviews for effort, and somewhere out on the lake a loon piped up with a sorry cry or a mournful heckle, we couldn't agree which.

Night falls as the bass rise

A man of the cloth, a man of medicine and a man of letters were afloat on the Susquehanna River one night, and the bass were coming up over the side of the boat like Olympians clearing their hurdles.

Rev. John Schaefer, who's usually in the pulpit at Grace United Methodist Church in Hummelstown unless he's out fishing with Dr. Mark Bates, was piloting the boat and doing most of the catching. Doc was manning the net. It was a little past 10, and we were bathed in Three Mile Island's weird yellowish-pinkish light. I was in the fore, doing some fishing but mostly watching for any obstacles we might be approaching. Every lure we cast, it seemed, instantly had a fish attached.

The whole scenario changed when a jet took off from nearby Harrisburg International Airport, and the smell and taste of fuel descended, enveloping us and our boat. Somehow TMI's odd illumination now seemed apropos. Just like that the bass quit biting. It was as if Rev. John's Boss had said, Amen, boys.

Quite a few amens later, I found myself in a back pew with Dr. Bates one Sunday morning, so you know who was up front. Between hymns Doc asked if I'd been out for trout. When I said no, he immediately inquired about my health, which admittedly hadn't been so hot – night sweats, dizziness, not much pep, that sort of thing.

"Seeing any ticks this spring?" he asked, passing the collection plate.

Well, I didn't think so. But I did have some swelling behind the right knee.

Doc motioned for me to roll up my pant leg, which I did with one hand while returning the plate with the other.

"Bull's-eye," he mumbled before being drowned out by a chorus of "Praise God from whom all blessings flow …"

Later, with head bowed, Doc was on his cell when the singing ended. This time all I caught was, "thank you."

"Now unto Him who is able to keep you from falling," Rev. John went into his windup.

Right after the benediction, Doc turned and said, "Stop at Rhoads (drugstore) on the way home and pick up your prescription."

"Think I should see a doctor?" I shot back.

"Doug," he said, "you just did!"

Watch your step

Something else I never saw coming was the way-over-my-head-deep hole I walked into one day while fishing on the Juniata River with Jason. We were after smallies in Watts Twp., Perry County, and had traversed a rocky hillside to reach the water.

Wading the Juniata – and the Susquehanna, into which it flows – is a tricky undertaking, even during low water levels. Besides aquatic growth that slickens the bottom, the rock outcroppings tend to form troughs that act like vises on fishermen's boots – they won't let go. So long as you keep going the direction the trough runs – usually straight across the river – you're OK. Just don't lose your balance or decide to turn upstream or down; that's when things can get ugly fast.

It had to be anything but pretty once I got headed downriver. With one foot free but the other stuck in the rocks, I nearly fell in. Regaining my balance, I took one more step.

That swept me into a pool big enough to swallow my F-150, probably without a splash, and my boots were turning into anchors as they filled with water. *These holes can be deep, but hopefully this one isn't too long. Just keep shuffling along as best you can. Lord, grant me breath.*

Still clutching my fishing rod, I emerged from the hole with the current nudging me along.

One glance at my all-of-a-sudden-silent partner revealed a white face in place of the sunburned one that I remembered. For a young man so obviously in need of quick reassurance, the best I could come up with was:

“That sure got deep in a hurry.”

One thing that was unaffected by what he’d witnessed was Jason’s rollicking laugh. When he lets loose it’s infectious, and anyone within earshot invariably goes along for the ride. Soon both of us were laughing so hard we had to sit down on a convenient above-water rock and let it pass.

The last laugh that day was on him because as we moved toward shore he, too, slipped and fell into a hole. And he took the tackle box in with him, as I quickly pointed out, glad for the perfect rejoinder I’d just been handed for whenever he’d retell the tale of how “That sure got deep in a hurry.”

Besides some dignity, the only thing either of us lost was my hat, now a distant dot riding the Juniata and steadily growing smaller. What led to laughter just as easily could have ended in tears, and we both knew it. *One more time, Lord: Thank You.*

Sickness in the Susquehanna

Some of the joy started to go out of bass fishing in the Susquehanna River when holes of another kind began showing up. These were gaps in the smallmouth population, as revealed in young-of-the-year studies by governmental resource agencies charged with monitoring river health.

Fishermen sensed something was wrong just a few years into the 21st century. By 2005 lesions and sores were showing up on some of the bass we caught. Another red flag: Too few juvenile smallies were winding up in landing nets. No youngsters, no future – it's that simple.

Obviously something was wrong, and angling's regulators responded in knee-jerk fashion by imposing the catch-and-release-only rule for smallmouth on nearly 100 miles of the middle Susquehanna and more than 30 miles of the lower Juniata, a main tributary.

Blaming overharvesting when something goes awry is tempting; after all, the impact of human greed on various fish species has been well documented. But focusing exclusively on anglers in the smallmouth saga is unrealistic, as they account for just a fraction of the 3 million-plus humans inhabiting the river basin.

Every minute of every hour of every day the Susquehanna empties 18 million gallons of water into the Chesapeake Bay – about half its total intake.

That's what Paul Swartz, then chief of the Susquehanna River Basin Commission, told me in a 2011 interview. About an ocean's worth must have flowed into the bay since then, eh, Paul?

But man is a frequent dipper, tapping the river to drink, bathe, and keep the lights on, golf courses green and businesses thriving, etc. While much of what we remove is consumed, a lot of it returns to the river – some in far worse condition. Examples of the latter are the residues of farming, mining and timbering, which exact a frightening toll on aquatic life downstream and then pile up in the bay. Natural gas fracking also vies for the monitors' attention, and rightfully so.

Doing the write thing

Among those taking pen in hand to defend the smallmouth was John Arway, executive director of the PA Fish and Boat Commission, whose July 2014 letter to the U.S. Environmental Protection Agency faulted "dissolved phosphorus" for ravaging river and bay. The letter I sent a year earlier pleaded with President Obama to show compassion for "the tens of thousands living in three states that can't read and don't vote but whose lives depend on a clean Susquehanna River – the fish."

I suppose letter writing is everyday stuff for many journalists, but not me. This was my way of remembering an old fishing friend, the long gone Mel Baker, with whom I'd often shared a boat. It was the way Mel once had employed the pen – not his fishing rod or trumpet, both of which he was much better known for – that led me to write.

It all started when Tropical Storm Lee struck the U.S. on the first day of September 2011. Locally, it killed two people along the Swatara while lifting the creek to record levels. So many basements and garages were inundated that as debris piled up at the curb it looked, in bulk at least, like the aftermath of a snowstorm.

One of those cellars, three doors down the street from ours, belonged to Mel's widow, Mim. There, high and dry on a shelf, was discovered a long forgotten boxful of letters he'd written as a soldier in Europe to his beloved during World War II. Mel's passion so touched their daughter that she decided to tell the tale in a novel and asked me to help with the editing.

Wading through Krista's manuscript brought into focus the huge sacrifice that Mel and so many others made for those of us back home. I was exactly 21 months old and living in Great Barrington, MA, when Mel wound up his Dec. 16, 1944, letter to Mim this way:

"Well, I guess I'll close. I'm heating some water to take my Saturday bath! Ha ha! (out of a helmet!) I'll keep on thinking of you – gee but you're wonderful!"

The Battle of the Bulge began that day in Belgium, France and Luxembourg, and back in Hummelstown, in a house about a 4-minute walk from the Baker place, Kay Frances Howell came into the world, later to become my bride.

Mel Baker's example of the power of the written word to reach out and make personal connections inspired my letter to the Oval Office. He wrote out of love for Mim while my words were born of anger over the plight of the bass.

Lofty intentions aside, all I got back from the Big O was a lengthy outdoorsy form letter in which the word "smallmouth" appeared not one blessed time. Maybe it was a mistake to point out that fish don't vote.

Even before Arway addressed the EPA, his agency had announced it would spend $800,000 – due from Exelon in the 2015 relicensing settlement for Muddy Run Pumped Storage Facility – to remove small dams on streams in York and Lancaster counties. There are hundreds of these structures, slowing creek flow and creating stagnant, nutrient-deficient and oxygen-starved water – no place for fingerlings to flourish, smallmouth or otherwise.

Demolishing such barriers is a two-edged sword, Swartz pointed out. Rich in so-called legacy sediments – dregs of the stream that pile up behind them – the demolition of such dams sends more junk into the already polluted Chesapeake Bay.

As for fingerlings, degraded habitat doesn't have to mean dirty water: When sediment fills riverbed holes, little fish have fewer places to hide from larger, hungry ones.

The hunger to know

In 2014 a different kind of appetite was affecting the Susquehanna's small-fry. The official hunger to know what was ailing the river assembled dozens of scientists and staff from a pack of state and U.S. environmental agencies and put the plight of the smallmouth on their collective investigative plate. By December, two separate lab tests detected cancer in a single smallmouth taken from the river.

About a year later, science confirmed what logic had long suggested – the trouble with the Susquehanna smallmouth was all about tainted water.

"Endocrine-disrupting compounds and herbicides, and pathogens and parasites" were identified by the scientists as most likely the culprits bashing the bass.

Somehow too many chemicals and possibly drugs, germs, viruses and a slew of other tiny but terrible organisms have gotten into our river. In part, at least, the Susquehanna's myriad life-forms are paying the price for our overindulgences.

The study started off in 14 different directions because that's how many suspected causes originally were listed for the illness. In a December 2015 update on the scientists' work, state Department of Environmental Protection Director John Quigley lauded advances in river monitoring developed along the way – tools, he said, that "we can use to ensure fishable, drinkable water statewide."

That, of course, puts the cart before the horse – or, in this case, the angler upstream from the fish – but let's hope Quigley is correct about the river's future.

To be sure, the sheer science of the Susquehanna's sickness is daunting. Throw in the political dynamics, garnish with personality conflicts and jurisdictional spats, and one could conclude that inertia seems to be winning out. A public frustrated at times by what some perceive as caretakers bent on studying the problem to death, rather than solving it, has been critical and impatient.

The bass seem to be bouncing back

Some front-line observers are suggesting that the smallmouth already is in recovery mode. Among them are Brian Shumaker, a principal with Susquehanna River Guides, and Halifax-based Edwin Cobaugh, a friend and former co-worker of mine at the newspaper, who both report seeing more small bass in client landing nets on the river.

"We've known for 11 years that something was wrong; even so, we've been catching more little ones the last four years. We're never going to see fishing like it was when I was a kid growing up on Fourth Street in New Cumberland, but it is getting better. Those small-fry are the big fish of the future," Shumaker told me in February 2016.

And the bass appear healthier, too.

"They never quit the fight," Cobaugh said over coffee that spring, "but there for a while we sure were seeing some ugly fish. Those growths are mostly gone now."

The river runs deep in boosters and defenders, as reflected in the response to the Save Our Susquehanna! campaign launched in June 2015 by the Fish and Boat Commission. The drive by October 2016 had netted $60,000, which was lumped with $50,000 from the agency and put to work reducing soil erosion and sediment and nutrient flow in Limestone Run, a Montour/ Northumberland counties tributary of the Susquehanna.

A lot of people have pitched in $10 apiece for an SOS button, and some much more. In the Harrisburg area, sportsmen's groups from Fishing Creek and Enola chipped in $5,000 and $1,000, respectively.

The river's friends are watching and waiting for science to identify the cause(s) and source(s) of its sickness, a process guaranteed to further test our patience. When it comes to affixing blame we are quick on the draw, but when it comes to a-fixin' what's wrong it's like someone keeps hitting the pause button. *Oh Lord, please grant the patience and courage we all need to make our river healthy again.*

The smallmouth bass was the second struggling species in the Susquehanna to catch my attention; the first was a fish I'd seen only in pictures.

Meanwhile, back at the office

According to a trio of guitar-playing co-workers, my job at the paper was "making chateaubriand from baloney." That was the refrain of their song at my 2005 retirement party, sung to the tune of Gordon Lightfoot's haunting ballad, "The Wreck of the Edmund Fitzgerald." Well, on a good day maybe, but I hereby confess to having served up plenty of the other kind, too.

I caught a break from my regular job – editing reporters' stories and writing headlines – by launching a seasonal audio feature for the paper in spring 2002. Called Angler's Report, it contained general information and personal observations about fishing. The weekly recordings were accessible to the public by phone. A sample:

"Hello, and welcome to Angler's Report:

"As you travel south the pinecones grow bigger; as you go north the deer get larger. Regarding smallmouth bass (and no doubt many other species), they tend to grow faster farther south, like the pinecones.

"Smallies will reproduce at about 1 foot in length, but getting through that first year is the key, biologists say.

"In the lower Susquehanna, a smallmouth might reach 8 inches in the year of its spawning and a foot by age 3 or 4, though some make it in just two years. The age at which they begin feeding on crayfish and other fish is the key, because that diet spurs rapid growth.

"Students of the smallmouth say it can reach 18-20 inches in 6-8 years in the lower Susquehanna, but require 8-9 years to get that big in the Juniata. A 20-incher in Ontario's famed Rideau River could be a teen-ager, maybe even 20 years old.

"A breeding smallmouth might average 7,000 eggs per pound of bodyweight. If at least 2,000 fry result, the nest is considered successful, which occurs 6 times out of 10 – again, on average.

"So killing a 17-inch, 2½-pound female smallmouth subtracts 17,500 eggs from the waterway, but harvesting one just a few inches longer could nearly double the loss.

"My question is – especially up north – why are we still keeping the very biggest ones? Take pictures and measure the fish to show friends, but don't take extra thousands of smallmouth lives. Let the lunkers live!

"Until next time, this is Doug Dohne, reminding you to always play it safe around the water."

By the third year I was running out of things to say and, yes, my wife was flabbergasted. Perusing the annual fishing digest put out by Arway's agency, I noticed a daily catch limit of 50 for the American eel. *Whoa! They allow 50 a day and you've never caught even one. How could that be? You should've at least snagged one by accident somewhere along the line. Check this out!*

My research spawned an article way too long for Angler's Report.

American eel as depicted by U.S. Fish & Wildlife Service.

Are we seeing end of the American eel?

Fewer make storied migration, putting their future in doubt

(Sunday, October 24, 2004)

Maple leaves aren't the only things that are changing colors and hitting the road this month. October is when the American eel begins its migration, and this fall's trip could be a last hurrah of sorts for the mysterious species, at least on the lower Susquehanna River.

You might call it the greatest migration story never told, because scientists cannot explain key parts of the life cycle of this continent's only catadromous fish. Just the reverse of its distant cousin, the anadromous American shad, the eel spawns in saltwater and matures in freshwater.

But fewer and fewer eels are completing their kind's remarkable journey, and the species appears to be in big trouble. Some authorities say the eel is verging on a resource disaster on par with the Newfoundland cod fishery collapse.

While some experts believe eels can live four decades, most biologists on the Chesapeake Bay's tributaries peg it at 24 years – which is how long it has been since young eels, or elvers, were last captured in Maryland waters and released into our leg of the river.

The most recent adult eel sightings during electrofishing by Pennsylvania Fish and Boat Commission biologists came in Trout Run and Big Spring Creek, tributaries of Cumberland County's Conodoguinet Creek. The last eels were recorded in 2003 in Big Spring and could represent survivors of the 1980 stocking, now ready to return to the sea.

As for elvers, the local evidence is equally thin but just as bleak. At York Haven's dam – whose fish ladder is the only one on the lower Susquehanna to specifically monitor eel traffic – no elvers appeared during this spring's shad run (April through mid-June).

Where we eat eels: Swatara

Long before the rivers were dammed and polluted by the whites, American Indians were well-acquainted with the autumn eel migration. Swatara, as in Swatara Twp. and Swatara Creek, is the anglicized word for a Susquehannock Indian term meaning "where we eat eels."

With a caloric value six times that of other freshwater fish, the eel was a prized catch, usually smoked for winter and "travel" rations. Weirs, or V-shaped rock formations pointing downriver, were fashioned to funnel migrating adult eels into basketlike traps. In some stretches of the lower Susquehanna, remnants of weirs can be spotted during low-water conditions.

The typical adult eel weighs a pound or so and seldom exceeds 3 feet in length, but they can get much bigger – up to 5 feet. The world record, taken in 1985 at Cape May, N.J., is 9 pounds, 4 ounces.

Long regarded as snakes

Medieval folklore held that larval eels sprang from the hairs of horse tails or the dews of May mornings. The ancient Greeks – Aristotle was first to observe that eels migrate downstream in fall – thought eels were serpents spontaneously generated by river mud. Early 1900s scientists still thought of eels as snakes.

The principal puzzle for years was, where did the eels spawn? A Danish oceanographer, Johannes Schmidt, searched it out in 1920, finding thousands of larval eels drifting near weed clumps in the Sargasso Sea. Eels go to that relatively calm water, in the northern Caribbean-Bermuda region of the Atlantic, from the United States and Europe. Just how their offspring know to which continent to migrate remains unexplained.

In its youth the eel is a hitchhiker, drifting north as larva from the Sargasso with the Gulf Stream up the East Coast to the North Atlantic. Each one somehow turns landward along the way at the stream or estuary from which its forebears came.

By now it has assumed the look of a tiny transparent or glass eel. After feeding along the coast, it turns opaque and distinct dark spots mark the eel's eyes. This is the elver stage. Less than 6 inches long, the elvers set off upstream.

Years later and just before leaving freshwater, the adult eel's eyes grow huge and round, enabling them to see better in the ocean's depths. They also undergo color changes – from yellow to metallic green to a bronze black sheen and, finally, a shimmering silver. This provides better camouflage from ospreys and other open-water predators.

A sexually mature female eel carries millions of eggs. After their three- to five-month return trip to the Sargasso, they spawn – at depths of 6,000 feet – then die.

More theories than answers

How eels find their way 2,000 miles to the Sargasso is unknown, but one theory is they follow geo-electrical fields generated by ocean currents. Another is that the eel relies on smell, differences in salinity or temperature, positions of the sun and stars, or a mix of such mapping systems.

Once on their way, almost nothing stops them. Silver eels have ceased feeding and will ignore watermen's baited traps. They are remarkably determined, able to surmount just about any obstacle by squirming over, around, through or under it. Protected from drying out by a mucous coating, eels can travel overland for short distances with the aid of just a heavy dew.

In 1989, scientists followed the eels to sea. Their research vessel had a computerized echo-sounding device on which they saw ghostly blips like those produced by eels in the lab. The blips also appeared at the center of the Sargasso on the nutrient-rich boundary between warm and cold water – just as experts predicted.

But were the blips really eels? The crew strained to capture one, employing nets and baited traps. Every net came up empty, just like science's every effort to grasp the secrets of this slippery species of stream and sea.

Decline is heavily documented

There is no secret about the eel's demise. According to a National Marine Fisheries Service survey, the recreational harvest of eels in 2001 was about 11,000, roughly 10 percent of the peak of 107,000 in 1982. Commercial landings slipped from a high in the mid-1970s of 3.5 million pounds to a low of 870,000 pounds in 2001.

Similar ratios are reflected in data from Lake Ontario, which had as many as 10 million eels two decades ago, but now holds only tens of thousands, according to Ontario's Ministry of Natural Resources. The ministry says the province's commercial eel harvest peaked at more than 500,000 pounds in 1978. Last year's take was just 30,000 pounds.

Ontario officials blame the eel's plight on overharvesting, migration barriers, climate conditions and hydro-dam turbines. Monitoring of the St. Lawrence River hydro dams reveals that 46 percent of adult eels exit the turbines dead.

Fish ladders in the seaway, such as those at towering Conowingo Dam on the lower Susquehanna, were built to boost shad and other herring, not to give elvers a lift.

Most herring are midwater forms not associating with bottom structure. Hence, they can be easily corralled into fish lifts or elevators for safe passage. The eel, by contrast, is a bottom hugger and tends to travel the edges, not the main channel. So he is unlikely to get any such boost.

Even with the so-called eel ladders on the St. Lawrence, the elvers' springtime upstream migration has fallen from 25,000 a day in the early 1980s to about 100 a day.

European eels are in decline for the same reasons as North America's, plus the introduction in the 1980s of parasitic swim-bladder nematodes via imported Asian eels. Since eels cannot be bred in captivity, Europeans turned to the largely untapped U.S. eel fishery to satiate their appetite.

With elvers fetching up to $500 a pound abroad in the mid-1980s, American greed quickly became the eel's enemy. The lure of big bucks drew a springtime army to New England's riverbanks to net the elvers. Shipped live to Europe or Asia, they are fattened on aquaculture farms and sold to restaurants.

In Pennsylvania, pressure on elvers persisted until 1997, when the Fish and Boat Commission banned their sale if taken by net. Recreational anglers are permitted to take 50 eels (8 inches or longer) a day with hook and line.

Clearly the American eel is in peril. Only time will tell if, like the Indians who once plied local streams in search of it, the eel will be forced from its native habitat by changes in the environment.

Enlisting in the eel effort

As the eels went to sea that fall, another chapter in their story was being written back on land. Two brothers were demanding federal protection for the species and – within a few days of its publication – the above story was incorporated into their lengthy petition. Though strangers to me, New Englanders Doug and Tim Watts became friends and allies in the campaign to find relief for the eel under the U.S. Endangered Species Act. I was their newest recruit in a battle begun years earlier.

What had galvanized these blue-collar brothers into the unlikely role of petitioners was simply too many blank stares and excuses from the authorities to whom they turned for help during their years of research and study of the American eel.

"We filed the petition because all scientific evidence shows the American eel is going extinct and nothing is being done to stop it. As U.S. citizens, we have the legal right and responsibility," Tim said.

The taste test

Tim's big-picture take on why we should rescue the eel contrasted dramatically with one I heard not long after right across the street from my home – "because it's good to eat, just like chicken, only bony."

I'd known the widow Betty Evans for years, but never as an eel aficionado. She became quite animated – I just knew Tim's ears had to be ringing – as she served up tidbits of her childhood history with the eel:

"My grandfather, Harry Jacoby of Carlisle, was a conductor on the Reading Railroad and took the early electric train from Harrisburg to Reading and back. Many times after his run he would take me and my sister (Anna Mae Moore of Susquehanna Twp.) fishing near a covered bridge on the Conodoguinet Creek between Carlisle and Newville.

"He had a toolshed out back where he cleaned the fish we caught. We often cooked eels for breakfast and, oh how they wiggled in the pan! They were good eating, not fishy at all."

And the largest eel she can recall?

"Bigger around than grandfather's arm, and a lot longer."

Big is the operative word when it comes to man's appetite for the eel: One pound of elvers would be going for an obscene $2,600 at market by 2012.

On the campaign trail

My newly minted role as friend of the eel in print led to a series of stories through which, as one office wag put it, I became "the eel guy."

Some of those little epistles appeared on news pages, others in the Opinion section. None ever ran on Page One because the eel's importance as a water quality monitor really just never registered. Not sexy enough, I guess.

In a nutshell, we need the eel in our rivers because this long-lived bottom dweller is the freshwater equivalent of a canary in the mine. If the eel can make it where heavy metals, toxins, etc. tend to pile up, that signals decent river health.

Had the eel been present and subject to monitoring, it's quite possible the Susquehanna smallmouth bass might never have gotten sick. Whatever is to blame might have been detected long ago after impacting the eel first.

But here I was, 29 months after enlisting in the cause, writing the campaign's obituary, accented by Tim's dark forecast:

"I think the states and the [Atlantic States Marine Fisheries Commission] will use this as an excuse to put their hands back in their pockets. We will see funding for an eel ladder here and there and some scattered data gathering, but sadly no coast-wide intensive effort to understand or address the issues of the eel decline. The plight of the eel will now fall off the radar screen."

On the comeback trail

True, the eel never was embraced in those federal arms a.k.a. the Endangered Species Act, but neither was it abandoned. In fact, the American eel was on an upward path, at least in central Pennsylvania, and a glimpse of its progress came during a February 2016 meeting of the Susquehanna River Anadromous Fish Restoration Cooperative.

Aquatic biologist Aaron Henning, of the Susquehanna River Basin Commission, told his Harrisburg audience that about 817,000 juvenile eels have been captured downstream from the big hydroelectric dams and stocked upriver since 2008.

Elvers migrating from the Atlantic often encounter hydroelectric dams in their path to the East Coast freshwater homes of their ancestors. For offspring of those that matured in the Susquehanna basin, towering Conowingo Dam, rising from the Chesapeake Bay tidal pool, is their first big obstacle.

This tidal pool is unfriendly territory for the eels. Here, trapped in concentrated numbers, they sometimes resort to cannibalism or fall prey to the striped bass or rockfish, among the bay's top predator species.

The main elver capture sites are at Conowingo and upriver on Octoraro Creek at Muddy Run. As a condition of relicensing by the feds, the job of trapping and stocking up to 50,000 elvers a day falls to the plants' owner, Exelon Corp. Helping to bankroll the eel relocation effort early on was the city of Sunbury, PA, which had $88,000 left over from a riverfront improvement project where the Susquehanna's north and west branches converge.

At Conowingo, the eel's path forward is a ramp, unimpressive in appearance and rising only about 20 feet – well below the dam breast. Its genius of design literally taps the elvers' instinct to climb by providing a stream of water – about as much as a garden hose delivers – trickling down the incline. This gets their attention, and soon glass eels are navigating up the ramp. Clearing the top edge, they fall into collection tanks and are trucked upriver.

The transplanted youngsters, judging by some that have been recaptured, seem to be doing well, according to Henning, who spends many summer work hours electrofishing. His description:

"Sometimes I wear waders and carry a backpack to work the shallow water, from downstream up; for the deeper spots we use boats. A mild electric shock stuns the fish, which are netted as they float on the surface. After a general health check, the fish are weighed to determine biomass, then revived and released ..."

Eel recapture efforts are focused below Colliersville Dam, just north of Oneonta, NY, and one of the eels snagged there was 100 miles from its release site. The total catch topped 2,000 during the best years to date for eel recapture, 2011-14.

River cleaners ride the eel express

Just as in the saga of the smallmouth, water quality is a central issue for the eel, which finally wriggled into favor once we recognized its vital role in river filtration.

It turns out that the eel serves as host for larvae of the Eastern Elliptio freshwater mussels that help cleanse the river. Since spring 2015, some of the elvers leapfrogging the power dams have been outfitted by biologists with an advanced stage of the mussel larvae in a bid to jumpstart that species' comeback in Penns Creek, Snyder County.

Spellcheck is certain to object, but here it comes anyway: At long last the American eel once again is flexing its mussels in the Susquehanna.

Young eels – and their precious mussel larvae cargo – maturing in the traditional freshwater of their ancestors are closely monitored by the U.S. Fish and Wildlife Service. Annapolis-based Sheila Eyler is chief of the National Marine Fisheries Service's American eel tech committee – with responsibility for the Susquehanna and Delaware River basins. *If she could use that job title as fish bait it'd be enough to choke a largemouth bass.*

“Fall 2014 electrofishing in Buffalo Creek (Union County) and the Big Pine (Lycoming County) turned up some silver eels,” she told me in 2015, adding that silvers also were detected downstream near Peach Bottom and Safe Harbor.

Killing one eel might wipe out 20 million

The eel’s journey up the Susquehanna as an elver has gotten easier, but its spawning run years later to the sea remains a treacherous trip. The out-migrating silver eel’s first challenge, getting safely past the York Haven Dam, is pretty tame, thanks to the presence of a gate designed to collect debris. A lot of eels wind up in it, too, sparing them from those killer turbine blades.

From there on, the gauntlet of the power dams grows grimmer for the incredibly fecund American eel. The death of just one individual on her spawning run means losing up to 20,000,000 eggs – that’s right, 20 million. So, how many make it?

Eyler cited a 2010-11 study in which FWS staff captured 80 silver eels from the Delaware River, applied radio transmitters, and released them into the Susquehanna above Muddy Run. Ninety percent made the trip to Conowingo and passed safely into the Chesapeake.

Seventy-two out of 80 eels surviving this ordeal of the dams sounds pretty good, until you do the arithmetic. If all eight eels chewed up in the turbines were females, as many as160 million eel eggs were lost, too. Kind of makes the 817,000 elvers that in the last eight years with human help have managed to get past the big dams seem like the proverbial drop in the bucket, doesn't it.

Actually, the feds already had settled a year earlier on a minimum 85 percent survival rate (and a loss of up to 12 eels potentially carrying 240 million eggs in the above scenario) for ocean-bound silver eels passing over the dams. That benchmark, a condition of Holtwood's 2009 license amendment as issued by the Federal Energy Regulatory Commission, represents a huge improvement from the eel slaughter that persisted until early this century.

Historically, the darling of Susquehanna fishermen has been the American shad, not the eel, and fish passage data therefore focused on the former. Just 33 to 53 percent of juvenile shad made it safely downstream to the bay in an early 1990s study. At the end of the 20th century, with adjustments by the hydroelectric plants, two-thirds of the young shad were surviving outmigration.

The eel's survival rate was lower than that, and here's why:

The shad – and every other migrating fish species in the Susquehanna but one – spawn in the river but relocate to the sea as juveniles. Only the eel does it in reverse, starting in salt and finishing in freshwater. So when shad fingerlings head downstream, they are more likely than the larger adult eel (3 feet or longer) to slip through those turbines.

Taking it personally

The Wattses were incensed by the frightful fee the eel was being charged at man's toll booths on the hydroelectric highways. In a news photo, probably snapped by Tim, Doug Watts stood waist deep in a Maine river holding the mangled body of an eel as others floated nearby, a dam in the background.

In a conversation right after petitioning the EPA, Doug discussed their motivation. Science be damned, the trigger was raw emotion:

"Tim said to me just the other night: 'People don't understand that when I see what is happening to the eels, to me it's like somebody attacking my family.' "

The season of relicensure

No one owns the Susquehanna, but lots of us feel like we do. We fish it, swim in it and boat on it. Some simply love to gaze upon it. Many others have commercial connections, chief among them the power dam operators.

Central to the process of relicensing is the opportunity that we who do not own the dams have to address those who do. Only when our negotiators and theirs stick to science – with reason and yes, even a little compassion thrown in – can any deal really work for both sides.

As official overseer of the nation's energy industry, FERC's job is often contentious and always complicated. The commission is a regular target of such ardent environmentalists as the Wattses, who nowadays champion the Atlantic salmon with the same passion once lavished on the eel.

For its part, FERC on occasion has been its own worst enemy. Its entire PR department must have taken off early for the holidays in 2015, for instance, because license orders for the York Haven and Muddy Run hydroelectric facilities were issued simultaneously on Dec. 22 – like Christmas cards, in the eyes of critics.

With the licenses of Holtwood and Safe Harbor good through 2030, that leaves Conowingo as the last of the big five hydroelectric facilities on the lower Susquehanna still negotiating with FERC. And water quality is front and center on the agenda, according to John Balay, the Susquehanna River Basin Commission's point man in the relicensing process.

Location, location, location

The byword in real estate sales also applies to the relicensing of Conowingo Dam. Because it is situated in Maryland, 10 miles upstream from the mouth of the Susquehanna near Havre de Grace, Exelon needs Maryland's OK on its water quality certificate while it seeks a new 46-year license to replace the 34-year-old one that expired in 2014.

The sticking point for Maryland is sedimentation, whose damage to the Chesapeake Bay has cost the taxpayers millions upon millions in restoration efforts. From a water quality standpoint, Balay said, it's primarily the nitrogen and phosphorus trapped in the sediments that are injuring one of America's most beautiful estuaries – not to mention its largest tributary.

In the spirit of its nickname – the Free State, dating to its 1919 balk at backing Prohibition – Maryland has become increasingly adamant in going to bat for the bay. Exelon is a huge player in this nation's energy industry with holdings that include both of York County's nuclear power plants.

The EPA threw another log on the Conowingo showdown in June 2016 when it called Pennsylvania the main laggard among watershed states in rescuing the bay from its phosphorus and nitrogen nightmare. Farm runoff once again was identified as a significant culprit in the choking of the Chesapeake.

Sediment buildup behind Conowingo Dam was estimated at 259 million tons in 2002, and a task force led by the SRBC (with Swartz at the helm) called its reduction critical and suggested enlisting U.S. Army Corps of Engineers' help to determine whether dredging was a viable option.

Full to the brim

The Susquehanna's other power dams, upriver in Pennsylvania, have been judged for years by the U.S. Geological Survey to be at equilibrium, or full, while Conowingo was considered still able to trap nutrients – and thus help spare the bay's health.

Ah, but no longer. The Army engineers' study has confirmed Exelon's worst nightmare: Conowingo's sediment storage capacity is indeed at full limit or nearly so. With Balay estimating it will take months for the study to wrap up, Exelon is caught like a guy at the end of a line of companions staring back at him as the prospect of dredging piles up at the FERC table.

Dredging is largely uncharted water for the Susquehanna's power-dam owners, employed in the past only on a small scale to ease marina boat traffic.

The remedy for Conowingo's reservoir-turned-sediment-pit figures to be salty. Even if Exelon agrees to pony up, can the already-ailing Chesapeake withstand the extra abuse? And what about the load of sediment – in some cases stretching miles upstream from the dams – that will be released if the other owners must follow suit?

The Conowingo talks generated a spring 2016 announcement by Exelon and the FWS detailing a 50-year deal to restore millions of shad and herring to their ancestral spawning grounds above the dams. Will the outcome this time be a real breakthrough or just more heartbreak?

Since the rise of hydroelectric dams early in the last century, the story of fish migration on the Susquehanna has been riddled with proposals and efforts that have fallen short. Nor has money always stood in the way: The power companies have chipped in tens of millions in a so-far-futile and decades-long effort to restore American shad and river herring to fishable numbers.

Hopefully, FERC and the state and other federal agencies overseeing river and bay health are standing firmly on science that will result in waters vibrant enough to fulfill a mandate enacted by the PA Legislature in 1866: Restore migratory species to the Susquehanna River.

That was a century and a half ago; wounds from the Civil War were barely beginning to heal, and what we know today as the PA Fish and Boat Commission was a newborn. Even for patient fishermen, it's been a long wait.

Water wisdom

Rivers are living, evolving things, and Heraclitus said it perfectly:

"No man ever steps in the same river twice, for it's not the same river and he's not the same man."

This Greek philosopher, preceding Socrates, also observed:

"There is nothing permanent except change."

Changes in the Susquehanna over the last century have shackled the shad and eel and bruised the bass and doubtless many other river creatures. To anticipate pulling off a one-eighty and bringing back the river of the Indian's day is unrealistic in this multi-use era of inevitable compromise.

The extent to which the river can be restored to its former glory depends on everyday people – not just those in titled positions of power. An example of the kind of individual I'm talking about appears in this Thursday, February 8, 2007, entry in my diary:

In awe of river
a boy spent his days;
too soon an old man,
she still owns his gaze.

Today I met retired ironworker George "Pete" Boyer Sr. of Middletown, who was baptized early on to 1930s life along the river. He was 5 in 1937 when his father, Hoke, took over operation of state-licensed Eel Chute No. 90 in the Susquehanna near Royalton. Two years later, son joined father working the dam or weir.

Boyer, who last winter built a model of No. 90, has taken some polite criticism from friends "for making a Cadillac" out of what "was more busted up and ragged" in reality. He just smiles and says he "wanted folks to at least see what it was like, how it worked."

How it worked was determined by when it worked. Eels are active mostly at night, and their spawning run starts late in September and lasts through October -- so that's when they're caught. An alarm clock sounded hourly, in case the thrashing of a newly arrived eel in No. 90's basketlike trap wasn't enough to awaken the attendant slumbering in the shanty above. The catch had to be secured or escape was likely, eels being frisky and resourceful critters.

V-shaped pattern on the river's surface near New Cumberland, PA, is caused by remnants of a dam built centuries ago by American Indians to trap migrating eels. Photo was taken in the 1980's by fishing guide Brian Shumaker.

By 1944, their catch down to four or five a night -- from 10 times that a few years before – the Boyers took No. 90's shack ashore for the last time that fall.

Nine adjacent eel weirs, each built of rocks in a V-shape pointing downstream, stretched east from Hill Island toward Royalton; the Boyers' was westernmost. Each dam had wings, 5 to 7 feet wide at the base on the riverbed, stretching 40 to 50 yards upstream and perhaps 100 yards wingtip to wingtip. Remnants of several weirs are still visible, especially when the river is low, says Pete, "but you have to know where to look."

Clearly this man reveres natural history. The home he and wife Eva ("Butch") share is a museum in all but name. Hundreds of arrowheads – gleaned by three generations of Boyers along the river – are displayed on its walls. One exhibit is devoted to broken arrowheads, fragments that fascinated their finders at first glance but disappointed upon closer inspection. He calls it "The Heartbreaker."

Will the animal whose noisy arrival excited the boy at Eel Chute No. 90 so long ago become a permanent Susquehanna heartbreaker?

Pioneer Japanese conservationist Tanaka Shozo (1841-1913) taught that:

"The care of rivers is not a question of rivers, but of the human heart."

One group whose hearts are full of reverence for rivers is my fishing buddies.

FOR ANGLERS, IT'S TIME TO GO ON LINE

(Saturday, April 15, 1999)

It's been said that fishing is nothing more than a jerk on one end of the line waiting for a jerk on the other.

In my first 50 years of angling, some of those jerks (at the underwater end) have been memorable; a few even qualify as outstanding.

The same could be said for those of us on the other end – specifically, my angling pals. Some have been impressive; a few even rate as unforgettable.

The arrival of yet another fishing season – opening day for trout in Pennsylvania is Saturday – has me musing not so much about the finned prey as about their faithful pursuers.

Sure, my regular fishing group is relatively small. But throw in the others -- the occasional partners, the one-time-only folks, the friends of friends who tag along, etc. -- and my angling fraternity swells to 62 members.

Their names seemed to surface more readily once I realized they were coming mostly from four groups: family, co-workers, friends and children.

Winter, now take your granddaughter
down by the lake – or white water

With 16 entries, relatives are well represented on my list of fellow fishers. And yes, three of them are granddaughters.*

My original fishing pal was little brother Steve. Together – before either of us hit 10 – we were entered in what so far has been my only fishing tourney.

The competition was strictly between us. Each boy was stationed on one of the two docks that stretched from the shore in front of Grampa Dohne's cottage on Panther Lake, not far from Syracuse, NY. Each was provided a fishing rod, a pail of water and an equal number of worms.

The object was to transfer as many of the sunfish as possible from the lake into the pail before your worms ran out. The winner would be resupplied with worms and keep on fishing; the loser had to help with the dishes from the noon meal. Funny, I can remember all of those details, but not who won the tourney.

We learned to fish with our father and other elders. Especially important in those formative years was Grampa. Half the relatives on this roster of anglers are, or were, older than me. Six of them are females; two have been wives and three are sons. One is a prison guard who finally broke away from that line of work and has been on the run ever since – as a truck driver. Another was a cousin whose IQ in the genius range was cruelly twinned with alcoholism.

Summer, with office pals you float
to stalk flatties out in your boat

An obvious pool of fishing partners is one's co-workers. Check off another 17 names on my list, including several who have been lured away from the newspaper. One of them answered the call of the ministry, while another was really into altar calls, the only guy of my acquaintance to marry the same woman twice. Several other members of this group are computer experts.

Fall, get your friends and go first class
while there's still time to catch some bass

My fishing companions who are separate from family and co-workers are 16 strong. Two of them are doctors, another a lawyer. But most are working stiffs in sales, carpentry, etc. One is a surveyor. Sure, there's a millionaire in there, but two of the others regularly seem to be unemployed – and always ready to go fishing. Another guy once asked for a loan to file his income tax return.

These fishing comrades include some hunters. One of them is descended from a York County gun-making family who built some of the so-called Kentucky long rifles, many of which actually originated in Lancaster. This fellow uses the spoken word so sparingly that many who think they know him are unaware of his family history – or that he is carrying on the tradition, producing miniature firearms (half the size, we kid him, but twice the price) and knives. And oh baby are they ever sharp!

A fishing chum will do almost anything for you – even give you his tickets to Penn State's biggest home game of the season when he can't make it. Such a gift might go over nicely with one of this freelance journalist's clients, so why me? "Fishing buddies," his answer flows with the serenity of a trout stream, "are special."

Spring, hit the stream with kids for trout
enduring screams that they let out

Special is probably the best word to describe 13 of my fishing friends who cannot yet be identified by occupation because they are children; five are grandkids.

There is something revitalizing about taking the young fishing. Their wide-eyed wonder, anticipation and curiosity are unmatched by adults. Each step of the way is fresh and exciting, threatening to explode as a memory-maker in a young mind. Your job is to make sure it's a good memory.

Even if one has only a rudimentary understanding of such a complex subject as marine biology, fishing with a kid offers a wonderful opportunity to share the knowledge, to plant the seed of environmental awareness and concern. You don't need a master's in oceanography to pass on an appreciation for nature's interconnectedness, a respect for its beauty and scope.

Properly presented, every shred of information will be devoured. For one brief moment, the new discovery will satisfy and may even seem all-sufficient. Then that insatiable appetite to know returns, often with these words, "But how does …"

After a day on the water, I'd pass up a whole boatload of the "Well, how many …" type of questions typically asked by adults for just one more "But how does …"

As for the gift of a new fishing friend, that can arrive anytime, anywhere.

Somebody new in your neighborhood, maybe someone who seems like the kind you might want to get to know better? Invite him or her along fishing.

Have a young niece or nephew whose main interaction with you seems to begin and (unfortunately) end with struggling over just how to address you? All that will change after you two go fishing together.

*Sometimes it's the other way around – the granddaughters take you along. Kay and I got to visit a beautiful Iowa lake in 2008 simply because Erin and Megan wanted to go.

Along with us and the young ladies were their parents, Kay's daughter and her husband, Jodi and John Mitchell of Bettendorf, Iowa, and the family puppy, Mojo, who though none of us realized it already was in training to become a fine school therapy dog.

The Dakota Sioux – to whom its name meant "great waters" – once thrived beside present day West Okoboji Lake. While some dispute that it is among the world's blue water lakes, Iowa's Department of Natural Resources rates West Okoboji's water quality as "outstanding."

The Hawkeye State's deepest (at 137 feet) and second largest lake, it is one of the links in a chain known as Iowa's Great Lakes and teems with black, smallmouth and white bass, bluegill, crappie, muskie, northern pike, walleye and yellow perch.

So after lugging my electric motor 1,151 miles (never would have guessed there were so many rows of corn in all of America) I rented a small boat and we went fishing.

Ringed by development, 3,847-acre West Okoboji is a busy spot in late July – and therefore a challenge for anglers, especially those limited to 30 pounds of thrust from a little Minn Kota. While sifting through our options, I spotted a weed bed and chose to try for walleye along its edge.

After some halfhearted hits, John hooked a fish and – great father that he is – handed the rod to Erin. As she reeled in a feisty smallmouth, I could have sworn her smile was as wide as the fish was long. But that would have made it 14 inches.

Rod 'n' reel create family bond

(Monday, April 12, 2004)

Goin' after one for the taxidermist this spring? Instead, why not consider creating some great memories by taking a child fishing.

Let me put it this way: Take a kid fishing, but don't go fishing with them. If that sounds contradictory, ask yourself how a youngster is going to learn anything if you're concentrating on catching fish.

Here's the first rule when taking kids fishing: Give your attention to them, not the fish.

In truth, kids don't give a hoot what they're catching -- as long as they're catching. For youngsters, who can start fishing as preschoolers, depending on temperament, fishing means action.

Rule No. 2: Take 'em where their chances of catching fish are greatest.

A favorite springtime midstate destination for adults with kids in tow is Cumberland County's Opossum Lake. With tons of trout extraordinarily hungry after the winter hiatus, your little Tom Sawyer or Becky Thatcher could catch the limit with a hook, worm and bamboo pole. Ditto at the Kids-Only trout fishing spot near Dauphin on Clarks Creek maintained by the Dauphin County Anglers and Conservationists at their clubhouse. One drawback here is that limited access can lead to overcrowding.

In selecting a spot, keep in mind that a kid is less likely to have a good time when confined to a small space, so go where they can run around and explore, maybe climb a tree. If the child is very young, you might want to consider avoiding the crowd that typically turns out on opening day of the trout season (Saturday in Pennsylvania) by instead settling for a sunfish outing – say, along the banks of the Susquehanna River or Swatara Creek.

Rule No. 3: Be ready to deal with a short attention span. Especially in the early spring when a lack of foliage opens the woods to inspection, it is easier to identify bird species and observe animal behavior. One thing I always keep handy is a bird call that's easy to operate, even for kids. Better yet, it always seems to work!

Hint: Leave the Gameboy at home. Snacks and drinks are always good. Bring along Animal Crackers or some of those individually wrapped power bars (so only one person's snack at a time gets wet).

Speaking of food, don't overlook the allure to kids of gathering fish bait. The excitement of finding worms, crayfish or crickets can sometimes outdo the fishing itself.

Rule No. 4: It isn't just about fishing. One good reason to take kids to the stream is to establish an activity that hopefully builds relationships strong enough to weather the changes sure to come.

The two little Mitchell granddaughters led me to the mighty Mississippi River one summer day made beautiful not so much by the fishing as our bonding. Oh, we hooked some panfish alright, but it was the hugs we shared that really counted. Megan was learning how to tell time and I was embracing my role as her teacher, as in:

"Sure, I'll put another worm on for you, Megan, but first I need my 3 o'clock hug – right now!" As for big sister Erin, she always seems to know when her pap needs a hug.

A discussion about wildlife encountered along the way helps to keep youngsters engaged. Squirrels swimming across long stretches to harvest acorns on the islands in Huntingdon County's Raystown Lake so fascinated my young companions that their attention was completely hijacked. So we put down the rods and picked up the binoculars to be amused by the swimmers' failed efforts to keep their bushy tails high and dry.

Sometimes you'll be surprised by what they point out – and how they describe it.

"Hey, look at the serpent!" shouted the younger of my two grandsons. Tyler had spotted a water snake making its way along a shoreline maybe 20 feet from where we were trying for sunfish.

While you're out there with little kids is the ideal time to think big, as the other grandson, Grant, once reminded me by catching a 10-inch sunny at the dock while I was getting our boat out of the lake and onto the trailer. He wasn't even using a rod – his had been stowed in the boat closet as we were done fishing, or so I thought. Grant was using a hook tied to a hunk of red carpet thread pulled from a pocket.

It's also a great setting to discuss fishing ethics, touching on catch-and-release, for example. Teach kids there are other people out there who also want to catch fish. Instill that they should respect all life.

So, does any of this stuff really penetrate young craniums? Sometimes, maybe. After one trout outing, Tyler's sister surprised the whole family by quietly recording her memories in a story that appeared in a middle school publication. In just half a dozen paragraphs Claudiea touched on water temperature, the creel limit, and the fresh smell of ferns along a trout stream.

Of Pennsylvania's 2 million anglers, about 600,000 are children. Why don't you make it 600,001 this season. And leave your fishing rod at home.

BEFORE YOU GO

Scout it out. Locate fish and generate a little excitement for catching them by selecting your fishing spot before the big day. Try to visit at least one dam – New Cumberland Borough Park has a dandy. A little patience might provide a glimpse of a rainbow trying to leap the roaring obstacle in its path while maneuvering upstream in Yellow Breeches Creek.

* Backyard casting. Use buckets set on the lawn as targets so you can concentrate on casting rather than the fish.

* Knot tying. This is another fun skill to cover before a fishing trip, especially if it's the first of the season.

* A license: In Pennsylvania, anyone 16 or older needs a state-issued license to cast for, retrieve or hook fish. So if the youngster you're taking along is too little to do those things, the job will probably fall to you. Be a good sport and buy a license (get a trout stamp, too, if that's your quarry). Chalk it up to conservation.

Bill Shearer takes no chances with grandson Scott set to cast.

Don, left, and Pete Sarvey share a passion for trouting.

Carl Dohne takes a spin in his father's boat with son Scott.

Jason gives son Tyler his first fishing rod.

As if there's any doubt, W.P. Dohne
indicates whose fish is bigger in Wisconsin.

(L to R): Doug, Grant, Claudiea and Tyler
after a Clinton County trout outing.

Doug with granddaughter Erin and Raystown sunny.

Megan inspects her Mississippi River catch.

Dennis Dohne and Grant with a Swattie sucker.

Christmas Eve call

Fast forward to Christmas Eve 2012, and the phone is ringing. It's Grant, now quite the adventurer and affectionately known around Kawaii, Hawaii, as Coconut Boy, since he supports himself largely by harvesting their fruit.

Grant, 22, apologizes for not returning my call earlier, explaining that he's been out of range while camping near Jurassic Falls – right, the one we saw in the movie – for several weeks.

The spot where the water pools is about 3,000 feet above sea level and, he says, necessitates a several-mile jungle climb to reach. Grant says the pool holds tilapia which, in the wild, are slimmed down cousins of what we buy at market. Quizzed about their taste, he admits he has yet to find out.

"But the smallmouth bass from the river (above the falls) are very tasty," he volunteers, as is the fruit he's been gathering from trees. That old standby fish bait, the worm, is abundant in the woods, he says.

Whether his hooks were attached to trusty red carpet thread from a pocket, he didn't say. Deep inside, I guess, a part of us never wants to see our young grow up.

The beauty of brevity

Tyler learned to shoot the pistol and rifle and the bow and arrow at camp, where he also helps out with mowing and loves to try for trout. Coming within earshot of a prowling coyote pack as we were deer spotting one night, he said, "You know, Pap, I've never been this close to nature. This is so cool!" He was about 10.

Twelve years later this master condenser was on a camping trip that brought him, his mother and her boyfriend within a few miles of Moon Valley Lodge. This time he struck in writing, leaving a corner of his note peeking out from under a chunk of firewood on the porch. When I arrived several weeks later for the spring 2016 gobbler hunt, the message was weathered but still legible:

"Hey Pap, it's me, Tyler. I came up here with Mom and Frank to show them the place where I was the happiest. I love you so much."

Squirming Potter County brookie catches Tyler's attention.

With spring upon us, fishing trips offer spiritual inspiration

(Friday, April 11, 2003)

Baseball is the first sport that pops up in the Bible – Genesis 1: 1: "In the Big Inning ..." (Major League version) – but fishing is the most mentioned (King James and all other editions).

The Old Testament contains a stringer full of references (13) to fish or fishing, my favorite being the story of Jonah running away from God and getting swallowed by a great fish. Nine other such entries surface in the New Testament, including Jesus' challenge to Peter and Andrew, James and John to follow him and become "fishers of men."

Spring is the season of renewal, whether we're talking about getting back to the ballpark or that favorite fishing hole. This also is the season of spiritual refreshment: Christians are nearing Holy Week, and Jews are about to observe Passover. The arrival of yet another Pennsylvania trout season (8 a.m. tomorrow, Palm Sunday Eve) seems like a good time to consider what makes angling so special that for some it rises almost to a spiritual undertaking.

Let's start with this animal we call the fish, which is the root word for 149 entries in Webster's New International Dictionary. Historically, these guys and gals with gills have symbolized fertility, because of the multitude of eggs, or roe, in a single spawn.

The fish served as an early Christian symbol. Its likeness was scratched in the sand by persecuted first-century followers as a secret sign. Scholars note that the first letters of the Greek words for "Jesus Christ, God's Son, Savior," taken in order, spell the Greek word for fish. Christ used fish to feed the 5,000 near Bethsaida. The symbol survives in the form of fish art that adorns the lapels and autos of the faithful.

Scientists believe that some species of fish have been around for hundreds of millions of years. That ranks fish among the most durable of all animals. This success at survival should inspire a reverence -- for the creature and for its Creator.

Hooking a fish is always exciting, and I never tire of re-establishing this direct tie with the natural world. For a brief time, past and present, land and water are linked. Often, just as dramatically as it began, the bond is broken, fin triumphing over finger, tail over foot.

Should the battle go the other way, I am privileged to touch, study and admire my subdued but still squirmy adversary. It's more like a peek, really, out of respect for the life that I hold in hand. A few seconds to delight in the perfection of its physical design and contemplate the colors, then it's back into the drink for the fish.

Those are good times on the water, days when there is action. But every angler also has to learn to deal with going home empty-handed.

Among the parallels between fishing and faith is that you're not always going to get what you seek. Sometimes the answer is no! Getting skunked at fishing is a humbling reminder that we must accept what we don't understand.

Faith is belief in that which we cannot see, touch, prove, etc. It's what lets me get up the day after being shut out on the stream and go right back to fishing, confident of a different outcome. To me, this has to be fishing's most spiritually reinforcing aspect, that even in defeat it nourishes.

Something else on which fishing and faith thrive is solitude. The opportunity for reflection while fishing can be an excellent preparation for prayer. I try to let it be a time of focus, of sorting things out, of coming to realizations.

Along the way, I've learned that prayer usually breaks down into one of three things – Please, thank/praise You or I'm sorry – and that one's prayers reflect his level of spiritual maturity.

For example, I can recall many times as a younger man, asking that an upcoming fishing trip be blessed with a good catch. OK, there were days when I prayed right there in the boat just to let me catch one fish. Any fish!

Later in life, it's still "please" and "thank You," though now the request is more apt to be for safe travel before, during and after the fishing and/or fair weather throughout. The good health that allows me to get out fishing with friends regularly rates a "thank You." The need for "I'm sorry" (for what I shouted when that last fish got away, for example) hopefully is diminishing.

A boat designed for fishing also works for reading, birdwatching, etc. Beyond that sort of thing, my boat is a place where friends can talk freely about anything. And there's always Someone to listen, even when I'm alone. After all, what better time and place to stay in touch with the One who can walk on water.

And speaking of being out there on the water, how many folks do you know who will tell you where the fish are biting? Even those who get paid – charter boat captains, for instance – sometimes can't deliver.

In John 21:5-6, there is a better example:

"He called out to [his disciples], 'Friends, haven't you any fish?' 'No,' they answered. He said, 'Throw your net on the right side of the boat and you will find some.' When they did, they were unable to haul in the net because of the large number of fish." Hey, talk about a fishing buddy.

Church connections

Like everyone else, I attend to worship my Lord and Savior, Jesus Christ, but church is also something of an aquatic crossroads in my life. Besides the head man and his close friend, the good doctor, this is where I met riverman Swartz and the Bakers. And late one night a few years ago around the kitchen table in a fishermen's cabin near Perth, Ontario, I found still another. Actually, he found me.

"Doug, you look an awful lot like a guy who goes to my church in Hummelstown."

The man was a new member, he said, and played in the handbell choir. Admittedly terrible on names, I'm usually a lot better with faces, but not the one of the fellow now rounding my side of the table.

"Hi, I'm Bob Laudermilch from Palmyra," the big redhead said, a smile galloping ear to ear.

Everyone else was grinning, too, especially when I couldn't seem to place him.

"Grace United Methodist?" I parried disbelievingly, rising to shake hands.

His steady rejoinder, "Yep," brought a chorus of laughs, this time mine included. The whole thing resembled an unofficial rite of initiation, this being my first time at their table.

I'd been introduced by fishing guide Cobaugh to the chief of this crew, retired banker Harry Minskey Jr. of New Cumberland, who graciously invited me to come along.

Hopefully, Harry said at the time, my first visit to this leg of the Rideau would outshine his. The bassing was lousy 50 years ago when a friend led him to the river, but Harry fell in love with its pure water and soon returned with his father.

"Dad borrowed my lure and caught a nice bass," Harry recalled. "Then he said, 'You know, I'd sure like to be up here catching fish with my grandson.' "

Taking that comment to heart, Harry and his wife, Bonnie, have been holding family and friends close for decades here in cabins owned by the Winton family. Through work and family ties, the group at times fills all four cottages, and the Minskeys never pick up their deposit, always letting it ride "for the next time."

The 10 men on this trip split by age – under 50 (or a tad past) and way over – into two cabins, but take all meals in the old guys' quarters.

The group's senior member is Harry's close pal, Gene Murray, who retired as fire marshal at the Army War College near Carlisle, but is still dealing with hot spots as the camp cook. They got to know each other at what today is Trinity United Methodist Church, New Cumberland, and Zembo Shrine in Harrisburg, playing in both organizations' musical groups and working together in food service at the latter.

Also sharing the house of the elders are Cobaugh and his son in law, Ed Maerkle, a retired heavy-equipment operator with a light touch in the bass boat, and myself.

Food and drink have a prominent role in this delightfully social group. In the middle of their table, mixed in with the pickle jars and an adult beverage bottle or two, is an assortment of hot sauces. And they all get used.

Cobaugh's Cabbage and Hamburger Soup is a lunchtime favorite, and chef Murray's Potpie, Turkey Burgers or Chili will make you forget all about a fish-weren't-bitin' afternoon.

Harry Minskey III, better known as Henny, joins Bob in the cabin of the youthful. With them is Rich Wright, who, after his days as Henny's roommate at Messiah College, married into a large Philadelphia family and learned to cook and make wine Italian style. Rounding out the under-50 roster are Harry's nephews by marriage, Mike Niederreither and Scott Bankert.

These fellas love fishing almost as much as eating and, with four boats riding the river, are all set to do plenty of both. The fleet's largest and fastest craft is Henny's, and he's often first to locate and start catching fish.

Mike and Scott man a boat they co-own but regularly trade seats with Bob and Rich in Henny's Bayliner, while yours truly bounces between the company of Ed and Ed and Harry and Gene.

The rationale for this musical-chairs-on-water routine is that all of us have our favorite fishing spots and tactics and this way, by the end of the week, everyone gets to do his thing.

Henny learned filleting at his father's elbow and with practice has honed his skills to the point that an entire bass banquet finishes without anyone finding a bone. Eat your heart out, Red Lobster!

While Henny's fillet knife is at work, former insurance co-workers Rich and Bob are at play, jousting gently over who gets to wear Gene's imaginary apron. Somehow they manage to serve the fish five ways: Plain, Salt-Pepper-Garlic, Lemon and Pepper, Cajun or Creole.

Another gastronomic highlight is the tasty Lasagna Rollups that Rich brings along from Philly. Made by his wife's grandmother, these morsels verily melt in the mouth. They're so good that even before they disappear Bob is quietly pleading for the recipe. Back and forth it goes; the more he asks the more Rich insists the old gal just won't give it up. Hey, Bob, maybe next year.

Fisherman's prayer

Catch me right this moment, Lord,
with thy oh so perfect cast;
fillet for me a future
unhooked from all sins past.

A tense day at the office and same on the stream

(Sunday, August 10, 2003)

What a difference a year makes.

At this point 12 months ago, any story about midstate trout fishing necessarily would have been mostly in the past tense. Drought-shrunken creeks and a relentless heat wave once again had combined effectively to cut the chase.

August 2003 finds the subsequent trout saga still very much under way. It's goodbye, dog days of drought, and hello, extended trout seizin'.

It's been said that timing is everything, and this trout season certainly is everything that its immediate predecessor was not, in terms of duration and quality angling conditions.

All of which set me to musing the other day, while challenging the finned fraternity of Dauphin County's Clarks Creek, about the role of time in fly-fishing for trout.

As a newspaper copy editor, I have to keep in mind the time element of any story I'm handling. If the writer jumps back and forth from one tense to another, it can confuse the reader and interrupt the story's flow.

As a trout stalker, especially when employing dry flies, I also have to pay attention to the tenses. Huh?

As I see it, the past, present and future are written by the stream's current. From my station standing in the creek, at the tail of a riffle in Clarks, I launch a No. 16 Adams on a brief flight upstream – into the future.

In dry-fly-fishing, as in life, no one knows what the future holds. It is impenetrable to the eye, a mystery that only the proper mixture of time and patience can solve.

Also as in life, the dry-fly angler's future is all about anticipation. You hope, but – unless you've been peeking, say from the bank overlooking the riffle before entering the stream -- you don't know whether there are any trout in your immediate future.

Will the fly alight, in flawless but futile presentation, where there is no fish? Or will its arrival trigger a wily brown to strike?

Visiting the future in this manner is a short-lived proposition, as the lure I've chosen, floating freely with no fish attached, drifts downstream toward me. In this, the present tense, I can see every stone on the streambed. I am intent, alert, focused. The eyes take over for the heart, which was so full of hope with the fly upstream in the future.

Anticipation ebbs as, spotting no trout on the prowl to inspect my offering, I decide that this cast probably will wind up just another dry run. Dutifully, nevertheless, I retrieve some line, stripping it through the fingers, shortening its length to stay ready for the quick reaction required should a trout strike.

But the little lure, on a mission best known only to itself and the water gods, bobs swiftly, silently under my gaze and passes from present tense.

Now in my wake – everything downstream from where I stand – it enters past tense. Visibility and hope sink as the chances of being spotted by nearby trout facing upstream (in my direction) rise. It's time to pay out the floating fly line now tightening in my grasp, letting the inexorable tug of the current prevail.

The graceful part of the fly's three-tense odyssey is nearing an end. Even after the line goes taut and the little Fenwick rod bends, the well-dressed fly defiantly hugs the surface, its several-second voyage complete.

Usually either of two things disrupts the future-present-past tense sequence of dry-fly-fishing. The first is snagging your lure on a tree limb, rock, etc. The second is hooking a trout. Then, if you hooked the fish in, say, present-tense water, he might take you back upstream into the future before revisiting the present and (if you're lucky) coming to net in the past tense. For a dry-flier, it's the time of his life.

To every rule there is an exception

Sometime after this story appeared – and again while out for trout – I came face to face with a challenge to my little treatise on tenses. Suddenly the past was upstream, not down.

I was trying my luck in Potter County's Freeman Run, and the few brookies in attendance were uncooperative. Sometimes when that happens I take a seat by the stream and try to figure out why.

From a convenient tree stump, I studied the massive remnants of a concrete dam that had burst a century ago not far from where I sat. It struck me that it wasn't the future I was staring into upstream – and moments ago had been casting toward – but rather history written in stone, definitely past tense.

The day panic punctured the peace

Tragedy struck this peaceful valley on the last day of September 1911. The Bayless Pulp & Paper Co. dam break is well chronicled on the Internet, in engineering and geological publications, and at least two 100th anniversary books.

Newspapers of the day were somewhat less reliable: The Harrisburg Telegraph, a competitor of The Patriot (forerunner of The Patriot-News), reported the death toll at 200, while The London Times got a little careless with the decimal point and made it 2,000. For the record, the dam breach killed 78 people in the towns of Austin, roughly a mile downstream, and nearby Costello.

This is a tale of greedy men who conspired in an environmental rape that ran terribly amok. It also is the story of a boy on a bicycle and a hooker out on bail whose quick actions doubtless spared many lives, and a grocer who regularly visited the cracking dam and prophesied its failure. The youngster sounding the alarm as he pedaled just minutes ahead of the floodwater survived it – as did the madam, who later got off lightly in court – but the storekeeper and his wife died in the deluge. He is remembered as the Jeremiah of Austin.

Survival was a test of bravery and courage for both the mill bookkeeper, her leg pinned beneath a large grinding stone as she pleaded for someone to grab an ax and free her by cutting it off, and the man who did just that, then carried her to a hospital where she recovered.

The dam builder paid burial costs for about half of the victims while offering to rebuild the mill and dam if survivors would forgo lawsuits. Both sides stuck by their deal, but the new mill fell to flames in 1933 and, nine years later, its replacement broke. This time no one died.

More than a century later, lessons continue to flow from Freeman Run. I'd failed to net a fish on my last visit, but the catch of the day was a dandy: There's a big difference between perceiving or observing something, and merely seeing it.

Within minutes I was making the mental leap back to boyhood, to the day I was learning that very lesson.

Seeing things through eyes of a wise man

(Monday, April 12, 2004)

Grampa Dohne was a quiet, self-educated man, a jack-of-all-trades sort who emigrated from Germany, passing as a boy through the Port of New York circa 1880. Late in life he passed on to me an understanding of the difference between perceiving something and just seeing it.

We were fishing for bass from a rowboat on Panther Lake in New York. It was dusk as we approached a rock pile, jutting out from shore. From about 15 yards away, we watched as one, then another big fish broke the water's surface just off the rocks.

Silently Grampa unfastened the trusty Jitterbug lure from my line and reached for a strange-looking plug from a little collection beside him on the seat.

"Forget the fish," he commanded, his pipe clamped between teeth and bobbing with each syllable, as if for emphasis. "Tell me what you see."

All I could make out were some small, oblong objects popping up and down by the rocks. My 10-year-old imagination put forth its best guess: "Mexican jumping beans?" (These were very big at the time as children's novelties.)

Whether he heard I never knew, for now he was intent on instructing my cast. The plug skittered off a rock and into the water. It wasn't there for long. Bam! A fish bashed it out of the lake, hooking itself in the process. The taming of the fish took all of what little daylight was left, and then some.

Wordlessly, he rowed back to camp. Under the porch light, the fish measured an even 2 feet. From its stomach two full-grown field mice were removed, tails still intact.

Mystery solved: What I had seen as Mexican jumping beans were really mice, imitated by the lure Grampa tied on my line. That day a little boy learned a big lesson for life, that someone older and wiser could see things he could not.

After the Freeman Run outing triggered that memory, it was time for a little help from Webster:

see: *to apprehend by sight*

perceive: *to become conscious of, to discern, realize; to recognize or identify*

observe: *to take notice of, to inspect, to see or sense, especially through careful analytic attention*

So, seeing involves the eye, but perceiving and observing require more brainwork. Humans are complex creatures, capable of amazing behavior. Take selective sight and hearing, for instance. We can dial down our senses by putting on invisible blindfolds and earmuffs to avoid that which offends, or don rose-colored glasses to see our wishes come true.

Our senses thus dulled, we delude ourselves that we are observing and perceiving when, in fact, we are merely seeing what we have selected in advance.

And what happens when we leave our defense mechanisms behind? That was the subject of an earlier column.

TROUT FISHING IN AMERICA

(Thursday, April 16, 1998)

Ah, springtime, and the outdoors beckons anew.

Most people answer to some activity or other that calls them outside during this season of change.

Gardening, mowing, or other yard chores are examples. It could be just washing the car or taking a walk.

The purpose in each of these endeavors is pretty obvious. No one's going to ask why you're putting out cabbage plants, or trimming the hedge. And everyone who sees it can appreciate the gleam of a just-waxed auto.

For the trout fisher, the answer might seem just as obvious. But there's more to it than simply catching a brown, brookie or rainbow.

It's the rest of the answer – or at least part of it – that I'd like to tackle.

What I'm aiming at is the opening of the senses that allows one to more fully appreciate – maybe even helps to define – such outings.

Many trout seasons ago, I noticed that the farther north I drove into the woods (and away from the city), the more likely my car window was down – because the air was fresher, I reasoned.

And on the way home, I noticed a tendency to raise the window to reduce the impact of car horns, blaring radios and other audio intrusions – in other words, plain old self-defense.

Sight is affected, too. I'm more apt to enjoy spotting an unfamiliar bird or a beautiful garden while traversing a rural area than I am in an urban setting. Because there are fewer dedicated gardeners in the city so such birds go elsewhere?

Of course not. I think the reason is because, like other folks, I have trained myself to close the mind, and therefore the eyes, to such things while I'm in the world of macadam and stoplights. Once in the woods, I am looking for those little treats. Here’s a sampling of this trout chaser's world beyond the rainbow – trout, that is.

Sometimes the attraction is man-made.

How far will a slightly crinkled 20-dollar bill float on the fast-moving surface of Larrys Creek in Lycoming County in late April? How about, at least half a mile.

Just such a bill was riding the riffles and, as though I'd been practicing just for the chance all my life, I snared it in my landing net. Curiosity pointed me upstream, now more in search of the twenty’s owner than trout.

After a good walk – and encountering no one along the way – I retreated to the car. The drive from the parking spot to where I’d exited the woods registered .6 mile on the odometer.

Sometimes it's right there in front of you, hopping around in the road.

It was after dinner on a Friday in May. We were driving to Potter County’s Lyman Run to battle the brookies. But there was a roadblock, the likes of which we’d never encountered.

Rounding a bend in the two-lane macadam road hugging a small stream, I hit the brakes. Jumping Jehoshaphat! The roadway was alive with frogs. Some were big enough to be seen from a distance; others sat just an inch-and-a-half or so high, barely discernible until you got much closer. The place literally was soaked with their song and movement.

Just how many there were was tough to say. A quick count within an estimated 10-foot square section of roadway came to 22. The amphibian phenomenon –

known ever after as Frog Friday to its three human witnesses – covered the immediate area and well beyond, a peek through binoculars confirmed in the fading light of dusk. We chose a detour on dirt roads rather than frog mayhem on macadam. It had to be frog mating season.

Sometimes you don't have to guess.

While wading a tributary of Sinnemahoning Creek, elsewhere in Potter County, something floating downstream bumped against my leg. Once again my netting reflex kicked in perfectly. This time a pair of snapping turtles came to net.

It was quickly obvious that they were mating. Just as evident was that, being netted wasn't going to interrupt the proceedings. The decent thing to do was to release them back into their watery world. Splash!

Sometimes it takes a little imagination.

"Christmas in May" and what I call the Mickey Mantle maple fall into this category.

"Christmas" arrived early in the fifth month one year in the form of a small but dazzling emerald snake in my path just as the scarlet sun was setting – a very special red-and-green package, indeed.

A large maple tree had fallen at the bottom of a mountainside in a windstorm, I suppose, smashing and splintering to smithereens near where I was fishing in Kettle Creek, Potter County. In the middle of the maple mess was a piece almost the perfect size and shape of a baseball bat.

Sometimes ... yikes, a snake!

A hungry snake is a clever hunter. A black snake had climbed a young evergreen along Clarks Creek, Dauphin County, to a height of about 3 feet, reversed course and wound itself around and around the sapling, positioning its head about three inches above ground. Not far off a rattler, spotted along the same creek, was lying parallel with – and very much resembling – one of several tree roots. Each was out to waylay a thirsty rodent – or one that had just taken its last drink.

Sometimes it takes a little longer for the senses to open fully – even years.

After going to the same cabin in God's Country for 29 years, on last spring's visit I noticed something previously overlooked.

Not terribly far from camp is a small but faithfully free-flowing stream, too tiny to lure most anglers but always a joy to walk along – especially in springtime on the way up the hollow to fish or hunt.

What I finally noticed was, none of the downed trees along that stream had a stump attached. Further, they all seemed quite straight, about the same size (6 to 8 inches in diameter) and length (6 to 8 feet). Then I spotted a rusted metal band around one of them.

Closer inspection revealed that inside, these logs were hollowed out and, on both ends, had been whittled so they could be joined to one another. These were leftovers of yesteryear water pipes, held intact by the mud and clay inside them.

Now, if you'll excuse me, I think I'll take my fly rod for a walk through some favorite woodsy spots. Never know what I might see. Or better yet, perceive.

What makes trouting special

The only broken bone of my life was suffered neither on the football field of my youth nor the motorcycle of midlife, but rather on a trout stream at age 60. Wading the East Fork, I slipped on mossy rocks and fell face-first, snapping the right little finger as it snagged in my belt buckle.

Instead of some distant doctor's office, I headed for the nearest spring and plunged in my hand. A thermometer from my fishing vest recorded the water at 44 degrees, and a 10-minute soak seemed to help arrest the swelling. Whittling away with my trusty penknife on a dried piece of driftwood resulted in a makeshift splint, which was secured to the purpling pinkie with Band-Aids from my wallet. *Now, Doug, it's a beautiful spring day. Go catch some trout!*

In the interest of full disclosure: My only arrest as a wildlife violator also occurred while trouting. I was fishing the Sinnemahoning, just below the mouth of Bailey Run, but had gotten careless and failed to do my homework. I was an easy pinch, breaking the law on a sunny afternoon right out there along busy Route 872.

One of the rules I hadn't read barred keeping trout caught in that section until sometime in May. Well, this was May, all right, but still two weeks before the applicable date.

It was ignorance of the law, so no excuse, and the warden was nice about it. Ignorance was something Jerry Crayton no doubt witnessed regularly. I had two respectable browns on the stringer, and he took one off, helped it to resuscitate and released it back into the stream.

But its companion was dead, so I was fined $35 for that one, which he confiscated – for supper, I somewhat enviously but silently concluded. Then, with a chuckle and a reminder about "reading the rules," he was off.

This deflating incident cast a pall that lasted the rest of the day and, as it turned out, well into the next one.

Visiting the Clarks ordinarily was a social and gastronomic highlight of our north woods sojourns, and by luck Chauney and I had an invite. I had just about finished letting myself off the psychological hook about the whole citation thing by the time we pulled into their driveway.

Self-forgiveness flowing from the fount of promised self-improvement is a healthy thing, encouraged when others are supportive. Chauney, a leader at writing up violators during his days with the Game Commission, had chided me yesterday but let it rest today.

Saying hello to the Clarks was like slamming the door on my budding reprieve. Inside with Eleanor and Ed were son Ken and his fiancé, Cherie, and they knew the whole story because, it turned out, the bride-to-be was a daughter of the man who arrested me.

Suddenly there were two seasoned lawmen, a wife, and a son and his sweetie – all lined up against a guy who'd been caught red-handed yesterday and was still red-faced about it today. It was all in fun – at least, I think it was – but trust me, I've been diligent about doing my homework ever since.

Trouting is its own special thing, distinctly different from other kinds of fishing – and not just because it can be dangerous or you might meet a waterways conservation officer under less than ideal circumstances.

The world of all things trouty

The Salmonidae family has two mandatory requirements for any neighborhood they swim into: It has to be clean and it has to be cool.

Mountain streams, such as the East Fork, are fed by seeps and springs. Their typically hard-rock base does little to offset the effects of acid rain. However, while trout can and do thrive in the pure waters of the high country in its north, Pennsylvania's most famous streams for brookies, browns and 'bows flow in the middle and south-central reaches.

Here limestone is king, and if there is a trout heaven, its pearly gates are made of this soft rock. Cursed by farmers and road crews who have to deal with the persistent and sometimes huge sinkholes associated with it, limestone teams up with springs deep beneath the surface to create slightly alkaline streams that stay cool in summer and mild in winter – ideal for trout.

Cumberland County is home to several renowned trout streams. Many fly-fishermen favor the Yellow Breeches Creek, while the more adept among them tackle the LeTort Spring Run. Noted for its wild brown trout and tough fishing conditions, the LeTort admittedly is not among my regular haunts. I'm more of a Yellow Breeches kind of guy or – in Dauphin County – a Stony Creek or Clarks Creek type.

To the west, rising near Newville, is Big Spring Creek, ranking among the world's most remarkable limestone spring streams with its brook trout population a worthy example of Pennsylvania's official state fish. The fishing here has always been good – so good, in fact, that in 1829 it spawned a law, perhaps Pennsylvania's first, specifically protecting trout. It was a local ordinance that set a creel limit.

Through the years I've come to recognize my fellow trouters as a special breed. Out-of-staters, some of them using vacation time to be streamside during a particular insect hatch, impress with their sacrifice. Seeing fathers fishing with sons, like the freckled pair of Maryland redheads I met on the Breeches one spring, always makes me feel better about the future of trout and those who stalk them.

Still life with fishermen

Most anglers are patient by nature but, near the end of one especially damp and cold late April week in the 1970s, I found two who seemed in danger of overdoing it. I stopped by Lyman Run State Park near Galeton on my way to camp for the gobbler hunt. It was a drizzly Friday.

Pulling up, I saw two fishermen in their 20s staring down at a 2-footer flopping at their feet on a raft on Lyman Run Lake. It was as though the light wind had rocked them to sleep. With the lunker's odds of escape looking better with each squirm, neither man moved.

"Hey, nice fish!"

The sound of my voice seemed to serve as some sort of reset button because no one looked up as four knees quickly hit the deck. Soon the big trout was on a stringer and savagely splashing its disapproval.

"This is our first fish of the week," the smaller of the two announced, fingers running through a scraggly beard as he pointed to a solitary yellow tent pitched in nearby woods. "We been here since Monday."

Now things were making sense: The persistence it had taken this dogged duo to finally hook and catch a fish had lingered as a kind of temporary paralysis when it came to the matter of what to do next.

Holly Blyler's lovely watercolor was a gift to the author.

Special delivery

A friend stopped by yesterday
with four not-so-fresh-caught fish,
frozen leftovers of spring
to delight as summer dish.

But my wife had just fixed up
BLTs with coffee hot
and yard tomatoes so fresh
our guest could refuse them not.

So it was that lunch today
I knew would rank exquisite –
the succulent treat of trout,
all due to Sarvo's visit.

The trout were caught by Grant; the tree was felled by beaver.

Grant can't resist climbing a tree.

Don Sarvey mans the grill at his cabin by the river.

We were joined by journalism in the 1970s when Don Sarvey came to The Patriot-News as a reporter and I was one of the copyreaders checking his stories. We've remained friends through four divorces, the death of a child, heart attack, etc.

When he landed at The Patriot-News, Don was just that – Don – and I was plain old Doug. How we became Sarvo and Dougo is a lesson in the significance of nicknames.

It all began when Mary Ormanoski, who took my place in the paper's York bureau, married photographer Jim Bradley. Our budding friendship endured even after I chose to go spring turkey hunting rather than witness their wedding.

Notice I didn't say, she forgot about it. In what became an every spring occurrence, she'd stop by my desk and say, "Gonna go chase turkeys around the woods again to celebrate my anniversary?"

She was a principled lady and fiercely independent, insisting on Mary O. Bradley as her byline. Now, a newspaper byline is the reporter's prerogative, but her nickname typically is for others to decide.

That she was called Mary-O in the newsroom and well beyond was a tribute to who she was, what she stood for and the classy way she always did things. All of which made it an instant honor when she began calling us Sarvo and Dougo. Mary-O was later taken by cancer, but she left behind some O so sweet memories.

I had a truck, and the purpose of the very first Dohne/Sarvey non-work related outing was to pick up a crib Sarvo had purchased for his as yet unborn daughter, Dana. We discovered the fisherman in each other and were planning a trip upstate for trout before we even reached the store.

Besides scrumptious brook trout meals eaten streamside, among my most vivid memories of Clinton County trout trips with Sarvo are the times:

• We fished under a full moon and came up with empty creels, nothing but crawfish clinging to our bait while several barred owls inquired relentlessly, "Who cooks for you; who cooks for you-all?"

• A black bear ambled downhill toward me the day Father died. Quickly climbing a stream bank in the opposite direction, I saw that someone had cooked there over a campfire recently. Ol' bruin had probably eaten the leftovers and was back for seconds. Maybe he thought I was the cook. At any rate, he went his way and I went mine.

• Wild turkeys chattered on the hill above as rising brook trout entertained us below. Suddenly a deer was on the dash to our rear, and with the ongoing concert of the cicadas we were experiencing nature all around.

• A rattlesnake, its girth shrunken during hibernation, recklessly crossed just a few paces in front of us on its way to the stream, hunger at the controls. We watched it pick a path through patches of snow that were retreating in pale April sunshine.

• We visited the hospital – after the fish stopped biting – for treatment of a wound suffered in a fall when the rod's finger grip punctured my right palm. The point was in deep enough that even with my hand open and palm down the little rod remained imbedded. I swear it never hurt until we quit fishing.

• Grant, about 10, tired of trouting and left the stream without telling anyone. Searching woods the whole way, we headed back to our vehicle. "Hi, Grampa!" The voice was loud and clear, but the speaker was nowhere in sight – until we looked high up in the hemlock shading our car and saw him waving. I suppressed the inclination to scold and merely returned his greeting in kind. *Thank You, Lord, for keeping your arm around this boy's shoulder when I couldn't.*

Rain Dance Weekend

Some memories refuse to fit into neat little nuggets. One of those unfolded on Memorial Day Weekend 1991, also known within the Sarvey clan as Rain Dance Weekend.

Dana, 14, and little brother, Peter, 9, helped pitch our tents along the stream, anticipating its voice would sing them to sleep later.

Dinner was something other than fresh trout because all we'd caught that day were five undersized brookies. Sunset was slow in yielding to moonrise, and low clouds quickly deepened the darkness. Oh, well, it was bedtime anyhow.

The first raindrops fell gently as though not to compete with but rather to complement the symphony of the stream. Soon storm was outshouting creek, and I was glad my tent was straddling a sandy crown of real estate. Many of my childhood nights – some of them quite damp – had passed in tents. Only two things mattered – the tent had to remain overhead, and I had to stay dry.

Meanwhile, things were less serene next door, and the situation was deteriorating with each clap of thunder. The kids were physically dry but emotionally drenched.

Spontaneity reigned as Sarvo and I staged an impromptu rain dance during a letup in the downpour. Lacking the campfire and feathered headdresses that automatically come to mind, our version of the Native American ritual also had a different purpose.

For a while our young audience seemed to be entertained, or at least distracted, as their elders circled the campsite, moving to the beat of unheard drums while loudly imploring the rain gods to relent. But the chiefs of the clouds weren't buying it – even if young listeners might be – and soon we were retreating to our tents as the rain resumed.

With neither sister nor daughter, I was ignorant of just how effectively a teen-age girl can convey her feelings of being terrified. Dana, bless her heart, now seemed determined to remedy my deficiency in spades.

It wasn't just the sheer volume, though I swear she could be heard above the thunder. Dana's anguish was bared in long wailings ending in screams that did to the ear what a knifepoint can to the chest. Her protest penetrated so deeply that at times she gave voice to what I came to realize were my feelings as well.

So magnificent was her struggle against the storm that I forgot how it all turned out. Surely we grabbed flashlights, sloshed back to our vehicle and retreated about 10 miles to the Sarvey family home in Lock Haven, right?

"Nope. We stayed the night," recalled my rain dancing partner, years after the fact.

Today Dana and Peter live near Boston and New York City, respectively. She is a doctor of adolescent psychiatry at Harvard's McLean Hospital and – with husband Jean-Michel Caruge – is raising little Olivia and Gabriel. Pete, a Purdue-trained mechanical engineer cranking out sales for iAutomation, and his wife, Amy, welcomed their firstborn, Adalyn, in autumn 2015.

Ah, more little feet to carry the next generation of explorers through the hills and tributaries of the Susquehanna River's West Branch above Lock Haven, a community and a family whose foundations are rooted in the woods.

Doug tailgates with Dana, left, and Pete Sarvey in 1988.

Fishermen dance around Clinton County campsite while imploring the rain gods to end heavy downpours in late May 1991. No, it didn't work.

The Sarvey story

Sarvo's great-great-great-grandfather, Christian Earon, left Wurttemberg, Germany, for America in 1821, settling on a mountain tract whose original deed conveyed it to Revolutionary War officer Edward Burd. Benjamin Franklin signed the document in 1787 as president of the Supreme Executive Council of the Commonwealth of Pennsylvania, but Burd never settled there. Earon paid $25 for the property known as Walnut Bottom in 1825, then built and operated a farm.

Nineteenth century lumberjacks lashed logs together into rafts, which they rode down the West Branch and put ashore at Lock Haven. For the logs the next stop was the mills; for the weary deliverymen it was off to the nearby Earon farmhouse for food, drink and lodging.

While lumber barons erected lavish homes in celebration of their wealth – some still lining the streets of present day Lock Haven – workers in the woods were developing calluses and courage.

Sarvo's great-uncle, Thurman Earon, labored in the forests as a boy, driving a horse team skidding logs for transport by rail along Tangascootac Creek, a tributary of the West Branch. When confronted by a burning trestle, he was able to extinguish the flames before the engine arrived, earning a reward of $10.

A brother of the fire hero worked as a railroader in the woods. W. Donald "Pop" Earon once retrieved a bloated body that was floating down the Scootac. Guessed to have been a lumberjack from a crew operating upstream, the stranger's remains were buried by the trainmen in a high bank along the creek.

Today the railroad track from which Sarvo's granddad made his grisly sighting is a dirt-and-gravel road. The unmarked grave is in a section of stream bank that still juts noticeably higher at that point. Dead Man's Mound, to passersby in the know, always rates a reverent mention.

Pop Earon gave Sarvo more than just his first name. This World War I veteran shared not only a glimpse of the conflict – "We fought across the countryside by day and slept in cemeteries at night" – but also what happened after his unit reached Paris: "I went down and rode the subway!"

Sarvo's dad also was a military man, serving in the Army Air Force as a B-24 radar man in the Aleutian

Islands during World War II. Richard Sarvey, a soft-spoken member of the I Bombed Japan Club, married schoolteacher Mary Jane Earon and became postmaster of Lock Haven.

Just as he led me to his favorite woods and streams, Don Sarvey also took me into his family's home. I was often a guest in their rambling house and grew fond of his folks and Pop Earon, who lived with them. Pop loved to welcome visitors by announcing that he was "just about to have some ice cream," never failing to ask if you'd like some, too.

Sarvo's other grandfather, Thorld Sarvey, resided in an apartment at the rear of the property and also had a connection to the woods – he was a retired paper-mill foreman. That resonated with me because of Father's history in the pulpwood industry as a paper chemist. Dad had worked at several paper mills in the South but, to my knowledge, not the one in Lock Haven.

Our old folks are all gone, but their essence survives in the hearts and minds of those who love healthy forests and streams. Just how big an influence the Earon-Sarvey family and their stamping grounds have had on yours truly is evident in the following account of a June 2014 visit to Black Walnut Bottom Camp. The cottage is several miles up the West Branch from Lock Haven on the site where Christian Earon built his camp nearly two centuries ago.

Leaving Sarvo and five other fishing buddies to their slumber, I indulged in a daybreak re-acquaintance with the West Branch, discovering:

View of the Susquehanna River West Branch from Black Walnut Bottom Camp.

A lesson on the road

Among my most cherished trout trips with Sarvo is one we made to Ludlow, VT, in late June 2007. Pete's employer had given the young biz whiz a week off and the run of an A-frame cabin in the woods. The first thing he did was to invite his father, three other fishing buddies and me.

Fond memories of that outing include spotting a young elk early one morning as I sat reading on the huge front porch, and reviving in the Jacuzzi out back beneath a full moon.

I value this excursion not because of the fish I caught (zero) but because of what I learned. Now wait a minute, I can almost hear you saying, you mean you traveled all the way to the Green Mountain State and didn't land one trout? Exactly!

Vermont truly is a verdant summertime vacationland. Second only to Wyoming as the least populated state, it is three-fourths forested and boasts many sparkling brooks and rivers to beckon anglers at almost every bend. Until, that is, you notice the no-trespassing sign posted on what seems like every third maple tree.

Besides the Sarveys and myself, our party included Tom Chapman, Bill McKee and Jim Weaver, veteran anglers all. We fished the Black River, then brothers-in-law Tom and Bill tried the Battenkill near the New York border, while the rest of us checked out Otter Creek before returning to the Black but at a different spot. Pete was the only one to catch a keeper all week.

Besides the obvious lesson – a wise angler researches the waterway before his visit – our Vermont experience helped us see how lucky we are to be Pennsylvanians when it comes to stream access. All but six of this commonwealth's counties are home to at least one state park each. That's because the father of the Keystone State's 121-unit system, Maurice Goddard, had this vision back in the Fifties: Place a park within 25 miles of every resident.

(L to R): Doug Dohne, Jim Weaver, Bill McKee, Tom Chapman and Pete Sarvey visit Vermont to challenge its trout.

Still more to learn out west

A few years later I made another out-of-state discovery about trouting, this time in Colorado. It happened during a surprise reunion with an old pal.

Retired by August 2010, Kay and I began a Western U.S. motor trip that would include exploring Yellowstone National Park.

We took a break from driving – this is a very large country, one learns day after day at the wheel – and rendezvoused in the Rockies with one of her sisters, Elsie, a.k.a. Ace, and her husband, Ed Stevens, Arizonans eluding the desert heat by summering along the Dolores River at Priest Gulch Campground in southwestern Colorado.

Among the fishing gear I'd brought along were several favorite dry flies and some in other patterns well suited to Colorado trouting. These latter I found at Bass Pro Shops after doing my homework – right, this time before the fishing trip – but after a few hours in our rental cabin I knew they probably wouldn't be needed.

The next morning we piled into the Stevens Jeep and set off for Alta Lakes, passing through tiny Rico and skirting the skiing paradise of Telluride before going off-road and climbing a dirt two-track for what seemed like an hour.

At the summit we entered an unofficial mining museum by fording a clear stream flowing past the remnants of a sluice box. Nearby stood the shells of what once were two small wooden bunkhouses used by gold miners. Our arrival startled the current residents, a trio of marmots now quickly quitting a sunny spot and retreating to the safety of the camp's ruins.

Close by and at about 11,000 feet elevation, the three little Alta Lakes glistened above the timberline. Since they freeze solid in winter, the lakes are restocked with fish each spring.

All of the Altas are fishable and, before wading into the most accessible of them, I paused to study its surface. The trout were feeding on top, and I was pretty sure what was on the menu.

Attaching a No. 18 Adams to the tippet, I walked a finger of land jutting into the lake and went on the attack. In half an hour four healthy rainbows graced the stringer – thanks to the little imitation mosquito lure.

Last night we had the cabin windows open, and there were no screens. Instead of falling asleep, I was swatting mosquitoes and thinking about all the trout I'd taken on the Adams back in Pennsylvania. Now, standing here in the lake, it was like I'd just shaken hands with an old and dear friend.

P.S.: Ed and Ace both limited out that day, too, using Berkeley's power bait (orange) and fishing the bottom.

Occasionally my passion for trout stretches the limits of literary license. A case in point is the following column, all 4 feet of which actually made it into print. (My editors must have had spring fever that day.)

IF TROUT COULD TALK ...

(Thursday, April 12, 2001)

Yo! Yeah, I'm talking to you. Don't see anyone else tail-walkin' like some kinda beached whale on my bank, do ya?

Jumpin' catfish, some of you guys are really gettin' outta shape. Hey, if we let ourselves go like that we prob'ly couldn't even go upstream. Our waist would be sticking out so far our fins wouldn't work right.

Yeah, I know we got some big uglies in here, too. But, hey, you guys got those huge brains. You're s'posed to know everything, man.

Well, if you're so smart, let's see what you know about Pennsylvania's only true native trout. You did know we brookies – and not those gaudy rainbows or the now-you-see-'em, now-you-don't spooky browns – are the state fish, didn't ya?! Is that your final answer? Oh boy, I never shudda asked.

Please, please just tell me you already know that trout are in the salmon family, live in salt and freshwater and migrate to spawn. God bless you!

There are two main groups of trout – chars and trout – but I can tell you already know that, too.

The chars, as doubtless you are aware, have both red and light spots on their dark bodies, rather than red and black spots on a lighter background found in most salmonoids (steelhead, rainbow and brown trout and many others). So, check me out: Being a brookie (a.k.a. speckled trout, hemlock trout, mountain trout and square-tail), I am a ... char. Right! Congratulations, you just passed your 2001 Trout Eye Test.

Hey, you know my cousin out West? No, no, Dolly Parton's the country and western singer. My cousin, the char, is Dolly Varden. She's been helpin' to fame the West for years by showing anglers such a good time that they sometimes sing C&W to her. Just kiddin'!

Look, I gotta admit, up till now these questions have been as easy as findin' worms on Day 2 of a three-day rainstorm.

To step it up a notch, I hooked two special interpreters, Dan Tredinnick and Tom Greene, from the Pennsylvania

Fish and Boat Commission pool, to monitor quality control.

As director of communications, Tredinnick is a true friend of trout wherever he goes because his creel is so stuffed with nouns, verbs and adjectives he has no room for what's s'posed to go in there. Greene runs the Coldwater Unit (think head trout honcho) and knows as much about us as anyone who ever stepped into a pair of waders. He's the one we trout gotta watch out for!

I'm cuttin' you a break by makin' it true or false:

1) The 2001 Pennsylvania trout season opens at 8 a.m. the day after tomorrow.

2) There is a pecking order among trout, but more so in wild ones. Size is the main determinate.

3) Hatchery-raised trout have almost a schooling instinct, while their wild cousins are more territorial and solitary.

4) Wild trout are relentless in driving off any new arrivals to their territory from the hatchery.

5) In fact, the potential for severe stress in both groups when they meet is one reason the PFBC prefers not to stock hatchery trout in streams already supporting healthy wild trout.

6) While trout fight mainly by harassment and threat display, they may resort to nasty nipping.

7) Wild trout rarely suffer more than a 50 percent population loss in a year.

8) Wild trout run about the same risk of being killed by anglers as those raised in hatcheries and released.

9) The old man of the hole in a Pennsylvania trout stream could be 10.

10) Trout feed daily, if they can, and grow throughout life.

11) A hatchery-raised trout may double the size of its wild cousin by 16 months of age.

12) Trout, especially the larger ones, might feed at night.

13) A trout could travel as little as a few hundred yards in one year.

14) On another stream and under different conditions, a trout annually might make a 5-mile or longer round trip.

15) Trout will feed in water 42.5 degrees or cooler, but they can't digest food to get energy at such temps.

16) Limestone streams have more constant temperatures than others and could stay in low-mid-40s during winter and the high 50s-low 60s in summer.

17) During June a 20-degree daily temperature swing, say from 45 to 65, is not uncommon on many Pennsylvania trout streams.

18) The optimum water range for trout feeding is 52-60 degrees.

19) Water temps in the mid-70s will test a trout's upper tolerances.

20) Trout have a brain, heart, lungs, liver, gallbladder, stomach, esophagus, intestines, etc., but no kidney.

21) Trout are creatures of habit but cannot be trained.

22) Just as there are trap-happy bears, some fish get hooked again and again.

23) Trout eyes work much like ours, even though they have no eyelids or tear ducts.

24) Trout have good peripheral vision, but ours is better.

25) In effect, trout are nearsighted, which is why they often swim right next to your bait, close enough to take it, before turning away.

26) Trout eyes lack the iris, which adjusts to differing levels of light. But their eyes are sensitive to movement.

27) Trout have a well-developed sense of smell, thanks to two pairs of nostrils on each side of the snout.

28) Trout have fewer taste buds than humans.

29) Trout have two different organs working to detect sound.

30) A trout's scales are actually hairs.

31) Just as we do, trout have an inner ear that aids in balance.

32) On both sides of most fish is a string of pores called the lateral line. Their pores are the openings of tiny tubes that help detect vibration.

33) Trout never sleep.

34) Brown and brook trout reproduce in the wild as 2-year-olds.

35) Brookies typically lay their eggs later in the fall than browns.

36) Rainbow trout reproduce in the wild on only about 50 miles of Pennsylvania streams, whereas browns and brooks spawn on thousands of miles of waterways.

37) The female digs the redd (or nest) and lays her eggs, the male fertilizes the eggs, and she covers them by stirring gravel with her tail

38) A 9-inch trout will lay 800 to 1,000 eggs, an 18-incher double that.

39) From 1,000 eggs, as few as just two trout may survive to spawn.

40) An average stream could be home to about 30 pounds of wild trout per acre.

The Answers

1-6) True

7) False. A 65 percent loss in one year is not uncommon for wild trout.

8) False. Wild trout are less likely than hatchery trout to be killed by anglers because generally fewer fishermen ply these streams, a catch-and-release philosophy probably is more prevalent among those who do, and such streams are often subject to special rules.

9-14) True

15) False. The critical temperature is 38.5 degrees.

16) True

17) False. A 10-degree swing in water temperature is more realistic.

18-19) True

20) False. The kidney is that dark mass hugging the backbone that is removed when cleaning a fish for consumption.

21) False. Hungry hatchery trout learn to bump a bar on the hopper containing the feed.

22-23) True

24) False. With eyes on either side of the head, trout have excellent peripheral vision.

25-27) True

28) False. Fish have more taste buds than a typical human's 10,000, and they are located on the lips and in the mouth.

29) True

30) False; however, trout have tiny hairs that help in hearing.

31-33) True

34) False. While brookies reproduce at 2 years, browns usually delay until age 3.

35) False. It's the other way around: Brookies usually begin the reproductive cycle in late September, with the browns following in a few weeks.

36-37) True

38) False. An 18-inch wild trout could lay 3,000-4,000 eggs.

39-40) True

Scoring

* 36-40 correct answers: The pinnacle of piscatorial prowess

* 30-35: You know your Pisces

* 20-29: New heights to scale

* 10-19: Sit in the back of the boat

* 9 or fewer: Hopelessly out of the mainstream

My best keepers

They wore neither scales, fur nor feathers, and they didn't make much of a splash or even try to run or fly. What they did was to enrich my life with friendship. In their wake, these departed pals of the outdoors left a boatload of memories.

A man of the woods

(Prepared for Roscoe's funeral, Oct. 24, 2012, but never delivered, due to travel restrictions)

Good morning.

My name is Doug Dohne, and I first met Roscoe Joseph Stiles 43 hunting seasons ago at his camp in Potter County.

No doubt you are going to hear a lot about hunting here today, and rightly so: To a great extent, hunting was what the man was all about.

Calvin Coolidge was in the White House when Roscoe started to hunt squirrels at age 11. The family had a .22-caliber rifle and, as he put it, "we went trappin'."

Roscoe and his brothers, Walter and Paul, got a $2 bounty on weasel, plus $1 for the hide. Their family depended on rabbit and squirrel for supper.

The boys had a terrier, Jack, a good brush buster. According to Roscoe, Jack could catch pheasants alive. Just in case that didn't happen, Roscoe saved up for a JC Higgins double-barreled 12 gauge, "$10, used."

Eventually he set his sights on deer and even graduated to bagging a moose in Canada, but Roscoe didn't catch turkey fever until he was 47 and visiting kin in Lycoming County.

Family was huge with Roscoe, so it figures that a nephew took him on his maiden turkey hunt. Roscoe scored with a single rifle shot and, from then on, turkey hunting fascinated him. It became a passion that filled and helped to extend his life. He died 85 days short of what would have been his 100th birthday.

Now, there are turkey hunters and there are turkey killers. That first group is quite large, the second much smaller. Roscoe belonged to both. Those in the know estimate that 250 to 300 turkeys fell to his hunting parties in roughly 50 seasons afield in Pennsylvania, New York and New Jersey. That's a lot of wings and thighs! In contrast, there are hunters who go at it for years without even seeing a wild turkey within shooting range, let alone bagging one.

By his third anniversary as a turkey hunter, Roscoe had recruited seven partners and built a cabin in Potter County. "We call it Moon Valley Lodge," he told me, "because the mountain blocks the light until the moon is almost overhead. By the time you see the moon, it's real bright, as though someone just turned on the porch light. All of a sudden you can see the whole valley."

It was at Moon Valley Lodge that I met Roscoe in May 1969, and much later was invited to join.

In the woods, Roscoe was the picture of patience. Here, in his words, is a glimpse of his early days as a turkey hunter:

"One time I was watching a hen dusting herself in a depression along a trail. She sensed danger, got upset and began to sound off. Eventually she left, but I held still even after that. Wasn't long and a gobbler showed up. She had called in the tom, and I got him."

Perhaps less patient with people than turkeys, Roscoe nevertheless was a natural instructor who delighted in sharing his knowledge. Among the many novices he helped along was yours truly. Two of his best surviving students are son Frank and Pete Michaloski, husband of Frank's sister, Susan. But there are plenty of others – some of them complete strangers – who crossed paths with Roscoe and came away better hunters.

OK, he was a knowledgeable and accomplished guy in the forest; so, did he ever get lost?

"Well, no, but sometimes I didn't know where I was," he admitted. Once he was "confused" (his word) while hunting in Bedford County. Then a far-away look crept across his face, and he said: "Sometimes it's just best to follow a stream out."

Speaking of those times when things go wrong, his 80s were especially tough on Roscoe. He lost his beloved Helen midway through that decade, a crushing blow that shook him to the core.

A few years later the left-handed shooter was forced to switch to the right side after his surgeon goofed while implanting a pacemaker.

"I wanted it on the right side – the nurse even marked the spot – but they put it on the left," Roscoe recalled. Boy, talk about missing the mark!

The awkward switch was depressing as his shooting success slipped, especially on deer. Here's how he explained it: "You can change shooting sides, but you can't change your master eye."

Most other hunters probably would have laid down their weapons in the face of such a challenge so late in life. But Roscoe Stiles wasn't just any hunter.

By the way, he considered other hunters encountered in the woods "my best friends. Fifteen minutes after taking a stand, they're cold or hungry or bored and on their way. I stay put and stay alert, and that's when I see the game."

The other side of that coin, Roscoe said, is that "liberal" deer hunting rules have made the woods more dangerous for humans. He felt that many hunters had become less responsible in identifying their targets and more apt to shoot too soon.

He had this to say about the hunters of old:

"When I was a boy, there was a camp limit of six deer. There were no scopes and few rifles – mostly we had shotguns and pumpkin balls. We knew what our guns would do, and we were better shots. We had to be – our families were counting on the venison."

Along the way one of those other hunters really did become one of Roscoe's best friends. But they didn't meet in the woods.

About the same time Roscoe was discovering the joys of turkey hunting half a century ago, a mailman of Portuguese descent in Newport, Rhode Island, was writing to the Pennsylvania Game Commission. Al Pedro was looking for someone to guide him on a deer hunt in the Keystone State in exchange for fishing from his boat off the New England coast.

Eventually Al's letter fell into the hands of the nephew who had introduced Roscoe to the wild turkey, G. John

Martin, then early in what would become a lengthy career with the Pennsylvania Game Commission. Chauney Martin is among my best friends and led me on my first turkey hunt, later doing the same for his sons, Bradley and Brian, who in turn took theirs.

Anyway, Roscoe and Al connected through that letter and began a lifelong friendship. Al was intrigued by Pennsylvania's whitetail, and Roscoe learned how to road-hunt for bluefish. Huh?

"It was simple," Roscoe explained, "Al would drive along the Rhode Island coast watching for swarming seabirds. Where they were really thick, he pulled over and we'd jump out, run down with our gear to the water and try our luck. We caught lots of blues that way."

One fishing trip found the two pals far from Al's home at night. Just as they approached the only motel along a rural road, its lights went out. Here's Roscoe's account:

"Al pulled up, looked over and said, 'Hey, there's a Portuguese name on that sign! You wait here.' He went over and knocked and I could see a woman in the doorway. I heard them, but I couldn't understand a word – it was all Portuguese.

"Soon Al was motioning for me to come on in. She was so hungry to hear Portuguese there was no way she was going to turn him away."

Roscoe was the fortunate type. How about hitting two turkeys with one shotgun blast and retrieving both without getting out of your car! That actually occurred one foggy day not long ago while Roscoe had a state permit to hunt from his vehicle.

He was driving a dirt road near Delaware Water Gap en route to his Camp Herman in Pike County. Yes, that's right, he had two hunting lodges. But back to the two-for-one-shot story, in Roscoe's words:

"I thought I saw a turkey head pop up through the grass as I drove by. So I stopped and backed up a little. A minute or so later the head came back up and I fired. It flopped around a bit, then came sliding down the bank.

"It was a gobbler and it landed right by my left front wheel, so I pulled up a little, opened the door, reached down and grabbed it. Before I even closed the door another turkey came sliding down the bank. I had to move the car about 12 feet to reach that one. Never got out of the car till I hit camp."

Not only lucky in the woods, he also was fortunate at the wheel and on the battlefield. As a young man, Roscoe fell off a coal truck while making a delivery, but managed to get up and drive home. Later it was determined he'd suffered a concussion. Another time, his vehicle T-boned a moving train, but his injuries were minor and he walked away.

He was a Seabee during World War II when a Japanese torpedo tore through the hull of his ship in Palau, the Philippines, only a few feet from where Roscoe was handling ammunition. The torpedo was a dud and didn't explode.

Roscoe rose from a humble home. After finishing eighth grade in a one-room schoolhouse, it was off to work on a farm. He graduated from high school at 16 and, weeks before the stock market crash of 1929, entered East Stroudsburg State Teachers College (now a university), earning a degree in health education in 1934. Siblings Sylvia (Chauney's mother) and Roscoe, in that order, were the first college grads in the family.

The Great Depression found Roscoe driving a huckster truck, peddling fruits and vegetables. After working as a carpenter for his Uncle John, Roscoe made his mark in the lumber and construction business that he operated with big brother Walter.

Wood was in short supply in the late Forties, but resourceful Roscoe was able to acquire government gliders, leftovers from the war.

"We weren't really interested in the gliders," he admitted. "It was the wooden crates they came in that we needed, and we got quite a few by rail. As the gliders piled up out back, those precious wooden containers were recycled as stairs, walls and roofs of new homes.

Through it all, he learned not to worry and to trust in God. "The Lord will call me when He's ready," he told me about five years ago. "I just keep on hunting while I wait."

His first rule of turkey hunting was, "Hunt where they are." By which he meant, scout BEFORE you hunt. And that's what he resumed doing right after each hunting season, keeping close track of any birds spotted at 40 to 50 locations he visited regularly. "Even (while) hunting deer," he told me, "I'm looking for turkey sign."

Now Roscoe has lots of new places to scout. Happy hunting, old buddy!

Mr. and Mrs. Roscoe J. Stiles

Despite – or maybe partly because of – our differences, two of my outdoors friends from the newspaper stand out in memory like black bears on a snowy mountainside. Life without contrast, after all, would be so dull.

Bill Shearer

Hunter/angler/computer guru smiled through it all

William R. Shearer Jr. (1930-2004)
(Saturday, August 7, 2004)

Like most U.S. families on Dec. 2, 1930, the one Bill Shearer was born into that day was struggling through what would become known as the Great Depression.

While times were difficult, the birth apparently was normal enough, once Bill's mom got to the hospital. It seems his dad in several tries couldn't get the family car to fire off that damp morning, and it wasn't doing anything to improve his mood. Shearer Sr. had planned to be in the woods with his rifle, as it was opening day of the deer hunt.

Informed that the pace of contractions had picked up and it was time to go, he wadded up some newspaper, set it afire and tossed it under the hood. This stunt resulted in a bang and a few flames that conquered the moisture so the trip could begin and Bill would be born in the hospital. Rifles, hunting and newspapers would become recurring themes in his life.

William Ray Shearer Jr. grew up a gentleman. He graduated from Lower Paxton High School but, though possessing the mind of a scholar, never got a crack at college. Undaunted, he pursued everything that interested him, a dedicated student of life.

One of those interests was woodworking, and he built many furnishings for his home near Dauphin. He and his musically talented wife, Dolores, assembled several full-sized, beautiful looking – and sounding – harps from kits.

Just days before acute leukemia and stroke would strike, the Shearers and others from Charlton United Methodist Church were on a mission trip doing carpentry work at the New Life for Girls facility near Dover. Bill died July 25.

Wherever he went, his smile brightened the way.

Bill was quick with a joke, but just as ready to listen to yours. He laughed at life and at himself. Perhaps his biggest gift was teaching others to do the same. He was a guy who insisted that you didn't have to start out before sunrise just to go hunting or fishing.

"They'll be there all day," he'd say of the fish and deer. "They live there, remember."

He was passionate about his family but wanted to hear about yours, too. With me, he ranked somewhere between big brother and father figure. Like any little brother, I wound up with the clothes he outgrew.

In 48 years at The Patriot-News, Bill endeared himself to fellow employees and bosses alike. We were co-workers for 30 years; he was in Composing and later the computer end of it. Someone told him that I had a pool table in the living room of my second-floor apartment. He thought that was funny and that I must have a sense of humor, so he offered to come over and teach me Kelly-style pool. He was a super shot.

We shared similarities – both had endured divorce and each had a strong-willed son named David – and interests, hunting and fishing.

But there were huge differences, too. Early on, I thought him rather strange politically, somewhere just east of Rush Limbaugh. I told Bill that as a bird he'd never have made it far from the nest, always using just the right wing to get around. He'd be going in circles – always to the left, I pointed out.

In return, he invoked the L-word, calling me a liberal loon with ideas so lofty that nowhere down here would be good enough for me to land.

Even when doing things together we had our own styles. Bill was a rifleman, a darned good one. He was a Korean War vet with medals to show for his days with the Coast Guard rifle team. His thing was distance shooting.

In the woods, I prefer the shotgun and the close action that goes with it. He called my Ithaca "a garden hose, a general-direction gun," requiring little skill.

In his eyes, I was an elitist for insisting on proficiency at turkey calling. I told him he was just lying in ambush and missing half the fun by not calling in the bird. Well, we both took turkeys, so call it even.

Ditto for fishing: We just thought, well, separately. I like monofilament line and an open-faced spinning outfit for long casts that cover lots of water. His tackle boxes were full of old-style reels, and he used shorter rods. His goal was accuracy, being able to hit the spot where he thought a fish should be. Well, we both caught fish, so rack that up as a draw, too.

The biggest fish either of us ever hooked while we were together was a northern pike, an Ontario beauty that was about 5 inches wide, shoulder to shoulder. Bill had tired this trophy and now played it into netting position alongside the boat.

As I tried to land it, somehow the rascal wound up balanced crosswise – just for a moment – over the mouth of the net.

Then came a mighty leap, a caper that had us craning our necks to catch the action as the toothy critter soared then crashed off the side of the boat, slapping Bill's face on the way down. We sat there, Bill wiping away a splotch of mucous left by the fish. For a moment no one spoke. Then we laughed, in unison, and nothing more was said about it.

Laughing always seemed to dissolve our differences. And that was a good thing, because differences were mostly what we had – except for the mutual respect that let us become great friends. Each gave the other room to do things his way, understanding that later it would be thoroughly re-examined, challenged and defended, probably over a beer.

You knew those conversations, on the phone or in person, were about to end when Bill said, "Did we miss anyone?"

Jim Conrad
Patriot-News photo, 1987

Just between friends at the trout stream

(Saturday, April 14, 1990)

Once again it's the day between Good Friday and Easter Sunday – midway between death and life, a minister might say.

In a collision of circumstance, today also marks the start of Pennsylvania's 1990 trout season.

What's this, a sermon? A fishing column? Neither, actually. Let me tell you about a friend of mine …

Jim Conrad was a career journalist, an editor and co-worker here at The Patriot-News. He was a solid wordsmith whose language skills were twinned with excellence in math. Jim would format Page One – down to the very last word of the final line – using a pocket calculator. He was the only guy I've ever seen do that in my 25 years in the newsroom. He was a natural cyber whiz and ran our computer system.

A remarkable aspect of our friendship was that, besides newspapering, we had little in common. In fact, our divergent views far outnumbered mutual interests. We were on opposite sides of labor politics, for instance.

One thing we did share was an attraction to speed. Even here, however, we went our separate ways: Jim was into airplanes and fast cars; I abhor jets but am moved by the motorcycle.

Fishing, ah, fishing was what bridged all that. Oh how we loved to fish!

A short time on the stream and all the gaps that necessarily separate any two people seemed to wash away. In fast fashion, we were hooked – on fishing together.

Predictably, even as fishermen we were dissimilar. I fish because I enjoy eating them, while Jim was out purely for the sport of it. He was a sensitive guy, the kind who filed the barbs off the hooks so as not to hurt (his word) the fish. It didn't matter to him that this made it easier for the fish to shed the hook before he'd get a chance to net it. Those he managed to catch were always admired – and just about always released back into the water.

No fisherman ever catches too many, but my friend's allotment proved anemic. He had a heart attack, his first, and died in January. Jim saw just 41 fishing seasons.

OK, maybe this is sort of a sermon because, like a preacher, I'm going to try to persuade you to do something right now.

With any luck, you have someone with whom to navigate life's stream, just as I had in Jim Conrad. What this fisherman is asking you to do is give a gentle tug on whatever line it is that connects the two of you. Just let that person know in some small way how you value the friendship.

I'd do it myself, but, well, you understand – it's opening day and like any avid angler, friend Jim has …

… gone fishin'

Miss you in the newsroom, but mostly on the stream;
there is where we authored a truly Page One dream.

We shared of fin and feather and oft witnessed splash,
when booted legs together would signal trout to dash!

Flies flicked upon fast water, grown men stayed yet boys,
sun for hugs, wind for kisses, fishing rods for toys.

Too young the heart shall fail as you, in perfect bloom,
wade hard along life's trail, unsensing of the doom.

Dawns that angling season, no limit to the creel,
all the time, no reason to forgo thy rod and reel.

Cast line in the shadow and count on this, my friend,
right back here behind you, I'm fishing round the bend.

Chapter 4 - *March!*

Why we walk
By design man moves upright
as his world keeps passing by;
in the end what matters most
is not where he treads but why.

WALKING IS SUCH a natural activity that most of us probably don't give it much thought – we just do it.

True, our first steps, arms flung wide for balance, may delight adult witnesses. But by the time normal kids walk, run, hop, skip and/or jump to the bus on their first day of school, no one is watching – except maybe for passing motorists, forced to keep one eye on the road and the other on those unpredictable little bodies.

While the distance of our daily walk might seem inconsequential, like compound interest it adds up over time.

"The journey of a thousand miles begins with one step."

That's what the founder of Taoism taught followers five centuries before Christ walked the Earth. He could have made it 100,000 miles, because that's the distance experts say an average person walks in a lifetime – about four times around the world.

After the newspaper route and school sports of my youth, for most of my college days I lived a mile away and walked to classes on Penn State's colossal campus. Then came farming and the development of a daily hiking habit, and all that hunting and fishing.

Surely by now I'm making at least my fourth pass around the globe – all on gimpy legs, one grotesquely twisted in football, the other with its quad muscle disconnected and never surgically reattached.

Its devotees will tell you that walking aids in weight control, improves digestion, is easy on the joints, helps shape and tone legs and butts, improves the quality of sleep, enhances the mood, etc.

Mother encouraged us to "vote with your feet" – to express dissatisfaction with something or someone, you simply walk away. Of course, it works in reverse, too: You stay the course with the things (and people) you believe in.

As an example of voting for something with your feet, I nominate walking itself as a natural pathway to enjoying the active life. There's only one question on the ballot: Shall we wear out while pursuing our favorite activities, or rust out in comfy seats over on the sidelines?

Walking's greatest attribute

As far as I'm concerned, the best thing about walking is the conditioning of the mind which I'm convinced occurs along with that of the body. It's like hitting a mental reset button. The closest thing I can cite as proof of this are the countless times that – either during or right after a walk – the answer to whatever's been deviling me the most just pops up.

Given that the brain is what distinguishes us from all other animals, shouldn't we be taking whatever steps – and however many are needed – to help it excel? Who's to say that maybe someday a lifestyle emphasizing walking won't emerge as a scientifically endorsed detour around dementia or Alzheimer's, for example.

A belief in the therapeutic value of walking led a York County native to the Appalachian Trail in 1948. Earl Shaffer became the first person to document a hiking trip over the entire AT, a 124-day experience that helped him deal with the dark memories of his World War II days as a forward-area radioman in the Pacific Theater. He reversed directions in 1965 – walking north to south – and finished in 99 days.

Meanwhile, a new reporting job that autumn led me from The Easton Express to the York bureau of The Patriot-News. With a quartet of newspaper offices, the White Rose City was a challenging beat for newsmen in the Cold War era, partly because one of the four was on the very short list of U.S. publications approved for reading in the Soviet Union.

The left-leaning Gazette and Daily was driven by J.W. Gitt, then near the end of a remarkable 55-year reign as its crusading owner/editor. So tight was his grip on the paper that news business insiders nicknamed it The Gitt 'n' Daily. And out in the community, before a source would answer any reporter's questions, he or she had one for you, typically: "Now, which newspaper are you with?"

Catching up with a trailblazer

Overhearing a snippet of sidewalk conversation about "that old hermit who walked the AT" eventually guided me to trailblazer Shaffer, who was neither old (47), nor a true recluse (I got a great telephone interview).

But he was given to changing his mind. While my editors in Harrisburg were busy planning to play the story atop Page One in the Sunday editions, my source was having misgivings. He called shortly before deadline to opt out – in his words, "Just kill it."

Well acquainted with the written word, Shaffer was a published poet and the author of "Walking with Spring," a hiking classic. He mounted a nostalgic "Spirit of '48" hike of the AT in 1998, finishing in 174 days and just weeks shy of turning 80. He died in 2002.

Other former soldiers with wounds deep inside are following in this AT hall-of-famer's footsteps. Among them is ex-Marine Sean Gobin, who served in Afghanistan and Iraq before conquering the trail after his discharge in 2012. The experience inspired Gobin to found the Warrior Walk "Walk Off the War" program that helps equip, supply and support returning veterans as they through-hike the Appalachian or one of our five other National Scenic Trails.

Doug and Dee Pee pause during a 1980s walk.
Photo by Karen Castelli.

$ome other dividend$

Besides its physical and mental health dividends, walking also can pay off financially, and I wish I'd had the foresight to maintain a piggybank so I knew the exact amount.

Admittedly, most of the coins I found while afoot were pennies, usually near parking meters. For a long time I thought they landed there accidently as drivers picked through their change to plug the meter. But there were so precious few nickels, dimes and quarters mixed in with the coppers that eventually I realized some folks just weren't picking 'em up.

There also would be some small bills in that piggybank – and a twenty plucked from the surface of a puddle where apparently the March wind had deposited it. This was a short distance downhill – and more tellingly, downwind – from the empty parking lot of a branch bank in Cumberland County.

Another carless parking lot – except for mine – was the scene of my biggest find to date. Returning to the car from a picnic break along I-81 in Lebanon County, I spotted something over in a corner. A wad of folded up bills apparently had dropped when someone pulled out his car key.

Regular church attendance was not my habit when this happened in the mid-Eighties, but suddenly a stranger had handed me 191 reasons to give thanks. And share.

Passing newspapers versus weed whacking in the cemetery

One deals in the latest,
the other what's quite past;
the first hurries to serve,
the second, not so fast.

When a paperboy walks
on the customer's lot
he finds out soon who minds
and who really does not.

The trimmer runs no risk
of hearing a complaint,
not even if by chance
he steps right on a saint.

Two routes to knowledge

Walking my newspaper route brought in a little money, and so did working as a cemetery groundskeeper. Both jobs kept me on my toes mentally, too. That first set of customers taught a boy how to deal with people, while the second showed a retiree how others had dealt with life – and vice versa.

The bully's assault-by-golf-ball that marked my early days as a paperboy capped a lesson in trust. It's right to treat people in ways signaling that you trust them – or want to – but wrong to ignore the dangers of turning your back. Trust is something to be earned; the onus is on the person acquiring it, not the one doling out his chances to get it.

I learned who was going to tip me, and who would try to give me the slip by turning out the lights as I rounded the corner on collection day. I had lots of tippers – in an era of six-day delivery for 30 cents a week, the last family on my route faithfully forked over a 50-cent piece – and just one or two consistently reluctant payers. And I learned to separate the tips from the rest, so I could balance my little book at month's end.

There was a friendly builder/farmer who sometimes dropped sweet corn into my paper bag when I stopped to collect. When it was in season, Mom always checked: "Any sweet corn from Mr. Gutai today, Douglas?"

Mr. G broke a leg falling off a roof and lost the limb to gangrene. And then he lost his smile, and pretty soon I lost sight of him altogether. He simply withdrew, from everyone.

The daughter with whom he lived took him to Atlantic City and sent him out in his wheelchair onto the boardwalk. One day as gloomy Mr. G sat statue-like along the edge, someone else in a wheelchair waved while rolling by. His gesture un-acknowledged, the passerby spun around and confronted his elder.

"You have one good leg, sir," said the man who had none, "and you're giving everyone who has to be in a wheelchair a bad name. Good heavens, man! Get up and get on with life – get an artificial leg!"

Which, in time, Mr. G did.

Dohne family's Christmas 1977 pig roast at Cly, PA.

The senior Dohnes navigate their craft through Florida's Dora Canal in 1989 postcard photo.

History by the acre

My lessons in the outdoor classroom a.k.a. the Hummelstown Cemetery began on May 10, 2013.

The previous day, and only hours apart, my wife and I both accepted unsolicited part-time job offers. Kay retired years ago, but her old job was suddenly open again, and would she please come in and help get the train back on the track until a permanent replacement could be found? Kay always enjoyed her work as a bookkeeper for SEIU, Local 668, so she said yes.

Kay & Doug Dohne in the 1990s.

My caller was Ray Topper, a fellow tenor in the church choir and close family friend who gave Tyler his first job, as a groundskeeper with the cemetery crew that Ray ran. Back trouble had sidelined Ray's longtime assistant just when he was needed most.

"Doug, I can almost hear the grass growing it's coming on so fast over here," Ray began. No weak attempt at humor, this was a sincere stab at gravitas. "Can you come over here for a few weeks and fill in with the trimmer?"

Besides thousands of gravestones in need of tidying up, the cemetery contains roughly 23 acres of history, some of it written centuries ago and some as recently as last week.

The first thing I learned about cutting grass in a cemetery was not to visualize those rows of gravestones as an army awesomely arrayed against me, but instead to focus on the individuals and attack them one at a time.

Digging in on the eastern front

My personal battle began on the eastern front where the cemetery had originated. In its first several centuries, the preference for family burial plots – like squads within a platoon – was strong.

One wanted to be buried alongside those he'd lived with and most likely shared toils in the fields – the people who knew him best. He respected and loved them, and they him. It was a simple but honest life, one that often knew hardship.

While the adversity of the past is paved over by the green of the present, here and there in the solitude of the cemetery survive hints of its severity.

Within his family's stone-fenced plot lie the remains of John Paul Nissley, who died at 45 in 1914. He and wife Caroline had a daughter, Jennie, who wed T. Burd Zell then died in 1885, just four days after giving birth to son J.P., who was stillborn. Jennie was 28.

A short distance away, in one of the more elegant family plots among dozens in the cemetery, lies another tough-luck story, this one with a touch of mystery.

The statue topping their monument depicts a lovely but downcast maiden, bearing her cross. The inscription reveals that John H. Balsbaugh, 73, and his wife, Mary, 72, died on Christmas Day, 1895. They had a daughter, Malinda, who succumbed in her first year, 1850. A star-shaped medallion signifies that Balsbaugh was posted in Lafayette, NY, and served in the Grand Army of the Republic.

While working in that section of the graveyard, I sometimes mused about the fate of Mr. and Mrs. B.

Perhaps she was terminally ill, and her suffering was destroying him … Maybe he was the sick one and, thinking her too frail to go on alone, picked up his Civil War pistol one last time … Or it could have ended in flames.

Actually, the predecessor of my old employer had the scoop the very next day. For the price of one penny on Dec. 26, 1895, readers found it on Page 5, sandwiched between stories about the antics of Christmas drunks and "an escaped lunatic."

In the quaint, less sensationalized nature of the Gay Nineties, The Patriot reported:

MAN AND WIFE DIE TOGETHER.

Mr. and Mrs. John Balsbaugh Asphyxiated by coal gas at Swatara Station.

Mr. and Mrs. John Balsbaugh, aged seventy years, were asphyxiated by coal gas on Tuesday night at their home at Swatara station. The aged couple retired on Christmas eve at their usual hour after bidding good-night to their son, who had come from New York to spend the holidays with them. Mr. Balsbaugh and his wife did not respond to the calls for breakfast and going to his parents' room to investigate the son found his mother dead and his father dangerously ill.

Medical aid was hurriedly summoned but the old gentleman died before a physician arrived. The coal gas escaped from a stove on account of a defect in the pipe. Mr. Balsbaugh owned considerable land and was considered one of the most successful farmers in Dauphin county. He was engaged for a number of years in the grain business and at the time of his death was interested in the Swatara lime and stone company. Mr. Balsbaugh was a director of the Hummelstown national bank since its organization twenty-seven years ago and attended a meeting of the board on Tuesday. The couple are survived by one son, Hiram Balsbaugh, a trusted employee of the Equitable life insurance company.

A flock of funerals

Throughout much of my life, encounters with birds have had a Jekyll/Hyde quality about them. Most avian visits brightened my day, but occasionally a terrible darkness would follow. What turned into a disturbing personal mystery began innocently the spring I turned 10.

A ROBIN PERCHED on my shoulder.

Beside me in the yard that day were my mother and her father, Doc Loope; we were planting shrubs. I was leaning on the shovel's long handle when the bird landed. Trying not to move, I glimpsed Mr. Robin's dance across my bicep and up a forearm. He launched from the thumb.

That night a neighbor several blocks down the street died in a fiery auto crash, but no one connected the two events in any way – and why would they? Any notion that the bird's visit and the fatal crash somehow might be connected wouldn't occur to me until years later, after a string of bird incidents, each punctuated by the death of someone usually – but not always – close to me.

I WAS AWAKENED by the voice of a barred owl one summer midnight in 1970 after leaving a window open. Mother called later that morning with the news that Doc had died.

Sometimes what you remember about someone is something he or she didn't do. I never saw Grandfather Loope in dungarees or work clothes. Nope, it was a suit, vest and white shirt every day – even when gardening or mowing grass. The only garment he removed was his coat. Maybe he'd roll up his sleeves, but just to the elbow. That's how he was dressed the day of Mr. Robin's visit, and I'm sure that's what he wore the day he died. Doc was 94.

TWO YEARS LATER I was archery hunting for deer in Susquehanna County. Seated beneath a small tree whose branches bent low enough to offer concealment, I had to hold the bow parallel to the ground when taking a practice draw. It would be an awkward shot, but this was the perfect setup spot along a well-used trail. I chose to stay put.

The chickadees whose arrival quickly followed mine seemed to re-energize in the shade of the tree's dense foliage. They chirped and flitted like schoolchildren at play. First one then another and a third alighted on my bowstring, departing the second I blinked.

Returning home, I learned that Grampa Dohne had died in Syracuse, also in his 94th year. Not bad for a smoker who kept Prince Albert in a can. *You really should quit smoking because you might not turn out to be as lucky as Grampa D.*

Incidents of bird encounters preceding the departure of people mostly in my inner circle peaked in the Eighties and early Nineties.

IT WAS FRIDAY, May 2, 1980, and I'd said my goodbyes to the missus and our sons the night before, as I'd be leaving for hunting camp after work.

With the first edition rolling off the press, I went to work on a feature page to appear later. That put me close to a large second-floor window with a view of the veranda, on which Composing Room employees were feeding starlings gathered around their picnic table.

I've always marveled at the synchrony of birds in a flock, how each foot seems to touch down at the same moment. Their eruption into flight also is accomplished in near unison, and instinctively I glanced up from my work in anticipation of this little flock's lift-off.

Nature isn't always perfect, of course, as one of its creatures was about to demonstrate. In the blink of an eye the unlucky bird slammed into the window inches from my face and fell to the roof, its neck evidently broken.

That night our Danny boy's life was snatched away upstairs in the barn that sheltered the swine and steers he loved to tend.

FIVE YEARS LATER, after divorce and remarriage, my new life was unfolding at a gallop, but that old nemesis was still hovering about.

We were living a horse lover's dream on 17 acres in West Hanover Twp., Dauphin County, and I was finishing a project on Jan. 5, 1985. Perched on the just-installed metal roof of a run-out shed in the paddock, I glimpsed a solitary crow struggling high above in a steady breeze and making little headway.

The next time I checked he was in a straight-down dive and only 10 feet overhead. My drop to the roof was instinctive but unnecessary. When I looked up again the crow was gone.

Later that day we learned that a co-worker at The Patriot-News, reporter Bruce Cutler, had suffered a fatal coronary while in the embrace of a girlfriend. The attack, his second, came on the heels of his only complete marathon. Bruce was 47.

IN THE LATE Eighties and after a second divorce, I was working nights on The Patriot copy desk. Though it was often in the wee hours when I got home, heading straight to bed just didn't appeal.

I was renting a second-floor apartment into whose living room my pool table just barely fit. Elderly Mr. Peterson on the ground floor never complained if I racked 'em up for a little practice at 2 a.m., but I soon learned that sweet Alice across the hall had perfect hearing. So instead of running balls around the pool table, I'd take a walk around Camp Hill to clear my mind.

On one such nocturnal outing, while walking in a poorly illumined alley across Market Street from the Sheetz store, I stepped on a dead pigeon.

Later that day an establishment in nearby Wormleysburg was held up. Police Officer Richard Phelps responded to the scene in time to pursue the robber out of town, west through Lemoyne and into Camp Hill. The chase ended when Phelps lost control and his cruiser crashed into a metal post shielding the Sheetz gas pumps, about 30 steps from where the dead bird lay. The policeman was killed.

A THAW IN January 1990 enticed me into taking a motorcycle ride by a swollen trout stream. Stopping to stretch and rest, I paused briefly to lean against a large dead tree along Clarks Creek. Within seconds a pileated woodpecker was showering me with bits of damp wood, some of which found their way down my shirt as he hammered away.

Co-worker and fellow trouter Jim Conrad died late that night – another too young heart attack victim.

MONDAY, JULY 22, 1991, dawned clear and cool on the Rideau River in Ontario. Bill Shearer and I were in the boat headed for a prime smallmouth fishing spot when we nearly ran over a pair of loons just off the bow. These large, distinctively black-and-white patterned birds are quick to dive from danger, and can swim underwater for great distances before resurfacing. The only thing was, this pair never reappeared. Despite making several large circles and stopping to scan the surface with binoculars, we never saw either of them again. My mother succumbed to throat cancer later that day in Mount Dora, FL. I found out the following week.

Figuring it all out

After struggling for years to find meaning in this depressing sequence of events, my conclusion offered no comfort, no relief. I was convinced that this was simply a curse, payback for all the feathered lives I had taken. *The truth is, bird-hunting captured your fancy as a boy and you're still at it ...*

I know what you must be thinking, dear reader: The solution is as crisp and clear as the crow of a cock pheasant – just put down the shotgun. But it wasn't that easy.

Whenever the idea of quitting the life of a birder struck, invariably I would recall the forced commitment in order to reclaim my boyhood bow. Sure, it was illegal to shoot the rabbit – and somewhat heartless, too, as my arrow was not tipped for hunting. But the chief's demand that I never again draw down on another living thing – in essence, become a non-hunter – was just plain wrong.

Shortly after Jim Conrad passed, I was browsing in an art shop and paused by the watercolor print of a female snowy owl in wintry habitat. Studying her piercing yellow eyes, I noticed that they seemed to follow me – no matter how far left or right I moved.

For a guy grappling with the dark side of all things avian, a picture on the wall of a bird returning his stare might seem an odd selection. Surprisingly, the snowy owl proved to be the harbinger of enlightenment, albeit still distant. For the time being, I peered into those owl eyes and pondered the past.

My Eureka moment came two hunting seasons later, during a quiet walk in the woods with a gentle soul whose wise counsel had nothing to do with birding. He was non-judgmental about my history with the feathered ones, and his advice focused solely on how I should react to a bird encounter.

We were at a men's retreat that he was leading in Warm Springs Lodge near Shermans Dale, Perry County. With the morning session over and lunch 20 minutes away, we strolled along rain-swollen

Shermans Creek as I recounted my saga of the birds.

Though he was then a neighbor and our associate pastor, this was the first time I'd raised the subject with the Rev. Bob Stokes. As he considered his response, a cardinal landed on a tree limb close enough to serve as the perfect prompt. A quick exchange of glances signaled we both knew it was time for an answer.

My counselor stayed right in character by suggesting – as any minister might – that I should immediately resort to prayer.

"Ask for protection for yourself, your family and then others," he advised, a twinkle of the eye promising that this concise, practical response would suffice whenever feathers ruffled heart and mind.

The remedy was being tested on the spot, of course, and happily, no friend or relative's funeral followed Mr. Cardinal's visit. More importantly, this marked the start of a steady decline in my bird-related incidents, the last coming years ago. *Thank You, sweet Jesus, for sending friend Bob to give me peace.*

Walkin' in the rain

As a year-round hiker, I've encountered various situations and all kinds of people. I've been harassed, long-fingered and nearly run over a few times. Many others politely waved or nodded. Most simply ignore me. It's every walker's challenge to keep an eye on his fellow man while not losing faith in him.

Another thing pedestrians must contend with, of course, is weather. When it's raining, especially after midnight, might seem an odd time for a walk, but occasionally it just feels right. One such outing in particular turned into an enduring memory.

Crossing paths with nighttime police patrols was a fairly frequent occurrence during my stay in Camp Hill. There were no incidents – I honestly don't even remember ever talking with any of the officers – but I knew they were watching. My imaginary probation period ended when we began waving to each other as they drove by.

On the damp, sleepless night in question, I decided to don raingear, grab a flashlight and head out to gather earthworms for an upcoming fishing trip. The street was awash in wrigglers, especially where it met the curb, and my bait container was filling up.

Suddenly a car whizzed by, spraying me as I knelt by the curb. A few seconds later a police cruiser pulled up and, instinctively, I jumped up and pointed in the direction the speeder had gone. Like the pursued, the pursuer took the corner on what seemed like two wheels.

Re-energized by the excitement, I wrapped up my lowly mission, placed the can on the porch, and went for a walk. I had returned and was headed inside when the cruiser reappeared.

This time the dome light came on as the vehicle drifted by and I could make out a man's figure in the backseat, head bowed as though in prayer. The whole wordless scenario ended as it began, with me standing in the rain near my apartment building.

Epilogue: The next night at work, while editing the police log, I came to an item about a hit-and-run in Camp Hill. And an apprehension!

What is apt to arrest the attention of walkers in the autumn woods is all that colorful evidence of the seasonal change.

Life and times of the lowly leaf

(Sunday, October 17, 1999)

Heard the one about the down-and-out leaf that missed his higher calling?

Couldn't stem his fall from grace.

OK, it's a lousy joke, but it hints that maybe, just maybe, the lowly leaf is more than simply another painted face in Mother Nature's annual strip-tease extravaganza, now staging a colorful return engagement in your local woods.

How about the leaf as a mood checker?

Let me explain: Studying the forest photo on a wall in my home, a friend commented that it offered a quick reflection of the viewer's mood. The photographer took his shot while standing in a dark thicket and aiming into sunshine filtering through the tree canopy. The result is a heavy, black frame surrounding a sunny spot on the forest floor

To check on your outlook, my friend suggested, just glance at the picture. Quickly, where is your focus? If you “see” the sunny spot, then you're “standing” in the dark beside the lensman, suggesting a dark frame of mind. Find yourself staring at the dark border and it might signal a brighter outlook that goes with standing in the sunshine. I've tried it on myself and others, and it's amazingly accurate.

It's also probably true that the best-known broad-leafed tree in Pennsylvania is the mighty oak, actually a member of the beech family. Fifty to 75 species of acorn bearers occur in this country, mainly the East.

The palm-shaped leaves of the maple also play a big hand in the flaming foliage phenomenon. About 20 of the 75 or so species of maples are represented on this continent.

At least one notable tree species -- the commercially significant American chestnut -- has disappeared from the scene since Charles II of England honored William Penn's father, naming England's new colony Penn's Woods. While an ambitious effort to restore the blight-victimized chestnut is ongoing, yet another species has come under assault by the blight in Pennsylvania, the stately beech.

Penn once referred to wood as "substance with soul."

Substantial is a good description of Pennsylvania's forests at the time of the "Walking Purchase" (part one) in 1683, when the Indians sold to European settlers all of the land "west to the setting sun." They meant to the horizon, but the white men figured that meant all the way to the Pacific Ocean.

At any rate, within 1½ days, Penn had all the land he wanted. And trees. Pennsylvania was about 95 percent forested in his day, and much of it still is. And yes, people occasionally still get lost in this state's wilds.

Autumn woods walkers know – or soon learn – the differences between crossing an oak forest and, say, a beech stand.

Oak leaves are larger, flatter and tougher -- and therefore easier to slip on (especially when wet or frosty). The smaller, narrower and thinner beech leaves, with their pronounced veins, tend to curl up. Especially in depressions where they collect, beech leaves provide a soft carpet for the walker, though they tend to uncurl and stick to the shoe (again, especially when damp).

If the life of a leaf were to be presented as a three-act play, the first two would be brief. A few days of budding followed by a few months of helping to nourish the tree are but a blip on the great outdoor stage.

Then comes the fall from lofty purpose to seeming disuse.

Nor should the leaves, as poet Dylan Thomas phrased it, "go gentle into that good night." Always, there is the twisting and turning in the wind, the heat of day and the cool of night.

Gone too soon is the gallop into green. Slowly but relentlessly comes the color change. From a state of chlorophyll to a state of decay, the fall itself is almost anticlimactic.

Once down, the leaf lands a new, more lasting role.

Death, wordsmith Wallace Stevens observed, "is the mother of beauty."

Thus it is for the leaf. The ground troops of nature will soak, tear, crush, bake and freeze the newcomer, thus adding it to the mix that is the foundation for life in the woods.

Later on, deeper into the year, comes another example of that awesome power to tear and crush.

Pine Creek wild turkey hen can't escape the lens of Carlton Hoke.

(L to R) at the Hoke family retreat in northern PA: Jim Edris, Gary Lyter, Carlton Hoke & Doug Dohne. (This is what can happen if men are left alone too long in the woods.)

Tracks reveal drama in the snow ...

If you have hundreds or thousands of miles to go, take a jet. If you have more time and fewer miles, jump in the car – or better yet, on a bicycle. To really get the feel of the land, just step on it. And put your cellphone on airplane mode.

It was late fall on the calendar but early winter in the air and on the ground during a visit to the Hoke family mountain retreat along Pine Creek near tiny Cammal, Lycoming County.

My host was Carlton Hoke, who also had invited retired computer programmer Gary Lyter and former public relations guy Jim Edris for the weekend. Usually when this foursome assembles the purpose is to build a play set at the high school or playhouse in Hershey.

This gathering had a different flavor. We raked leaves, cut firewood, cleared debris from the creek shoreline and cooked Hobo Suppers over an open fire – sort of like a churchmen's retreat, which it could have been because at one time all of us sang in the same church choir.

Next morning I left my comrades in camp and took a walk. A dusting of overnight snow was starting to melt, but only in sunny spots. In 10 minutes of hoofing I spotted rabbit tracks here and there, as well as those of fox and coyote – but no footprints, meaning I was this morning's first man on the macadam.

With limited experience as a tracker, I was happy just being able to differentiate the fox's tracks from the coyote's (later confirmed in the library). As for when they were made, that was beyond me – initially, anyhow.

I spotted the rabbit tracks first, then the fox's and finally the coyote's had joined in. For a bit all three sets went along in the same general direction.

Out ahead the path bent slightly to the left, away from the creek. There the deteriorating rabbit tracks veered off to the right and so did the coyote's, but now the latter animal appeared to have been in full stride. *So the rabbit passed through either before or after the coyote.*

Continuing my walk, no fox tracks met the eye. *Must have gone uphill for whatever reason, maybe in pursuit of prey.*

Backtracking, I revisited where the three sets of tracks were last together, on the uphill side of the path. There the rabbit had moved several yards away as if headed uphill, then turned and crossed back over the path and off to the right. Its tracks appeared to be spaced the same as they had all along, conveying that it sensed no imminent danger.

Nor did the fox tracks seem to hold any hints. Then they simply ended. *Now where did he go from here, and how did he get there – he has wings?!*

Retreating a few paces to where their tracks showed the coyote and fox headed in the same direction, I noticed one coyote track where a fox print should have been. *So the coyote must have come along afterward and stepped on the fox track. Hmmmm.*

From there the coyote prints paralleled the fox's on the left, continued slightly past them, then made a hard right and portrayed an animal bounding toward the creek. *Now why'd he do that?*

Looking up from where I knelt to study the tracks, I saw something on the trunk of a small tree 15 feet off the path. A closer look revealed what seemed to be blood droplets.

If the coyote had managed to grab the fox from the side and shake it violently, perhaps fatally, that would explain the blood spatter – not to mention the abrupt ending of the fox tracks – as well as the 90-degree turn of the coyote as it ran off, presumably with the fox clamped in its jaws.

Snow was melting on the far side of the tree, erasing any sprinkling of blood that had cleared it. Soon the animal tracks – and mine, too – would vanish. But for the bloodied bark, no evidence of the fox's last trot would remain.

... as wind puts the tooth in winter's bite

Partly because it tends to keep others indoors, cold weather is the friend of those in search of solitude and reconnection with nature.

I love the starkness of the season and the way it shares itself so intimately. Winter reaches right inside your coat to make its icy point: You, friend traveler, are woefully underdressed!

The wind-orchestrated clattering of branches brushing against one another is a harsh attack on the ear, contrasting with summer's gentle, relaxed rustling of the leaves. To me, the former seems like a statement of protest. Ahhhh. Maybe the trees are grumbling about having to stand out there all winter with bare limbs.

This period of shortened daylight demands that pedestrians stay vigilant for icy spots, but chances are they'll notice even more of something else they'd rather not – trash.

Wind is a willing accomplice of the litterbug, and with farm fields stripped of their crops and trees of leaves, the result is a sorrowful sight. In the season of brown and gray, nothing serves so effectively as an icon of our ignorance and carelessness as one of those little white shopping bags waving wildly from the branch on which it is snagged.

I take this dance of plastic in the breeze as a personal invitation to be the change I'd like to see in my little patch of the world. Whether Mahatma Gandhi said so or not, it's good guidance, and when and where possible I simply grab the bag and start loading it with litter.

OK, some of us are simply not going to discard our trashy ways, but somehow I always feel better while turning those little containers into vehicles for change, albeit on a miniature scale. It beats turning a blind eye.

Grampa Dohne once observed that "a coat of paint covers up a lot of sin; an inch of snow does the same" – and so does the brand new carpet of green that Mother Nature rolls out each spring. Sin, be gone!

The reappearance of galanthus cheers winter walkers with its promise that the spring equinox is coming. But there might be quite a wait: This little white flower on a short shoot, a.k.a. snowdrop, often waits to coexist with snow until mid-February. The earliest snowdrop I've ever seen in bloom was right out front of Mayor Miller's home in Hummelstown on New Year's Eve 2015.

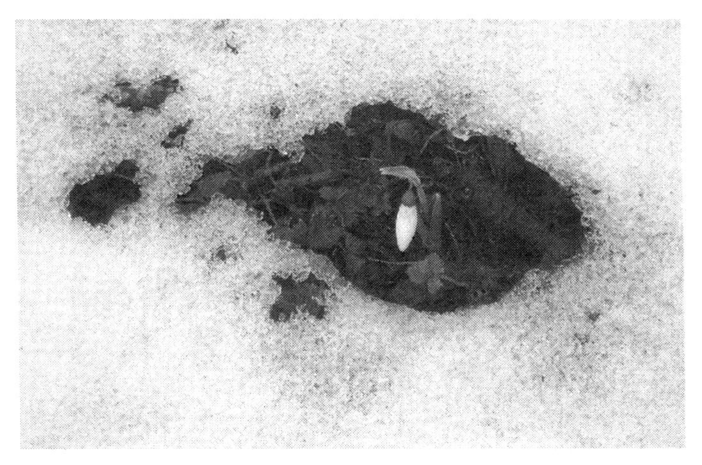

Galanthus blooms on Lincoln's birthday 2015 in Hummelstown.

Spring comes a-calling

(Thursday, March 1, 2001)

The first day of spring and the first spring day, we seem to have to relearn annually, are two different things.

The latest evidence that winter still wields the whip arrived in a Washington's Birthday whitening several inches deep.

It's a fickle and fitful process, this matter of spring's arrival.

But make no mistake, blossom by blossom, for sale sign by for sale sign, spring is on its way. Both are going up in my neighborhood – the former on crocus plants, the latter on more and more homes. Both are sure signs of spring.

If winter comes, as Shelley asked, can spring be far behind?

The farm fields seem in no mood to wait. They have been greening up early this year.

The daffodil plants on the south side of the house are nearly a foot tall. Though flowerless they may be, the hint of yellow in their swollen pods promises longer and warmer days ahead. Mind, this by Fastnacht Day.

You know you're bearing down on spring when the potholes open up to greet you. The springtime variety is especially memorable: just big enough so you won't forget 'em on your next trip, you'll steer around.

Another street sign announcing spring is the road-kill. A dead skunk, an opossum and a groundhog lay in mute salute to the season along a 2-mile stretch of Route 322 in Derry Twp. a week ago Sunday.

All were on the north side -- the "warm" side of an east-west highway. It's warmer there because the banks on the north side, facing south, more directly catch the sun's winter rays. This explains why snow often melts faster on the north bank, why vegetation regularly returns to life on that side first.

It might even help explain why the unlucky trio had been on the highway's north side: It perhaps offered a better chance of finding their last meal.

A few blocks north of 322, in Hummelstown, the crocuses were in gorgeous bloom, right on the north side of east-west running Main Street.

If nature is so often dependably predictable, man just as dependably isn't. Farther up Main, three boys walked side by side – in shorts – contrasting with their much more appropriately attired (long pants, coats, etc.) passers-by on the sidewalk. For the record, the trio in shorts was on the south ("cold") side of the street.

Though the forces of nature often collide, only one at a time can prevail.

To the east that same windy day, a huge flock of Canada geese bucking into a northwest gale over the Lebanon County landscape – a departing flight from Middle Creek – was making hardly any headway. The best the winged migrators could do was to circle, go with the blow and try to come around again – hopefully into a weaker wind.

Twenty minutes later, four deer stick tight together in a winter wheat field within sight of Hershey Medical Center. They're definitely not in that luscious but only several-inches-high green growth to hide!

The river shed its frozen skin more than two weeks ago. Sadly, already a fisherman is missing. His boat was found anchored in the river just north of Shuck's railroad bridge on Feb. 9, a day after his 49th birthday.

Someone took a noontime motorboat ride up the Susquehanna from City Island one day last week, and a bass boat on a trailer was parked in The Patriot-News lot that afternoon.

Elsewhere on that lot, a male pigeon was busy performing a mating dance, his neck feathers erect as he circled several other pigeons.

The robins have been back for quite a while, though this bird watcher spotted his first of the season only last week.

You see the robin, you think of the worm. You see the mud, you know the worm's not far below. Spring, after all, is the season of mud. Ask any child's mudder.

The ants will be in her kitchen any day now.

Viva la fleur

Spring is synonymous with blooming plants, of course, and walking with a grandchild in tow is a great way to savor your neighborhood's burst of beauty.

"Hey, Claudiea, how about a flower walk?"

"Sure, Pap," she beams, her brown eyes opening slightly wider than usual. "We haven't done that in way too long." It's late July 2013 and she'll soon be 18, a veteran of many such outings.

While five of the grandkids have been on flower outings, this activity predictably appealed less to the boys than the girls and – with Erin and Megan living out of state – that left Claudiea as my regular walking companion. She has an older stepsister, but Emily seldom seemed to be around.

The format was simple enough: Wander the town streets, identifying and counting any blooms we spotted. We might be at it an hour or more. Our longest flower outing was about 3 hours, which had Gramma on the verge of calling the cops just as we showed up.

The recordkeeping part of these walks, at times inconvenient and tiresome, gained luster when this teller of “old Indian tricks” realized he also was pretty good at making up flower names. When it got to where we were negotiating names for plants neither of us actually knew, it became deliciously obvious that she saw my floral fabrications for exactly what they were.

Young Claudiea noticed other things, too, such as names on mailboxes and various signs we passed. Once long ago we walked by a home with signs at opposite ends of its lone small garden – “Welcome, Friends” and “Beware of Dog.”

She struggled a little sounding out the words, then gave a look that had me silently vowing to revisit later, much later, the subject of the two signs that now spelled confusion on her face. The topic would be juxtaposition, and already I was savoring the prospect. The sweetness of that moment lingers in memory like the aroma of honeysuckle on a warm evening.

Little kids loom large when it comes to grabbing adult attention. Accompanied by Claudiea, I met and heard the stories of some folks whose houses I’d been passing for years – suddenly strangers no more.

A typical icebreaker:

“Hi, I’m Doug Dohne, over on South Landis, and this is my granddaughter, Claudiea. We’re out for a flower walk.”

And the response:

"Oh, yes, you've walked by here before. Ever seen a peace rose? C'mon over here and I'll show you one my grandpa planted. He was a rosarian. ..."

Or:

"Well, what kinds of flowers are you finding? Wanna get out of the sun and sit in the shade a bit? Hey, Daisy, bring out two glasses of lemonade!"

The impact of this kind of chance encounter on Claudiea was clear. Reserved but not shy, she simply began to, well, blossom. Interacting with strangers really seemed to help her personality open up.

She's come a long way since the day she wandered outside and began to pick wildflowers on her first visit to hunting camp. This was a grass-cutting mission, and when I was finished and came indoors there were three bouquets on the table – one featuring white blooms, another orange and the third blue.

While flowers can help brighten the way as young and old get better acquainted, they also can lift the spirits of the bedridden. Sometimes just a solitary flower can do the trick sight unseen.

A friend was battling cancer, so a message of cheer seemed in order. Walking back to the newspaper from the card shop, I nearly stepped on a dandelion that had risen through a crack in the sidewalk.

The thought of that little weed in bloom though surrounded by concrete just wouldn't go away. I put aside the coping card in favor of a personal note, then decided to go whole hog. I called my friend.

As a hockey writer covering the Hershey Bears, Steve Summers understood the difficulty of performing with excellence on a hard surface. When I mentioned the little yellow flower, he managed a chuckle and, as if on auto pilot, quoted legendary college football coach Joe Paterno:

"What counts in sports is not the victory, but the magnificence of the struggle."

It was the last time we spoke.

City stroll reveals nature's glory // Wildwood Lake lotus colony a spectacular sight

(Saturday, August 12, 2000)

A hawk swoops, a sparrow falls.

A school of minnows suddenly scatters as the "rock" just below turns into a large – and of more immediate concern to them, obviously hungry – turtle.

An opossum, suspended by its tail from a tree branch, swings in the breeze.

This is everyday stuff in the boondocks, but in Harrisburg? Yes, sharp-eyed nature lovers see all this and more on city strolls.

A sprawling example of natural beauty, just a few stone's throws from our urban area, is the American lotus plantation at Wildwood Lake. This somewhat rare water lily is now in spectacular bloom.

Although the police might frown on it for safety reasons, drivers on Linglestown Road who turn onto Routes 22/322 East have a perfect overview of the lotus colony from the berm at the high point of the entrance ramp. It's worth a moment's pause.

While the grounds immediately adjacent to the lake, overgrown with tree branches and vines, seem to cry out for silence, the din of highway traffic invades. Something about the thick canopy evokes one of poet Robert Frost's favorite themes, that of nature's relentlessness, its drive to seek out and overspread any unattended works of man.

A look around hints that the local ducks and other waterfowl don't seem to mind the noise, so maybe it's best to stifle over-sensitivity.

To the lake's south, within the city proper, Paxton Creek courses through one of Harrisburg's larger industrial and commercial sections of yesteryear. Simply put, the creek's rape by pollution has been ugly.

In its persistent way, nature has fought back, and regular flooding has helped clear the creek of clutter.

That is why one occasionally is able to spot a turtle or a school of minnows so close to traffic-crammed Cameron Street. Or a trio of fat carp swimming upstream, or a solitary skunk or groundhog working the stream bank.

Butterflies and swallows frequenting the exposed steel girders where the Paxton flows beneath Market Street add a dash of movable color.

In case you're wondering, the hawk attack, featuring the small but colorful kestrel, was witnessed in Riverfront Park, as was the suspended marsupial.

When it comes to wildlife in the city, often it takes you by surprise. Sort of what poet Emily Dickinson had in mind when describing a snake. Its notice, she wrote, "suddenly is."

Nature struts on an urban stage

During one lunchtime walk – downstream from Wildwood Park in the city's heart – I paused on a bridge overlooking the Paxton. Beneath a slightly oil-slicked surface, minnows were going upstream single file in the shallows.

Rounding a small rock to their right, one by one the little fish veered sharply away from shore, as if in some aquatic curtsy to an imaginary official on a reviewing stand, the stone.

There was a flash of splash as a crawfish – hidden by the rock – made a one-clawed catch of a minnow like an NFL tight end snaring a bulletlike blast from his quarterback. As the crawfish crossed the stream bed still wrestling his prey, it was plain that he had but one arm.

Nothing unusual there, given the violent lifestyle of crawfish. Still, the whole thing made me think about how difficult life must be for the residents of such a severely soiled waterway.

The crawfish and the snapping turtles, waterfowl and other species observed through the years in or along Paxton Creek are no less determined to succeed than their cousins in more pristine surroundings. These city critters play the game of life right where they are, regardless of the odds. And their chances dwindle when human neighbors ignore that they are just one part of something larger.

Another lesson on the same subject unfolded in a chance encounter on a restaurant rooftop in Pearl City, Hawaii, in 1978. My instructor was an Asian bonsai gardener who was tending the 150 or so specimens in his collection, some standing just a foot or so tall in their third century of life.

After graciously explaining various techniques of bonsai, this middle-aged man told me that the garden had been in his family's care for six generations, and that the youngest of his four sons (a teen, now at baseball practice) would be taking over eventually.

Later, reflecting on our visit, it struck me that I didn't even know the names of my ancestors five generations back. And I certainly wasn't championing any enterprises that they'd begun, let alone helping 150 little lives to hang in there for a few more decades. Or maybe another century.

What follows is a mix of miscellany and random thoughts on some of the bigger-than-you realities of our changing environment.

1) The state of *Penn-saw-drill-ia*

Geologically speaking it's the Marcellus Shale field, but a more descriptive name for roughly the northern half of the Keystone State might be *Penn-saw-drill-ia* because sawing down trees and punching up natural gas from deep below their roots account for much of what goes on here.

Half of Pennsylvania – 17 million acres – is forestland. This state has a $5.5-billion-a-year hardwood products industry employing 90,000 and supplying 10 percent of the nation's total output. Seventy percent of the woods are privately held, with the rest in state and federal hands.

My wish for the woods under government control is that they get the same break we give our rivers – by increasing transparency in the process by which our forests are being mowed down like batters in a no-hitter.

In runs, hits and errors, baseball sums itself up after every game. At least once a year, government should do the same when it comes to harvesting the public timber – give us a line in the general budget showing income (the state's and that of the loggers it hires), acres cut, and any violations committed in the process.

Mining is a $2.9-billion-a-year undertaking here – most of it targeting coal – and Pennsylvania ranks fifth in annual raw steel manufacturing with 5.5 million metric tons.

At least partly because of coal burning, the Harrisburg-York-Lebanon metro area in 2016 slipped into the bottom 10 in the American Lung Association's national rankings.

So the move to add natural gas generation to the coal-fired Brunner Island power plant in York County comes as a literal breath of fresh air. Once a dual-fuel operation, Brunner will produce less smog and enjoy better relations with its neighbors as far away as Allentown, a few of whom have practically been breathing fire over poor air quality for which in part they blame the plant.

While the old one-two punch of lumbering and mining continues to pummel Pennsylvania's vast forests, there's a new kid in the hollows these days – the natural gas fracker.

Gas wells are old hat in God's Country – there was one behind Pat Neeley's home in Costello, producing enough to pay his heating bill. What's different today is the technology of fracking, in which a nasty cocktail of elements is forced at great pressure deep into the earth to dislodge and harvest its trapped treasure.

This process sometimes mixes gas and contaminants in amounts that, unfit for sale, are simply burned off at the wellhead. At times resulting in an above-the-treetops flame, the frackers' version of throwing out the baby with the bathwater can be downright frightening to a first-time witness after midnight.

Besides precious fuel, gas crews in their large, ubiquitous vehicles also produce a lot of inconvenience for other drivers on those typically narrow roads – not to mention the potholes that proliferate in their wake. One very objectionable thing about the frackers, at least to anyone who loves peace and quiet, is all the noise they generate. Boy, talk about an invasive species.

And they certainly hit the woods in droves back in '04, didn't they. Driven by soaring energy prices, they zeroed in on Pennsylvania because it lacked an extraction tax (still does), going at it 24-seven, lighting up the nighttime hollows like Yankee Stadium.

Producing a glut of natural gas in their first decade, the drillers helped to fuel a bust marked by sinking stocks and lost jobs, a tale well documented by The Patriot-News, which noted along the way that six of Pennsylvania's environmental secretaries in the last 20 years later went to work for those they formerly regulated.

2) Briefly, a little relief at DEP

They left behind a department so crippled by the loss of tens of millions in budget dollars and nearly 700 positions (since 2008) that the U.S. Environmental Protection Agency twice in 2015 cited DEP for failing to meet its mission.

In less than two years as DEP's chief, Quigley demonstrated a better grasp of the larger picture than some who preceded him. After Gov. Tom Wolf in 2016 announced new rules that the gas drillers griped would cost billions extra to follow, Quigley was asked if the regulatory process had taken too long to catch up with the realities of gas drilling's impact. Here's how he began his reply:

"We're roughly a decade into what could be a hundred-year" natural gas extraction. By that yardstick, the harvest in Pennsylvania is in its infancy.

In a classic example of the contrast between errors of omission and those of commission, Quigley took a different approach than his predecessors in office who promoted themselves into lucrative energy industry jobs: He set out to fix what he thought was wrong, and there was plenty of that.

All of which made John Quigley that rare bird on today's political scene, a passionate leader for a just cause that he ranked above his party's, and his own, good. The secretary's resignation in May 2016 had more to do with the pitiful state of Pennsylvania politics – on both sides of the aisle – than any deficiency on his part.

Quigley was the third pro-environment voice to fade from the still-young Wolf administration, following policy secretary John Hanger and Katie McGinty, who quit as the governor's chief of staff to run for a U.S. Senate seat.

Wolf disappointed environmentalists in June by signing a half-a-loaf bill on new oil and gas rules, and a measure allowing the state to delay implementing the federal Clean Power Plan.

While Wolf strayed from the main environmental trail, Quigley stayed the course, counterbalancing fracking's pitchmen on environmental safety and economic issues in his new post as a teaching/ writing senior fellow at Kleinman Center for Energy Policy at the University of Pennsylvania's School of Design.

A few months after his fall, Pennsylvania's Supreme Court overturned Act 13, a 2012 overhaul of gas and oil rules favoring industry – the same regulations Quigley had opposed, and a good example of the kind of legislation that helped make Tom Corbett a one-term governor.

Something the natural gas lobby doesn't say much about is water quality in the lower Susquehanna. Common sense hints that fracking just might have at least a little something to do with the condition of that sweet spring water from northern PA by the time it passes Harrisburg en route to the Chesapeake Bay.

Besides fracking, mining and timbering, the river also is impacted by the activities of some of the 62,000 families who earn $6.8 billion a year farming 7.7 million acres in Pennsylvania.

3a) This lady can take a punch

In spite of all that, the natural world's resilience – far and away her most stunning attribute – remains on full display. You can see it in the leek fields that faithfully pop up low on sunny mountainsides each spring, and in the schools, herds and flocks that populate stream, woods and sky.

To Mother Nature, the advent of global warming is old news. Things have been heating up for the last 10,000 years or so, and this isn't the first time either. Earth has weathered five known ice ages – and the warmup that followed each.

Our changing climate is characterized by a lengthening growing season, evidence of which has been piling up for decades right outside our hunting camp. Here are some gleanings from our springtime visits to camp (starting the last Saturday in April or the first in May, 1969-2016, coinciding with the spring gobbler hunt):

It was so cold on our Seventies visits that the mice and moles were still nesting in the outhouse, making a mess of any toilet paper we'd carelessly left dangling from the roll the previous fall. By the Eighties, our initial spring trips to camp found the little rodents out of the privy and busy tunneling before we arrived. The telltale mounds of dirt in the yard signaling fresh passageways beneath also indicated that frost was leaving the ground earlier than usual.

Change was afoot topside, too, as things were greening up a bit earlier with each passing spring. Soon we were wearing cotton, not wool, as snow in May became the exception instead of the norm. We are much more apt to sweat than shiver in the 21st century springtime turkey woods.

As his world of white melted into one of green, the ice man picked up spear and atlatl and moved on. In a word, he adapted, and so must we.

b) Our ticket to change at camp

One of my personal adaptations to the new climate was forced by the exploding deer tick population and the threat of lyme disease that came with it. This little parasite has made Pennsylvania the nation's leader in confirmed lyme cases.

Though regularly bitten by ticks, I've never tested positive for the disease. One side effect of taking doxycycline, the antibiotic of choice vs. lyme: you're ineligible to donate blood for six months.

Tick-repelling powders and sprays seem to work, but they should be removed immediately after use. That calls for a shower, and our camp didn't have one, not even running water.

Well, let's just say that coming home from a week at camp to a wife pinching her nostrils shut while pushing me toward the shower ended in the spring of 2015. The camp's long dry run concluded with the installation of an outdoor shower engineered by brother Steve.

Climate change led camp to install outdoor shower.

4) Predators are on the rise

Besides the deer tick, some of the new climate's other big gainers in the woods include the wild turkey, white-tailed deer and the black bear, as measured in hunter harvests that reached record levels in 2001 and 2002 and 2011, respectively. Along with the black bear and coyote, such other predator species as the fisher and bobcat are also making strides.

The same thing is happening out west. After decades of managing a Yellowstone-area grizzly comeback, the feds proposed in March 2016 to lift a hunting ban on *Ursus arctos horribilis* in parts of three surrounding states but not the park itself. Six people have been mauled since 2010, and 59 grizzlies were killed in 2015, many by wildlife managers protecting ranchers' livestock.

Another bruin on the rebound is the Louisiana black bear, which inspired the teddy bear of retail fame after Theodore Roosevelt declined to shoot one while hunting in Mississippi. The teddy bear's population jumped from a low of about 150 in 1992 to an estimated 500 to 750 by 2015, when its legal armor was removed.

The Obama administration appears determined to set a record for delisting recovering species (including the gray wolf) from the laws protecting them.

Obviously, things could be better on central Pennsylvania's waterfront. Those monsters of the midway, the big hydro dams, still confront the migrating shad and eel. And while the smallmouth bass shows early signs of bouncing back, the sickness in the Susquehanna continues to afflict the river's many life-forms.

In August 2016, DEP warned the public about high bacteria levels, but still wasn't ready to designate the Susquehanna as an impaired river – a step the Fish and Boat Commission has been urging for years. Later that month the two agencies spoke with one voice, awarding $200,000 in grants to boost river habitat by reducing tributary sediment in York and Lancaster counties.

Also on the plus side are increased recycling and efforts to improve ag practices. We will know the Susquehanna is doing better when more of its tributaries qualify as Class A wild trout waters.

That's Mother Nature – always switching things around, sometimes in hurry up mode (think hurricane) but more often in slower, less dramatic fashion (just a drizzle). Meanwhile, every species – whether flying, swimming, rooted or freestanding – exists in the presence of all the rest.

Man wallows in ignorance when he fails to embrace nature's interconnectedness. We do not live apart from the natural world; we dwell, work and play at its very core.

Realizing that we are just one part of the whole means little unless it directs our behavior. We cannot afford to play on a team that saves the stadium's grass for game day by turning the practice field into a muddy mess every other day. With apologies to Shakespeare, all the world is a stadium, and The Big Game is played right here every day.

5) Best offense is still a good defense

It always has fallen to those who cherish and respect the outdoors to rise in her defense. It is everyone's responsibility to help check the greed that too often results in raping nature's beauty in order to reap her bounty. Any chances that our grandchildren's offspring have of seeing healthy amounts of green in both wallet and forest depend on the restraint we show today, and it's discouraging when we fall short and the shad, eel, bass *et al* must suffer.

Nor are lower life-forms the sole victims when, with callousness and stupidity in charge, too much lead winds up in tap water in Flint, MI, or raw sewage from Camp Hill is discharged 97 times into the Yellow Breeches and Conodoguinet creeks (2013).

When the environmental news depresses, I imagine myself in the wilds of Potter County at Gilly's Nose, a mountain point magically transformed into a spiritual gathering spot for all who in life loved the outdoors. Some of their names appear in this book, many others do not. The shade that forms their collective frown yields to a smile as sunshine's return signals that nature somehow has withstood our latest transgression.

Standing with the Wild Boy is the Indian for whom this glade was named. Nearby is Ferdinand Vandiveer Hayden, the Civil War-era physician and geologist who prevailed upon Congress to create the world's first national park (Yellowstone, in 1872). Naturalist/philosopher John Muir huddles beneath a huge oak with John James Audubon and Izaak Walton. Of course Gandhi's here, and later on there will be room for you and me, too, provided we apply his wisdom – live simply so that others may simply live.

I take heart in the U.S. Supreme Court's autumn 2016 refusal to hear a challenge to the Chesapeake Bay cleanup plan by 22 states and a bushel of farm interests.

And the pope's self-assigned role as emissary for the environment qualifies as downright uplifting. Francis grabbed my attention by choosing that name and then courageously living up to it. In the spirit of St. Francis of Assisi, patron saint of animals and the environment, forward into battle!

Flora and fauna forever!

Made in the USA
Lexington, KY
22 December 2018